POSTCARD HISTORY SERIES

Northwest Georgia

in Vintage Postcards

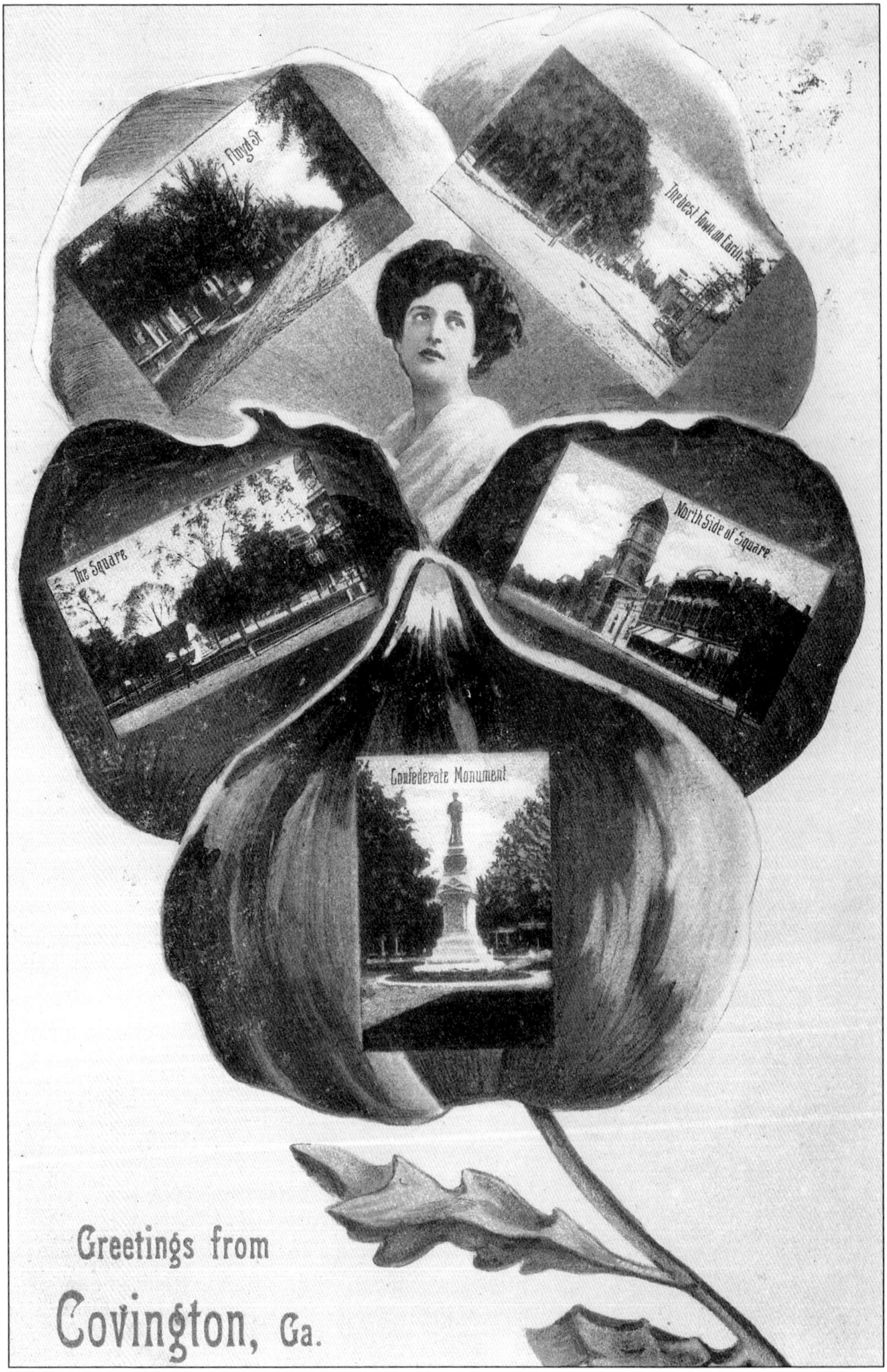
Floyd St.
The best Town on Earth
The Square
North Side of Square
Confederate Monument
Greetings from
Covington, Ga.

POSTCARD HISTORY SERIES

Northwest Georgia

in Vintage Postcards

Gary L. Doster

ARCADIA
PUBLISHING

ISBN 978-0-7385-6892-8

Published by Arcadia Publishing
Charleston, South Carolina

Printed in the United States of America

Library of Congress Catalog Card Number: 98-86669

For all general information contact Arcadia Publishing at:
Telephone 843-853-2070
Fax 843-853-0044
E-Mail sales@arcadiapublishing.com
For customer service and orders:
Toll-Free 1-888-313-2665

Visit us on the Internet at www.arcadiapublishing.com

For Faye Thomas Doster,
my sweetheart since May 30, 1956

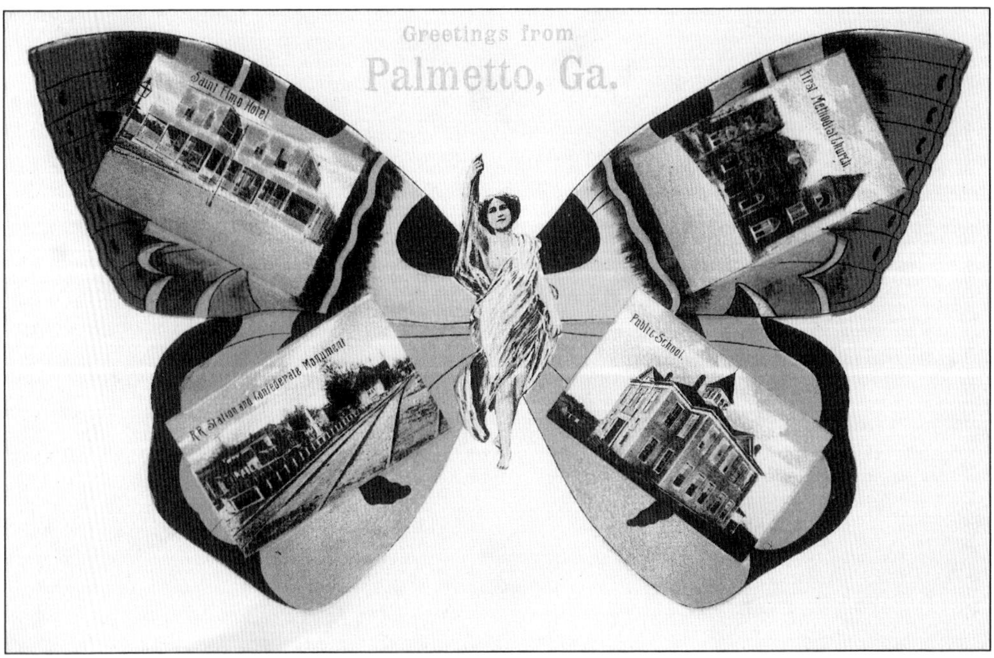

Contents

ACKNOWLEDGMENTS

For help in various ways, including advice, information, and post cards, I wish to thank the following people:

Carl Anderson
Bob Basford
Jim Dunn
Nell Dunn
John Kovalski
Jerald Ledbetter
Ernest Malcom
Dan Marshall
Bill Moffat
Edwin Oldham
Hershel Reeves
Gordon Sanford
Sue Fan Tate
Jeff West
Bill Wheless
Charlotte Marshall
George Marshall

INTRODUCTION

We are indeed fortunate that post cards* were invented and were so popular during the first several years of this century. In the clamor to satisfy the almost overwhelming demand for more and more post cards by the public, literally thousands of scenes were photographed that were never captured on film for any other reason. Over time, many of the homes, depots, courthouses, stores, and other buildings so pictured have disappeared and these early post card views are the only images that remain. Two particularly interesting facts that were discovered while selecting and compiling the cards for these books concerned Georgia's Confederate monuments. A great many monuments were unveiled or dedicated on Confederate Memorial Day, April 26, and few of them remain on their original sites. The ladies of the United Daughters of the Confederacy and the old veterans themselves usually selected some prominent spot in the middle of town, almost always at the intersection of two main streets. Invariably, as automobile use increased over years, the monuments became traffic hazards and were moved to another part of town. Consequently, many of these post card views are the only pictures of them in their original locations.

Also of great interest are the views showing the intrusion of the automobile onto the scene. It is fun to note that the earlier post card views, those before 1907 or 1908, usually have horse- or mule-drawn wagons, buggies, or carriages in the street scenes (a few even show mule-powered streetcars!). Then, from that time to about 1912 or 1914, these views will typically show a mix of the animal-drawn vehicles and early automobiles. After this time, a wagon or buggy is only rarely seen, and the number of automobiles on the streets increased rapidly.

*Throughout the book, I have chosen to use the older spelling of the word, i.e. "post card" versus "postcard."

The collecting frenzy that swept the world began in Europe in the 1890s, crept into this country before the turn of the century, and erupted a few years later. Many of the better quality post cards were produced in Europe, particularly Germany. Some of the post card factories in Germany were the size of cotton mills in this country, and they employed hundreds of people. For example, one German plant in 1909 had 112 cylinder printing presses and employed 1,500 workers. During the peak years of the post card collecting fad, more than a million people in Germany were employed in the post card business. In the three-year period from 1907 to 1909, more than 85,000 tons of post cards were imported into the United States from Germany.

In the Images of America book series published by Arcadia, the major effort has been to render pictorial books on individual towns or counties. And these are wonderful. Those of us who have an interest in preserving whatever we can of our past are hungry for books like this and they serve a valuable purpose. However, there are hundreds of smaller communities across every state that offer only a limited number of views of life of yesteryear that also are striking and important. Some medium-sized towns may have a handful of good views that show what their community and its people looked like nearly one hundred years ago. Many of the very small towns may have only one or two representative views. All of these are important, but none of them can support a book alone. Hence, this series of six volumes was conceived to provide a vehicle whereby a collection of early Georgia post cards from numerous small communities could be exhibited.

It is important to note here that this set of books is not intended to be any sort of scholarly work. It is merely an attempt to provide access to a selection of early views of Georgia that are not available in any other form, most of which have not been reprinted since their original publication. Many of the captions we provide in these books are no more than the caption printed on the cards when they were produced. Some additions have been made to some cards when the author had knowledge of some facts regarding the view in question. Other information came from the few reference books listed in the bibliography. To have researched each view and provided a comprehensive caption for each would have taken a lifetime of research, and then would still have been incomplete.

The author is a lifelong Georgian and has collected all manner of Georgiana for most of his life. Some of his other collecting interests are obsolete currency from the Colonial period through the War between the States, early letters and other documents, slave bills of sale and other items pertaining to slavery, Confederate letters and documents, old photographs, trade tokens, and Native-American relics.

One

Atlanta Proper

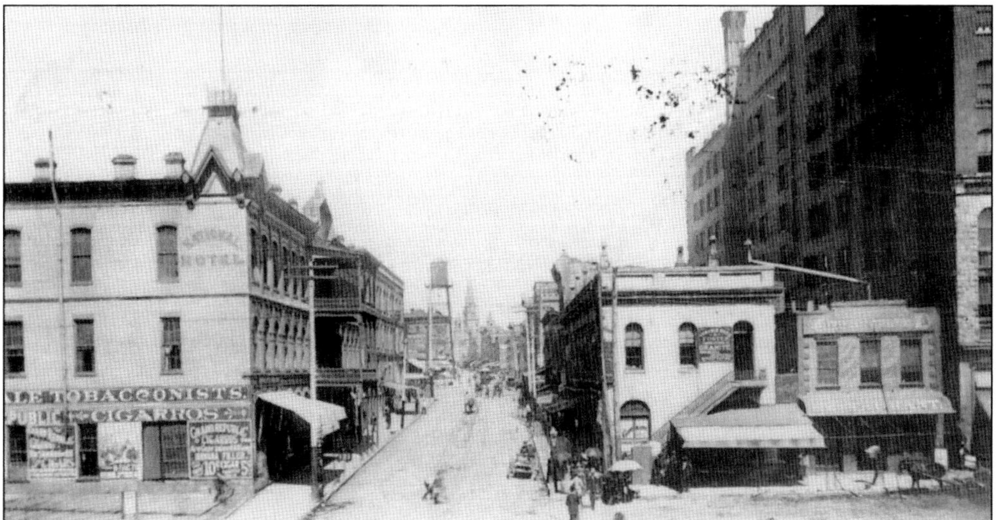

Long before Atlanta became the center of the New South, it was a bustling town that featured unpaved streets. The scene here, from 1887, when the city was still recovering from the Civil War, shows Peachtree Street.

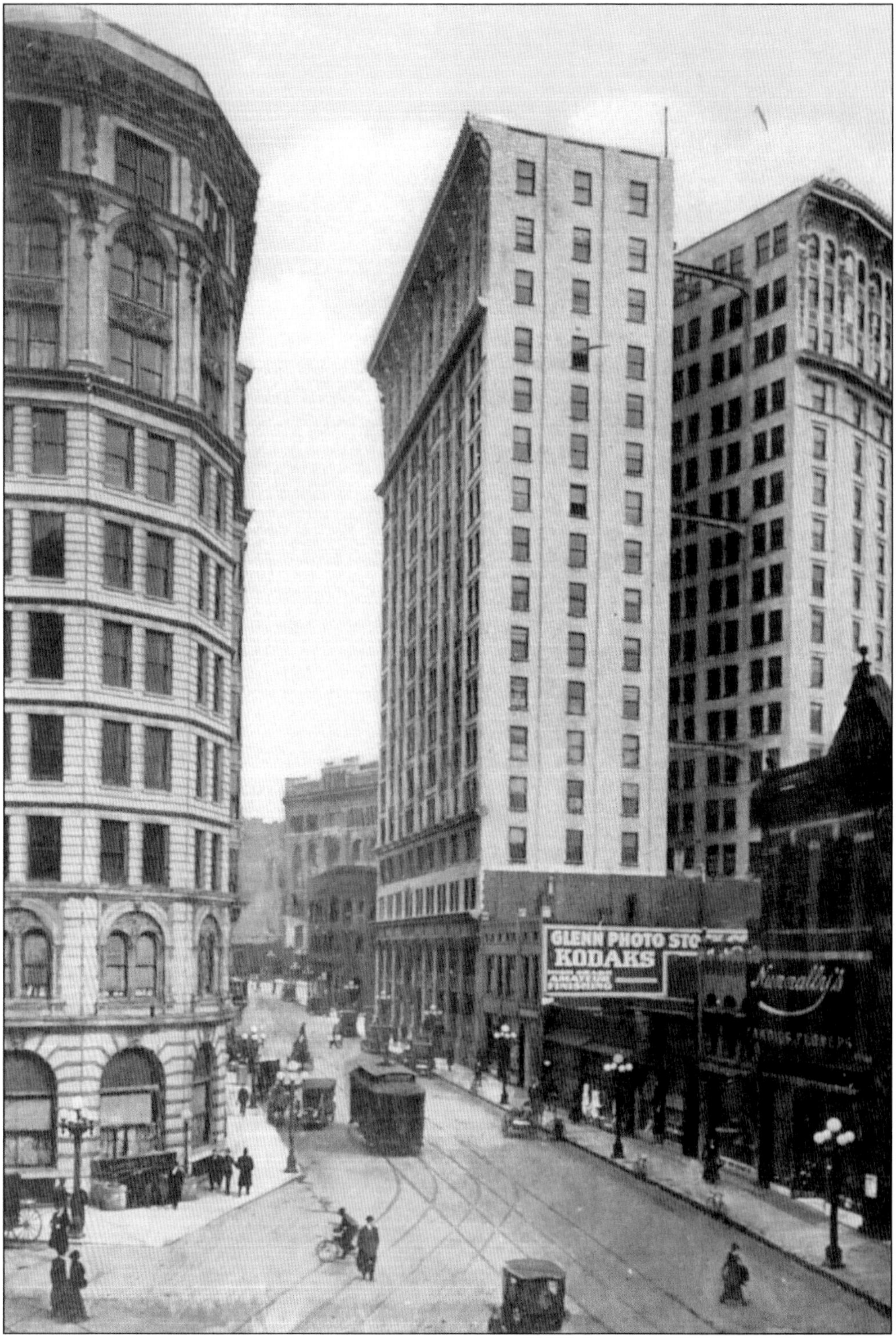

The Leighton and Valentine Company of New York published this view of Peachtree Street, including the Candler Building.

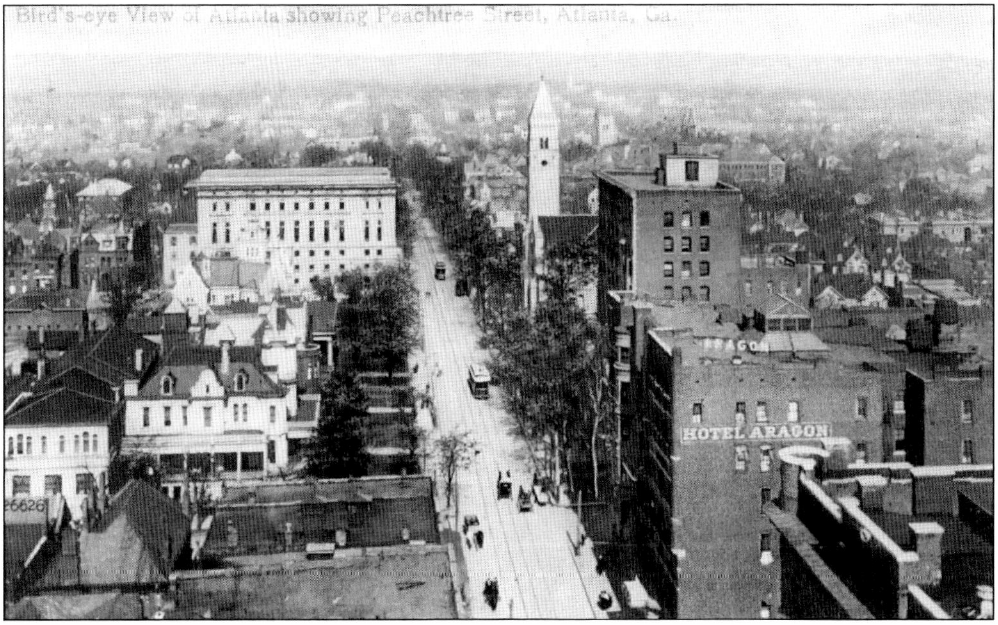

The sign for the Hotel Aragon is prominent in this view of Peachtree Street. The sender, who signed his name "Loafer," sent this card to an acquaintance in Ariton, Alabama, with an approximation of the first two lines of John Howard Payne's "Home, Sweet Home."

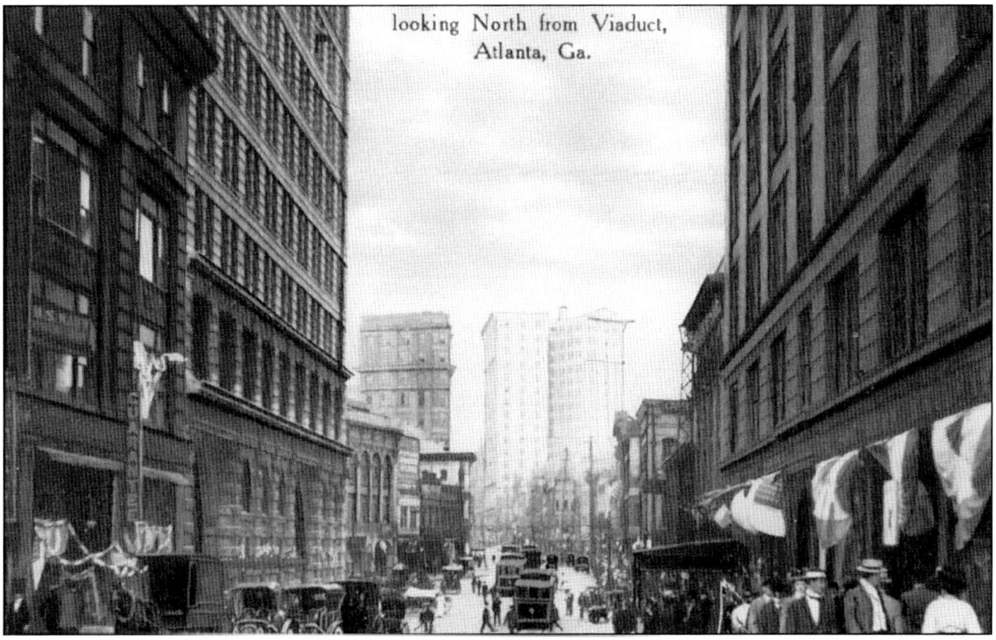

This is another view of Peachtree Street, looking north from the viaduct. Note the festive bunting on the right side of the street.

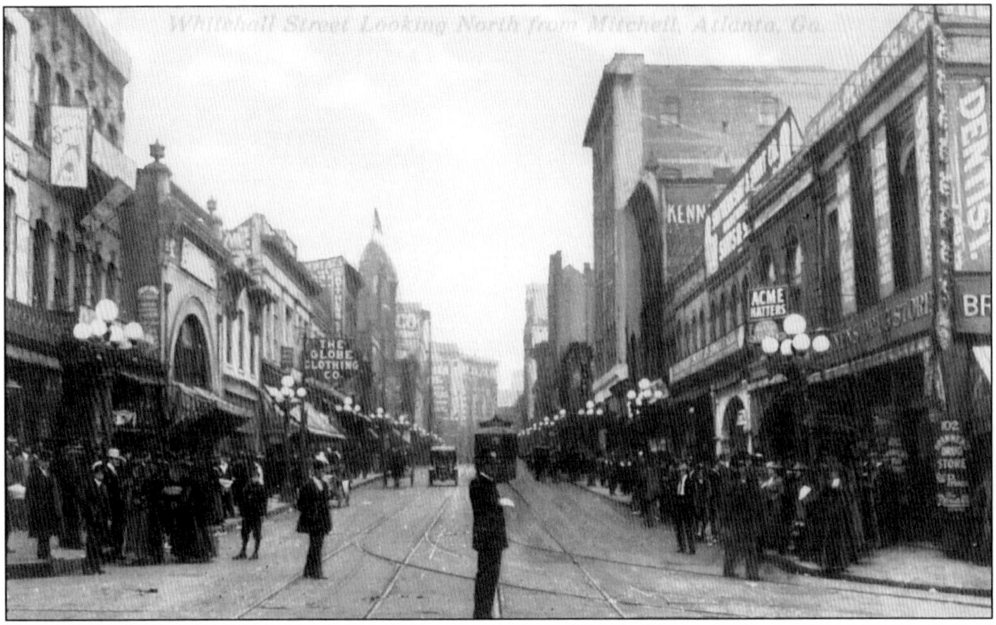

A white-gloved policeman stands in the middle of Whitehall Street at the busy intersection with Mitchell Street.

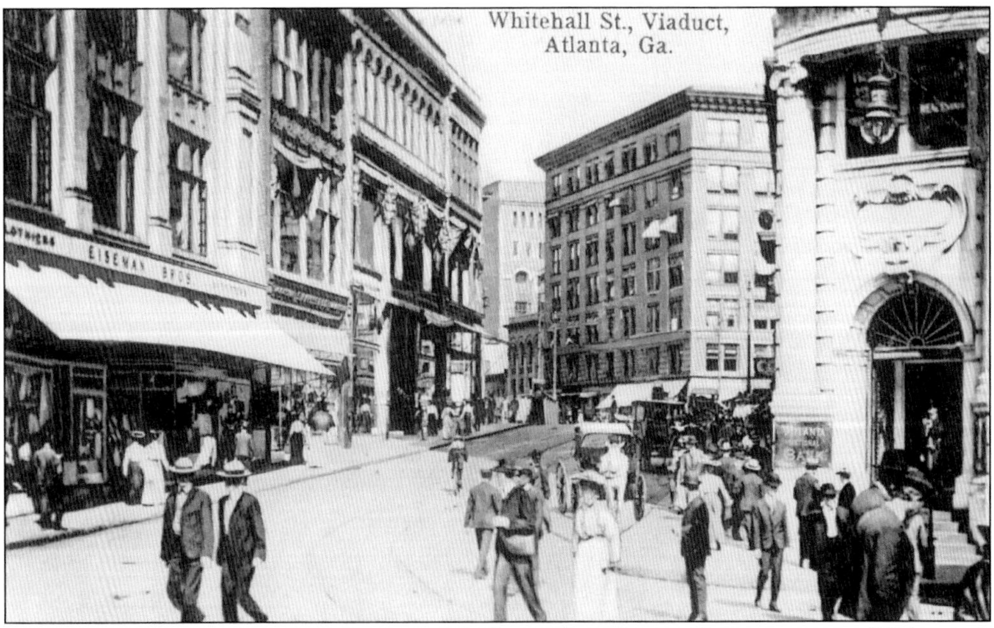

The Atlanta National Bank (on the right), located at the northwest corner of Whitehall and Alabama Streets, opened December 19, 1865, and later became the First National Bank of Atlanta.

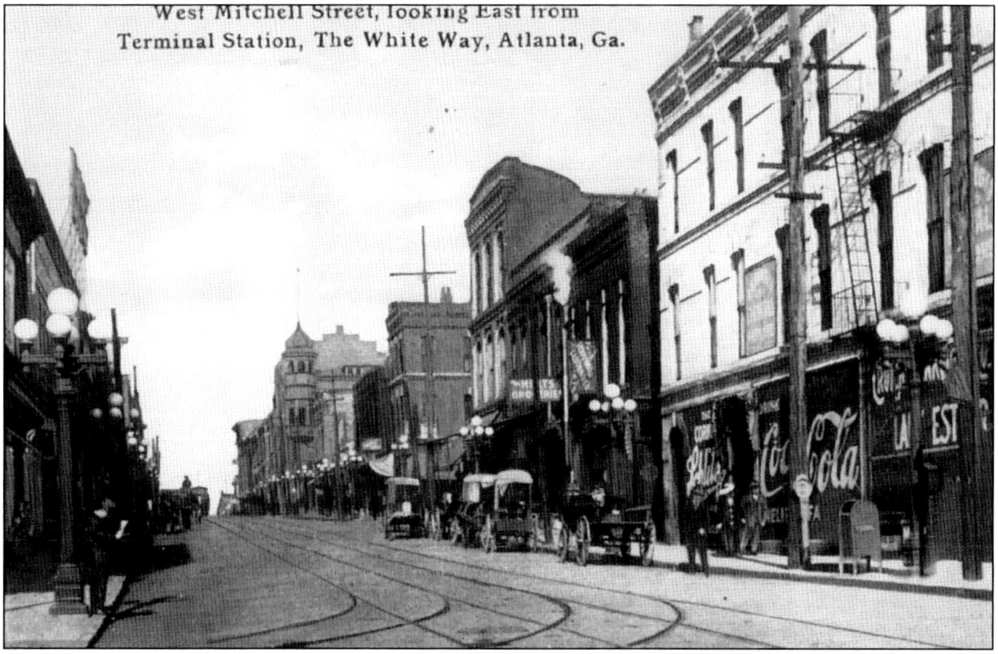

In this view of West Mitchell Street, an early advertisement can be seen for what would become one of the world's most recognized products—Coca-Cola.

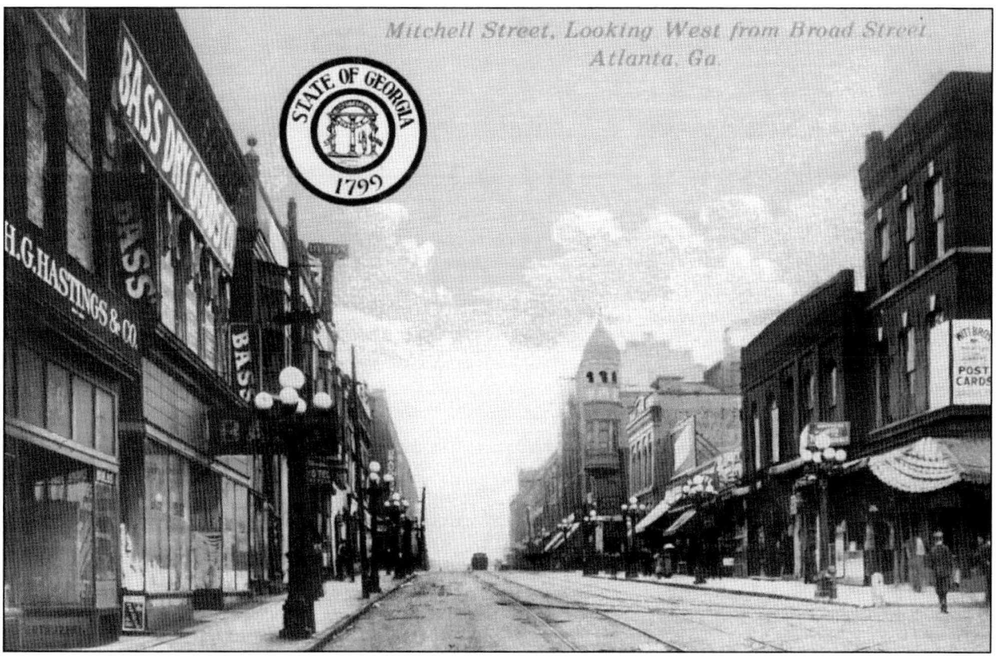

Witt Brothers, the publisher of this and other post cards, managed to include a sign for their company in this view of Mitchell Street. H.G. Hastings and Company and the Bass Dry Goods Company are also visible.

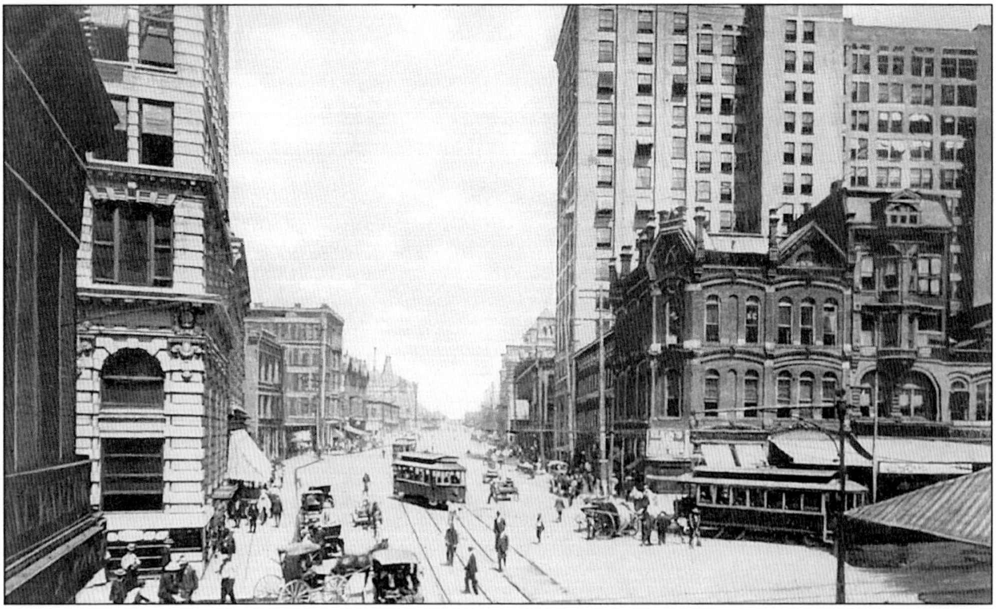

This card shows a busy Marietta Street, including streetcars, pedestrians, and horse-drawn buggies.

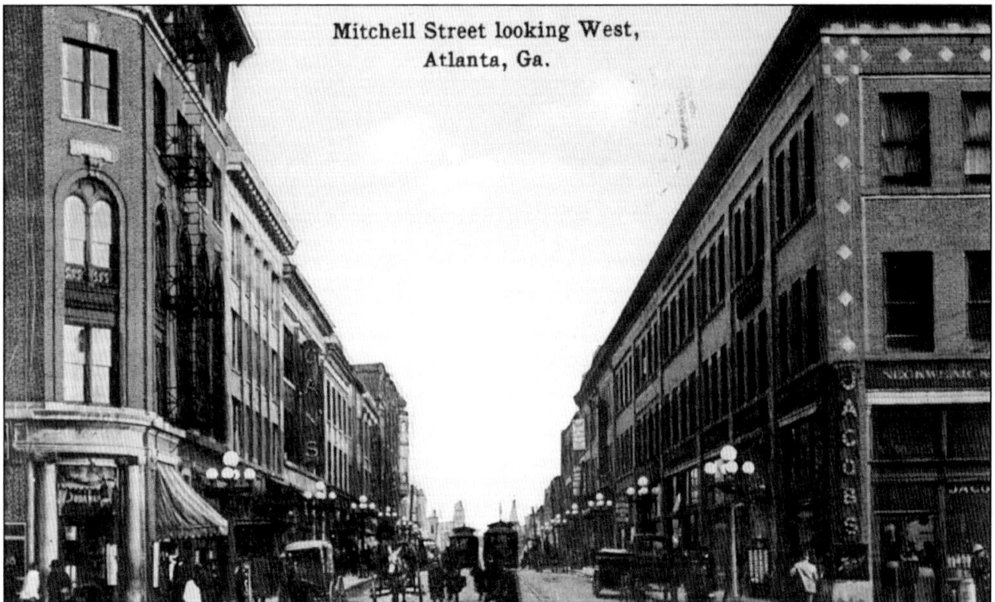

The sender of this view of Mitchell Street wrote: "Atlanta Ga-Dec 1-1919. We are here almost three weeks. The weather is fine, can sit on the porch almost every day. Like the city fine and am more than contented to live here. Ross is doing fine, all wrapped up in his new work, he has a fine organization. The children are fine. We had James' tonsils removed just before we left Det. and he is fine, he is getting so fat since we are here. Thomas was sick for a week due to the change of milk but is fine now. We have a furnished house for a short time. Hotel no place for babies. Will write again. Lovingly, Irene."

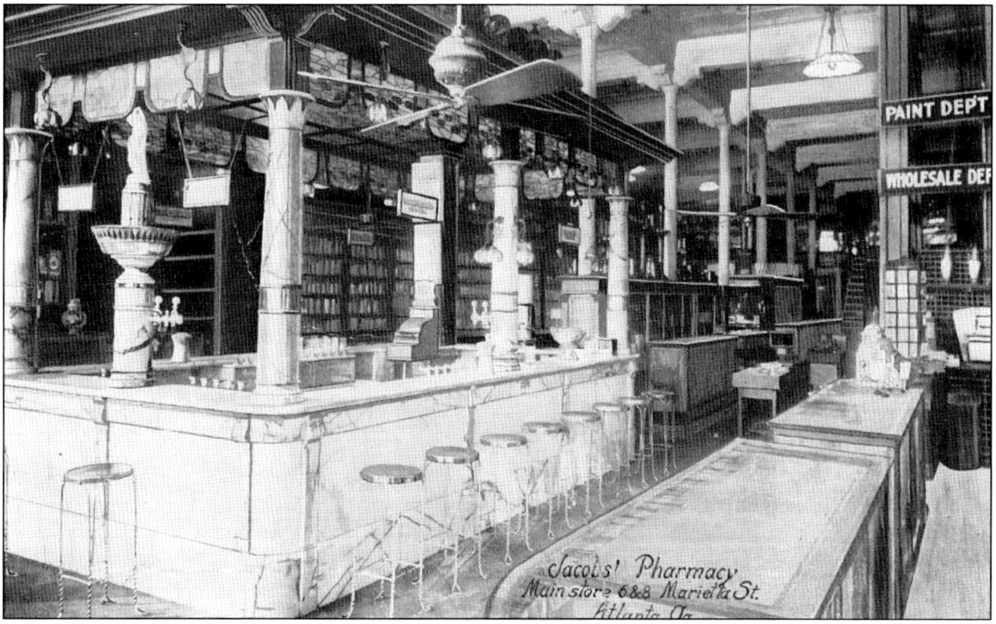

The elaborate interior of Jacobs' Pharmacy on Marietta Street can be seen in this card postmarked May 22, 1912.

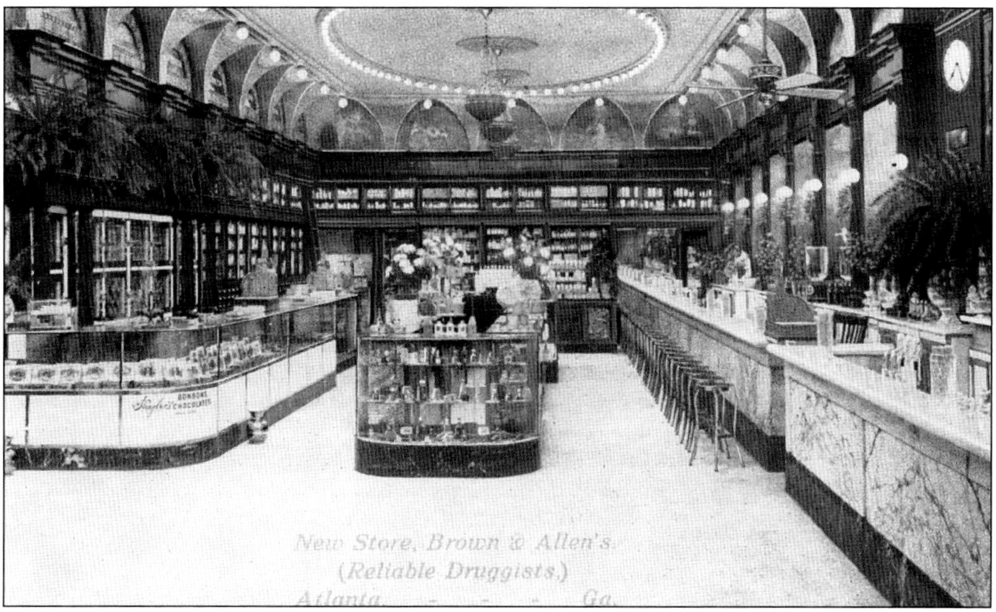

Another elaborate Atlanta drugstore, the "New Store" of Brown & Allen's, is featured in this card. In case the reader needed reassuring, the card stated that Brown and Allen were "reliable druggists."

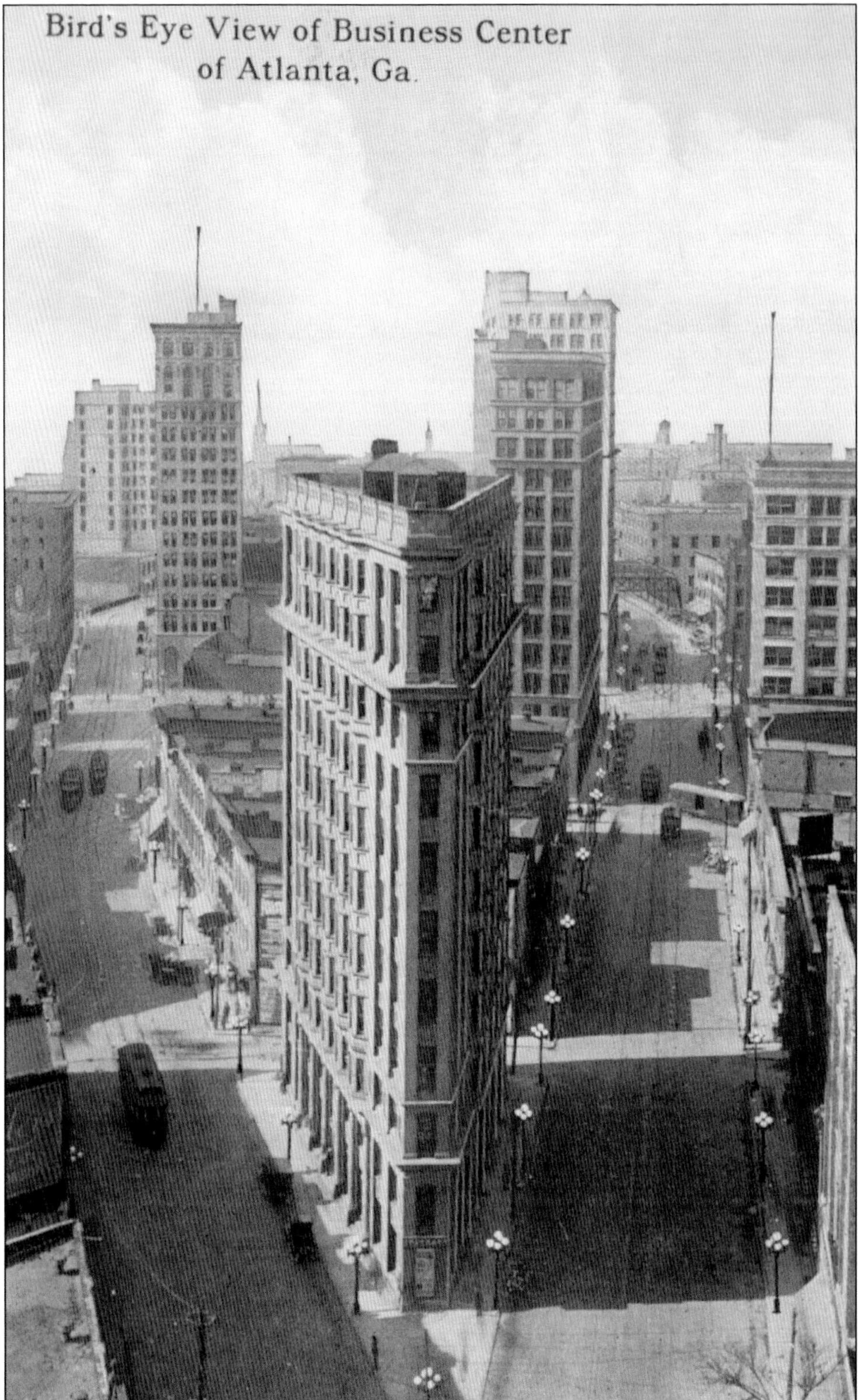

An inkling of the urban landscape that would soon be Atlanta is visible in this card showing the Flatiron Building at the intersection of Peachtree and Broad Streets.

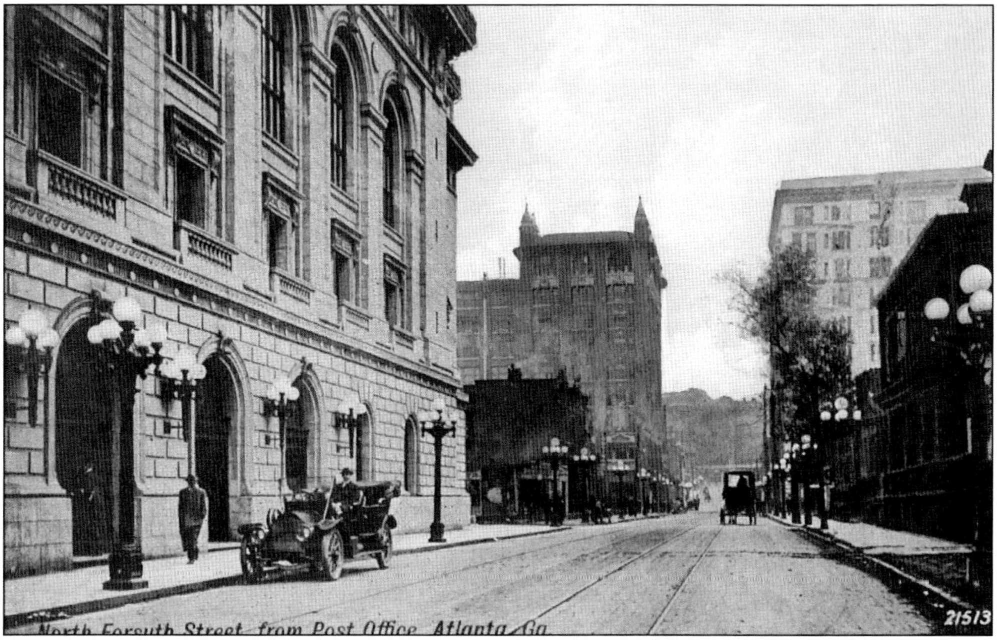

In this view of North Forsyth Street, both a horse-drawn carriage and an early automobile are visible.

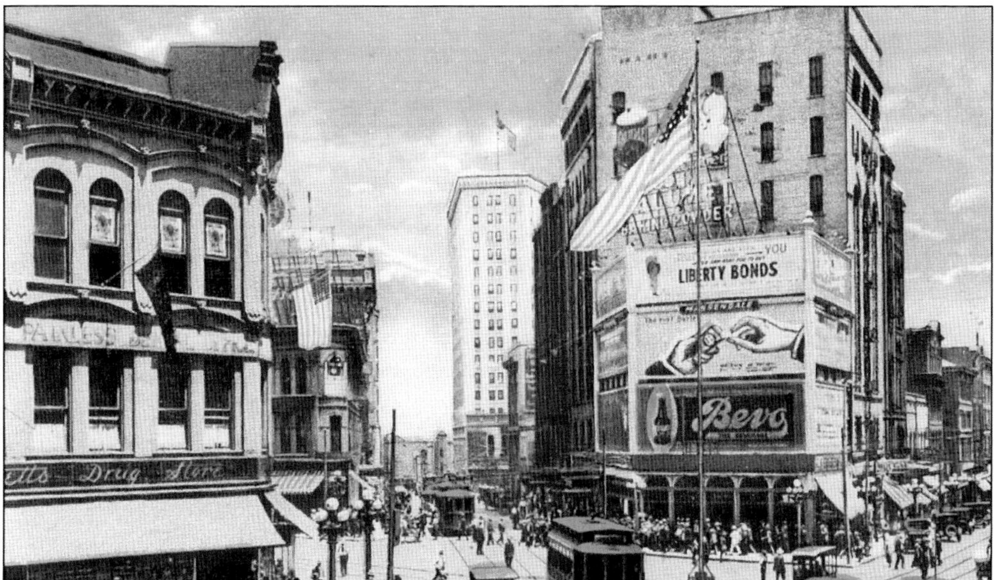

This view of Five Points made during World War I shows advertising for Calumet Baking Powder, Bevo the Beverage, and the all-important Liberty Bonds.

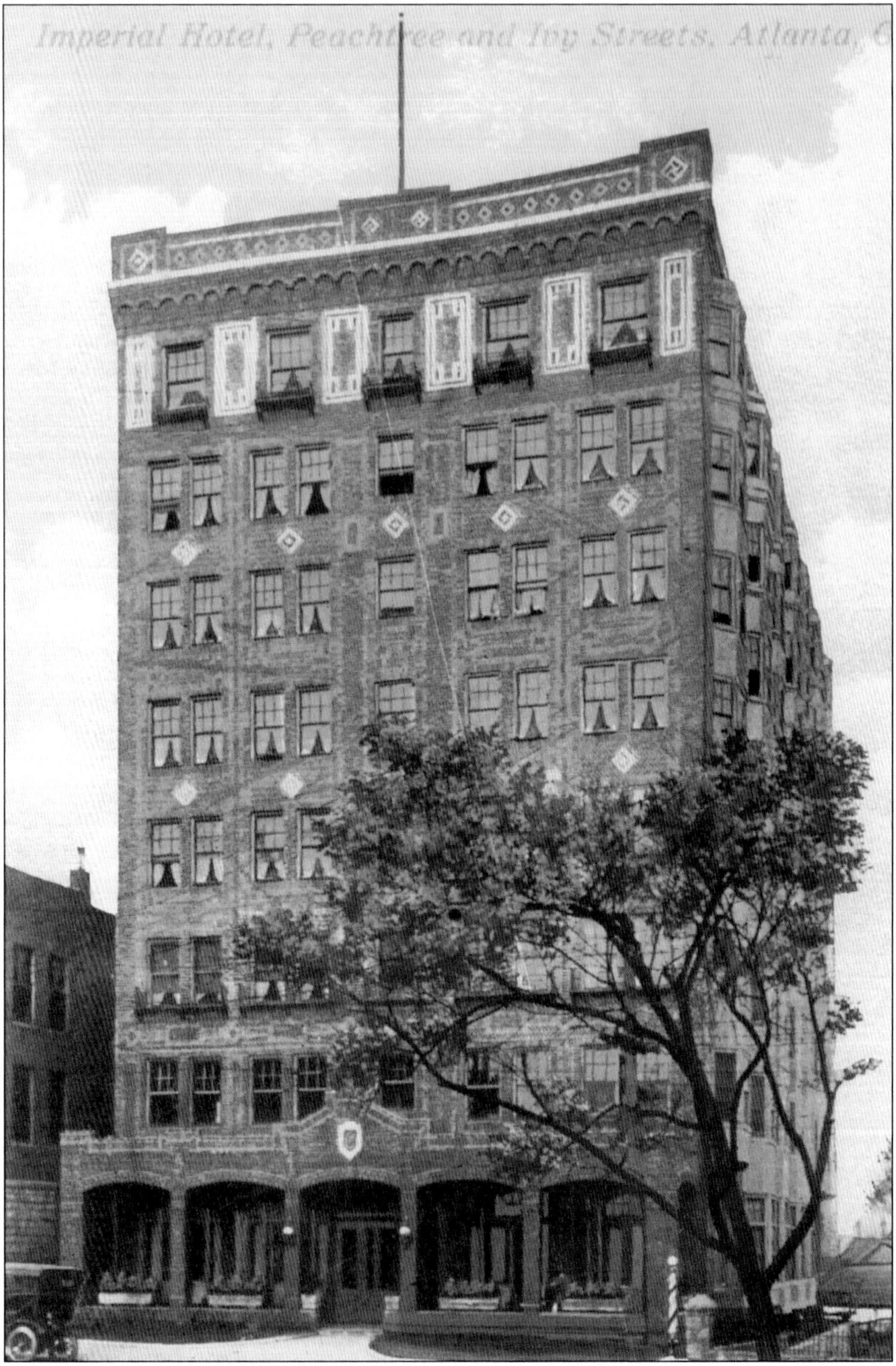

The magnificent Imperial Hotel at Peachtree and Ivy Streets is shown here.

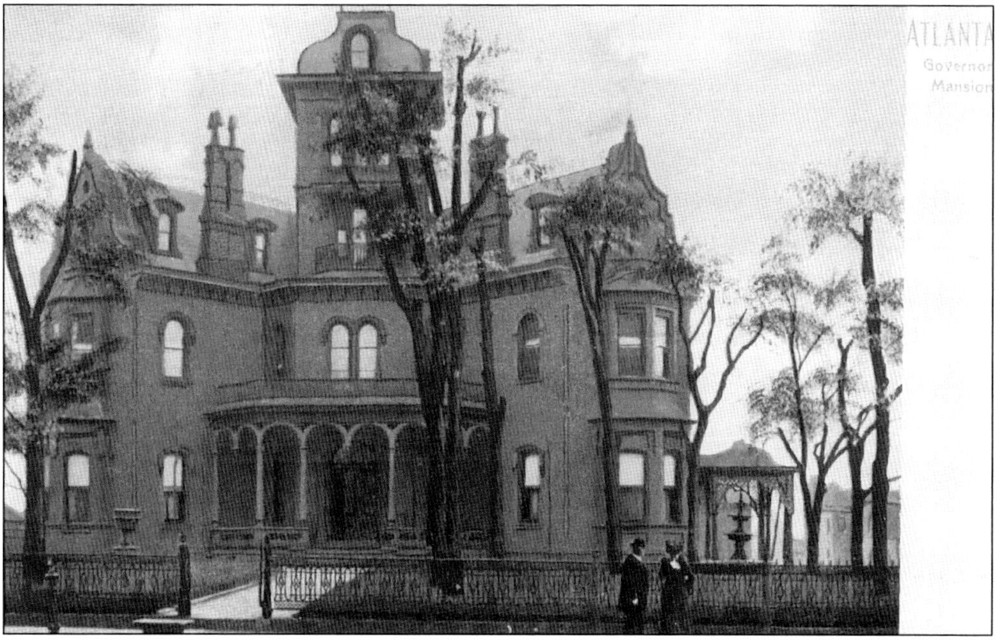

Raphael Tuck and Sons, "Art Publishers to Their Majesties the King and Queen," published this view of the Governor's Mansion.The copy on the back states: "The Governor's Mansion is an old house built in the early Seventies by John H. James; it was afterwards purchased by the Government, and has since been used as the residence of Georgia's Chief Executive."

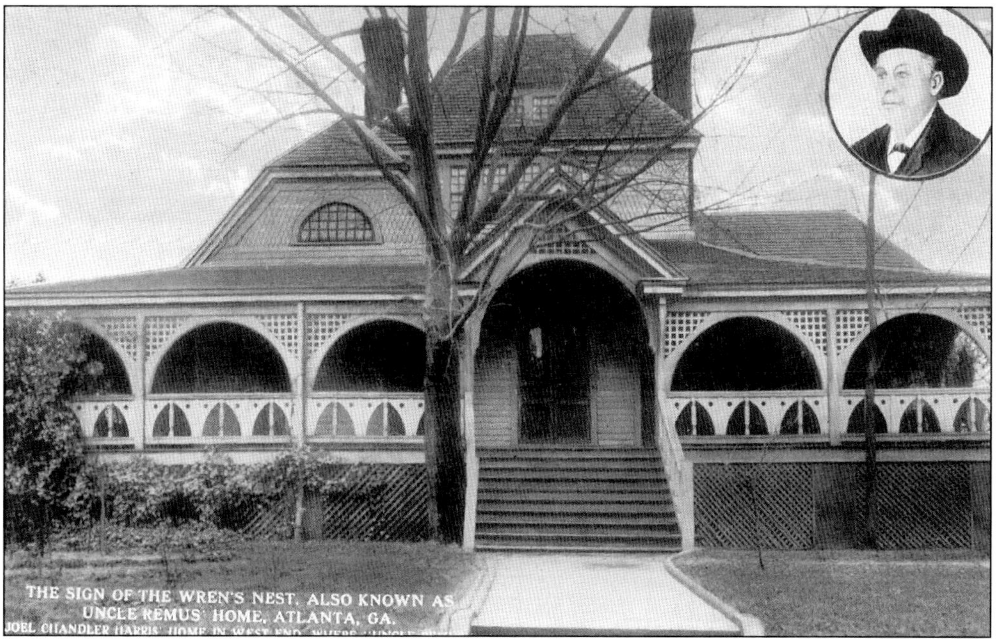

Joel Chandler Harris, the creator of Uncle Remus, lived in The Wren's Nest, which is shown in this card. The bottom of the card reads: "The Sign of The Wren's Nest, Also Known as Uncle Remus' Home, Atlanta, GA. Joel Chandler Harris' Home in West End, Where 'Uncle Remus' Drollery And Philosophy Were Written."

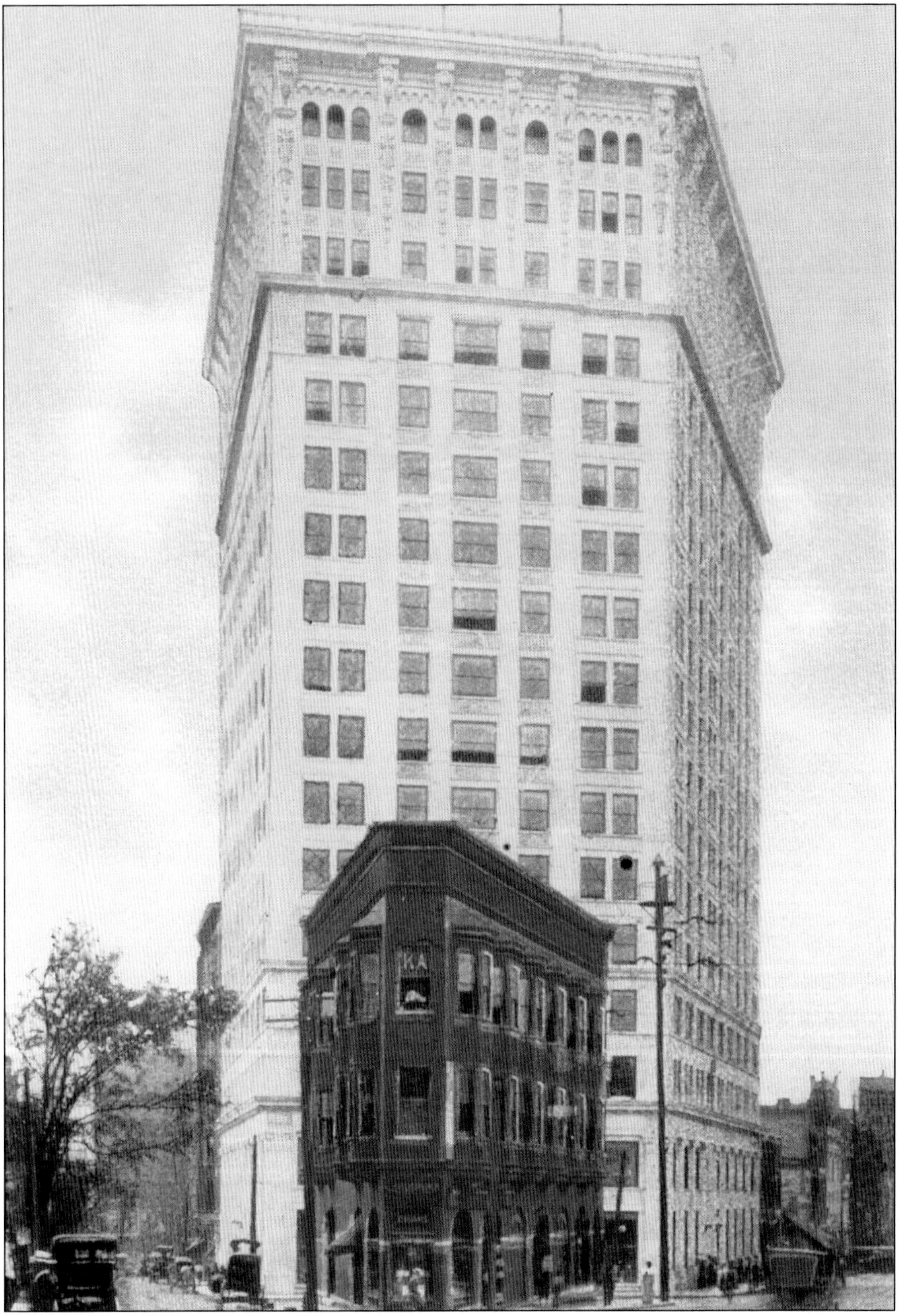

The streets seem to part to make room for the Candler Building, completed in December 1906 by Asa G. Candler of Coca-Cola fame. The building occupies the triangular block formed by Peachtree, Pryor, and Houston Streets.

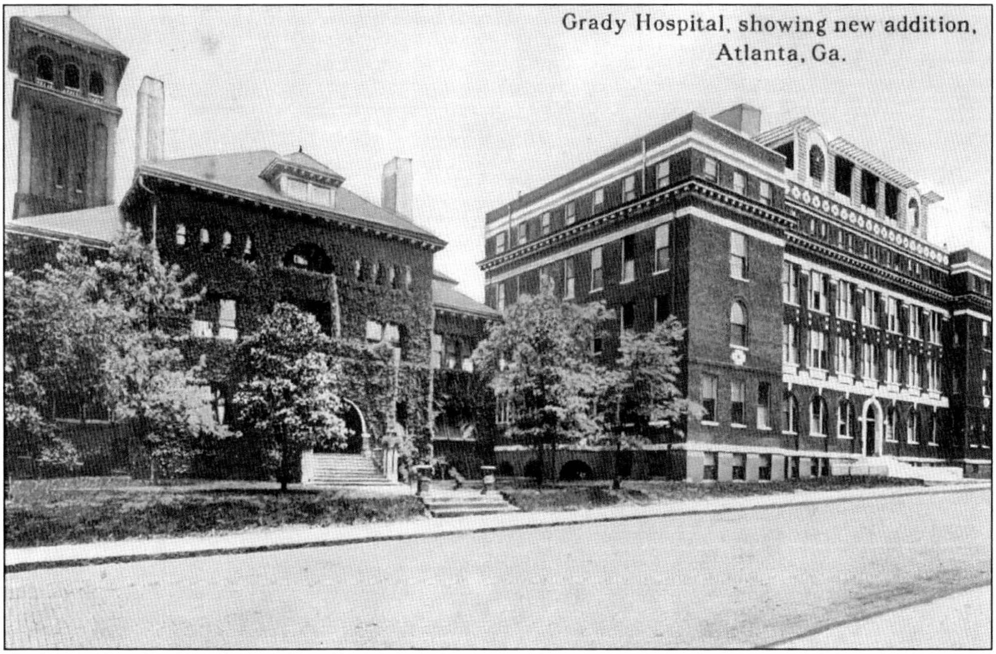

Named for famous Georgia journalist Henry W. Grady, the hospital opened June 1, 1892. A children's ward was added in 1896, and in 1903 a maternity ward was opened. This view shows the new pediatric clinic, which was built in 1908.

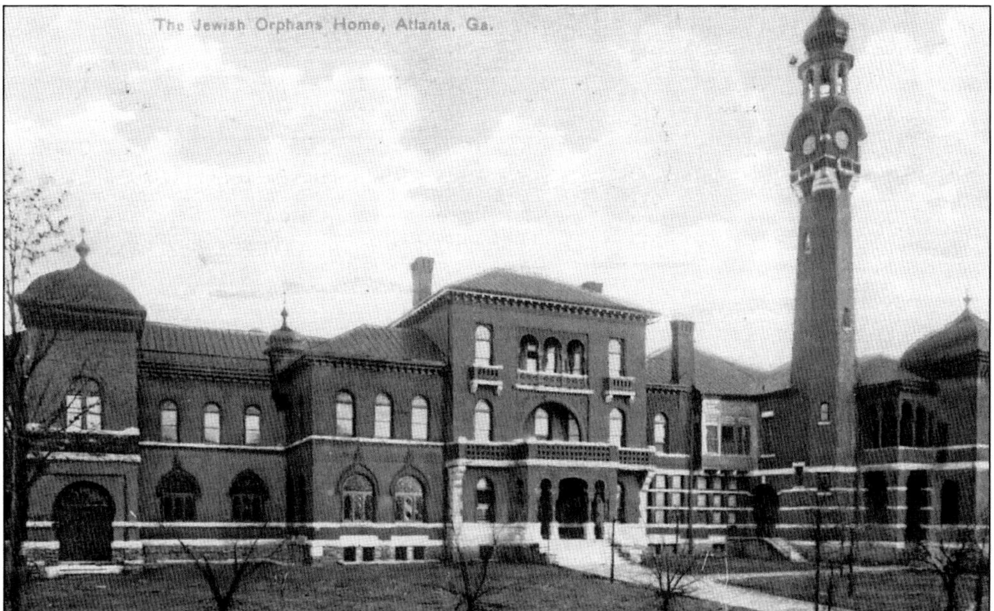

A major benefactor of the Jewish Orphan's Home was German-born Jacob Elsas, who came to Atlanta in 1869 and made his fortune as founder of the Fulton Bag and Cotton Mills.

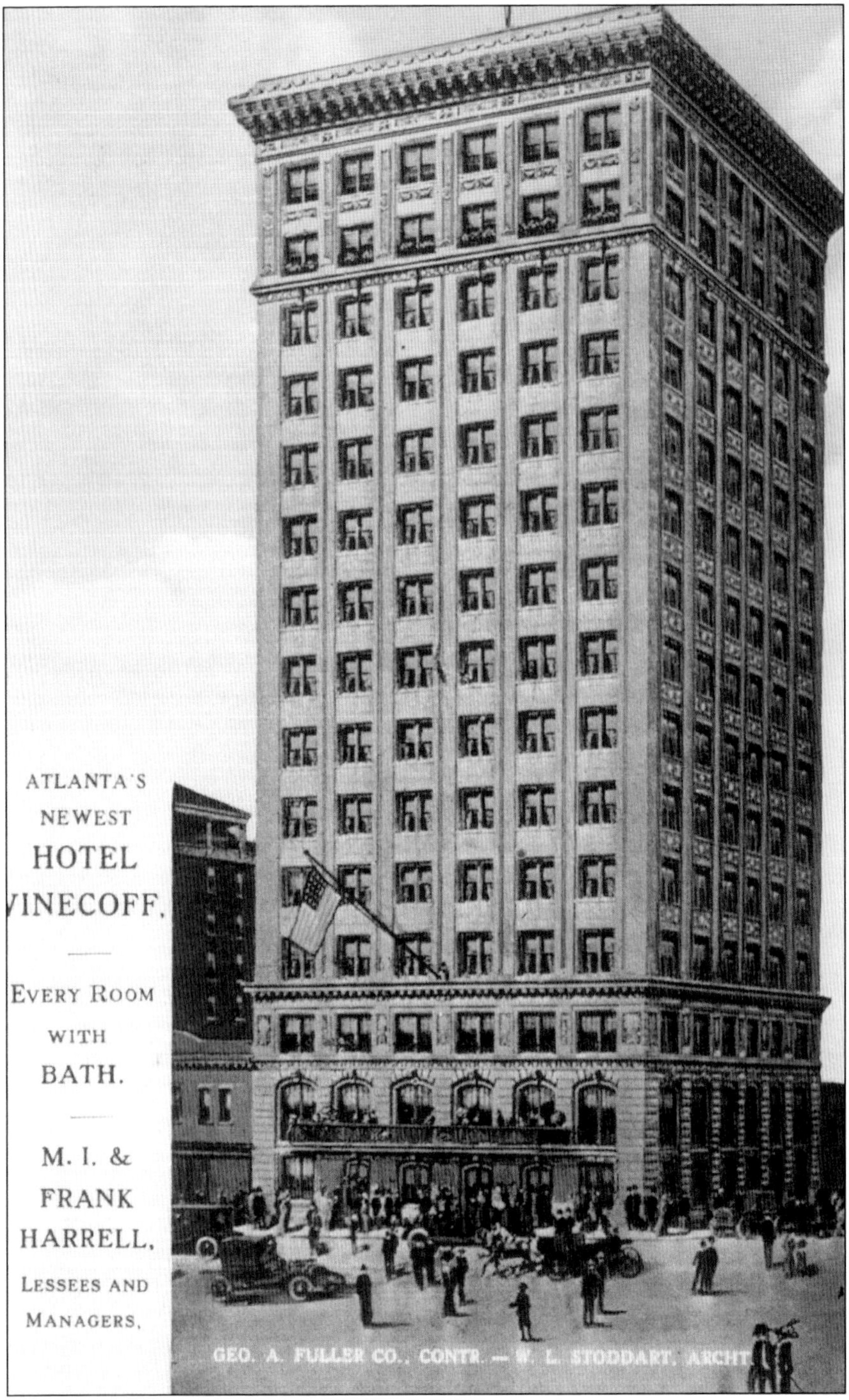

William G. Winecoff began his famous hotel early in 1913 and opened for business on October 30 of that year. The building burned December 7, 1946, and 119 people were killed, including Winecoff and his wife, who were permanent residents. The burned-out building remained standing for several years before being renovated and reopened in April 1951, as the Peachtree on Peachtree Hotel.

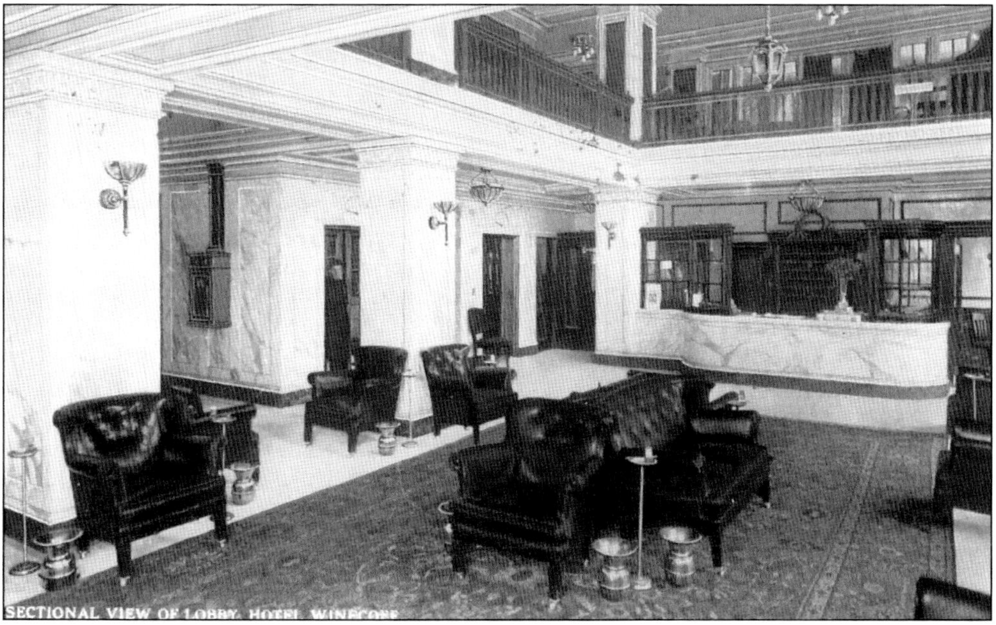

Another card featuring the Hotel Winecoff gives details on the back of the card. The back copy reads: "Hotel Winecoff, Atlanta, GA. 20 rooms with Private Shower Bath $1.50, 75 Rooms with Private Tub Bath $2.00, 75 Rooms with Private Tub Bath $2.50, 20 Parlor Bed Rooms and Bath (Suite) $3.00, 20 Special Equipped Sample Rooms."

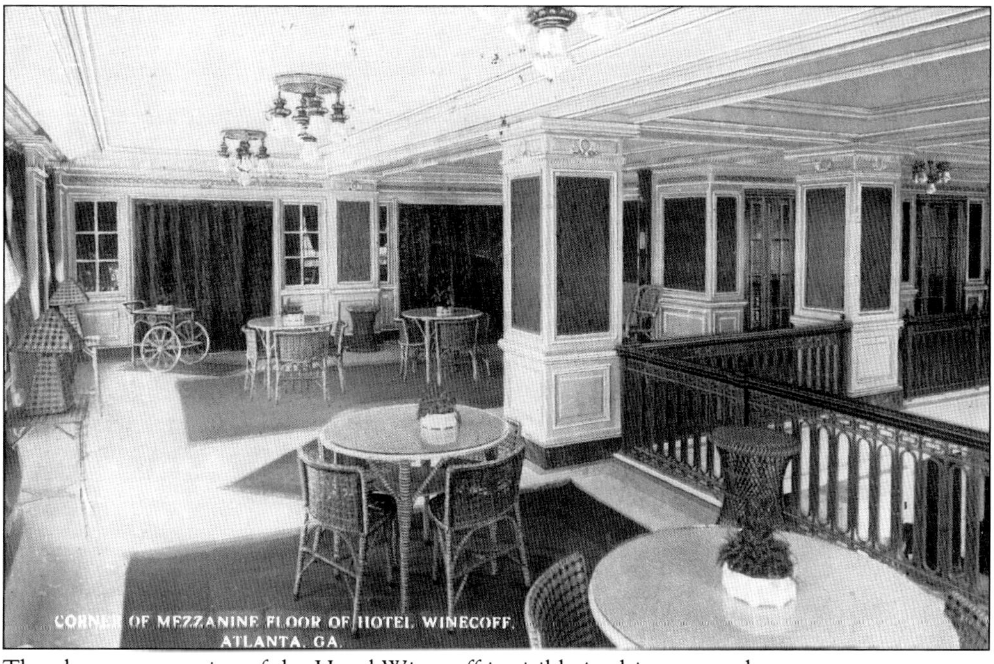

The elegant mezzanine of the Hotel Winecoff is visible in this post card.

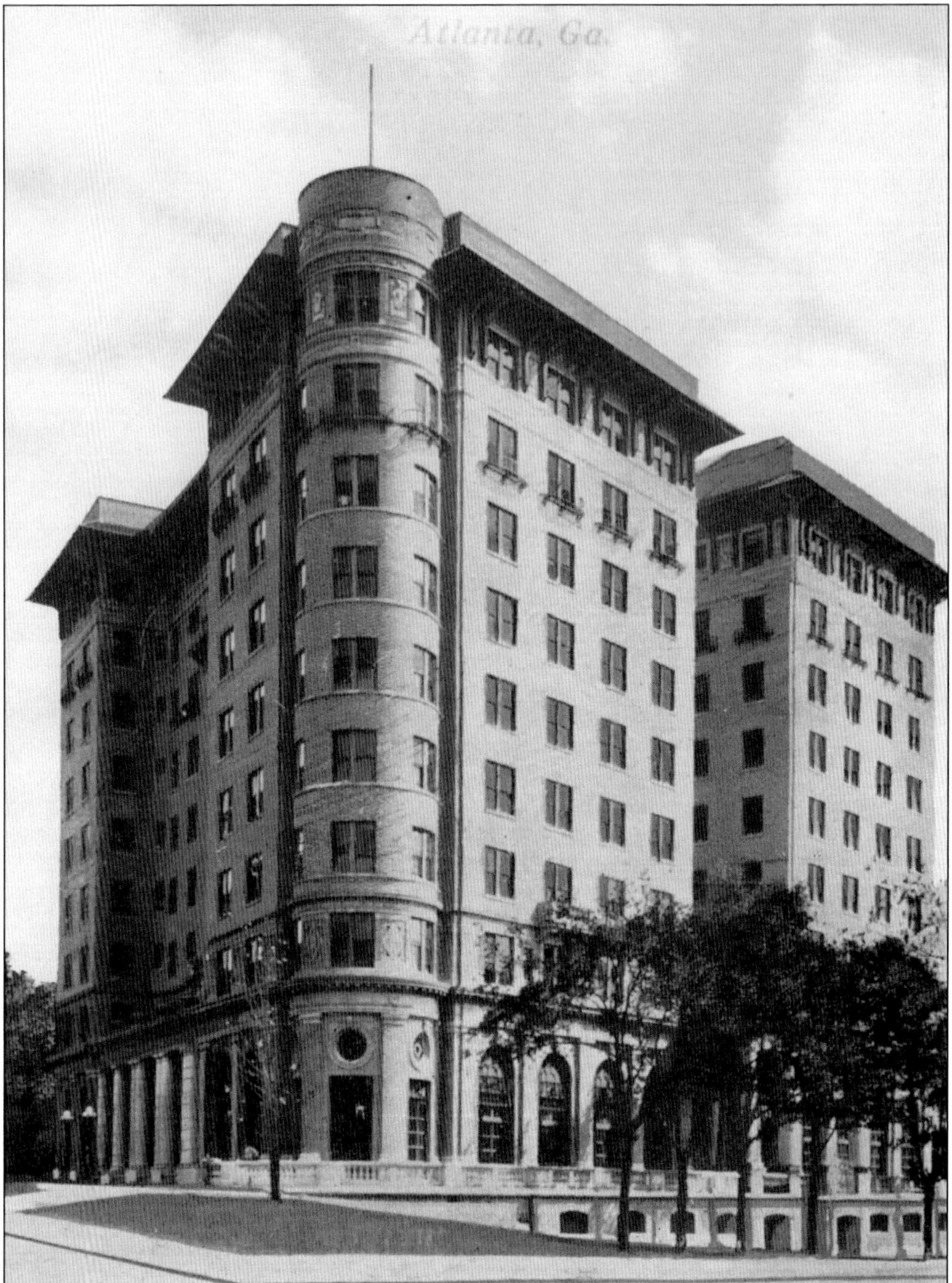

The Georgian Terrace, at Peachtree and Ponce de Leon Avenue, was completed in October 1911 by Joseph F. Gatin, a native Atlantan and son of an Atlanta pioneer. The 10-story, $500,000 structure had marble columns, murals, and fine furnishings and was recognized as one of the finest hotels in the South. Many notable individuals have stayed here including Enrico Caruso, Warren G. Harding, Calvin Coolidge, and the stars and producers of *Gone with the Wind*.

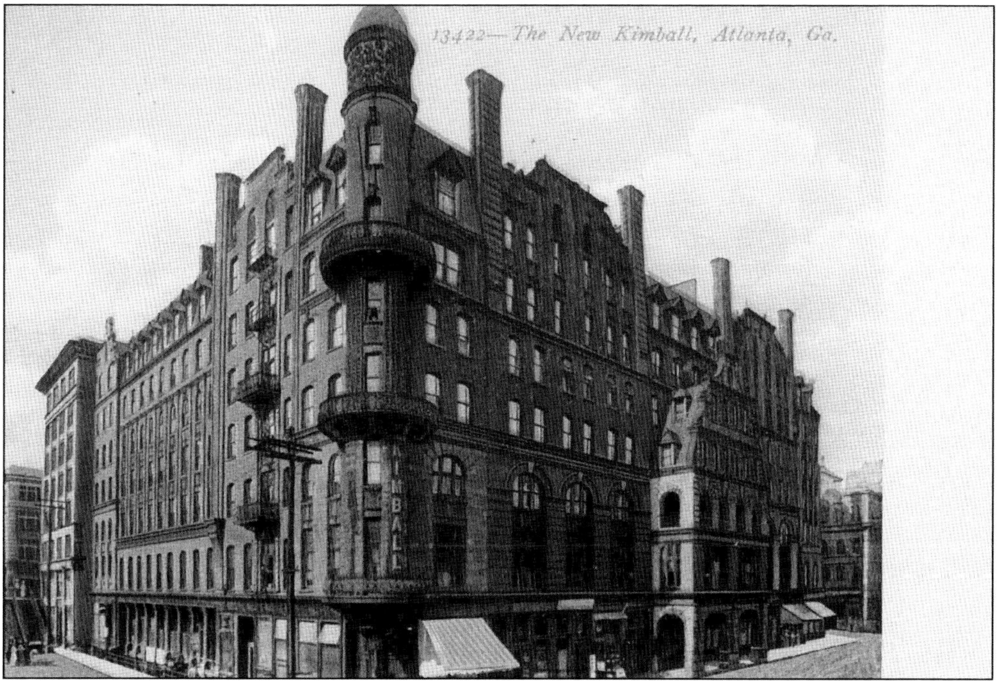

Another beautiful Atlanta hotel, the Kimball House, was built by H.I. Kimball in 1870. The hotel was completely destroyed by fire on August 12, 1883. Although more than 300 guests were staying there, there were no casualties. Within 90 days after the fire the rubble had been cleared and reconstruction had begun. This new 7-story replacement was completed in April 1885 with 357 guest rooms, 31 stores and offices, and 22 public rooms, in addition to kitchens, a bakery, and storerooms. The Kimball was demolished in 1959.

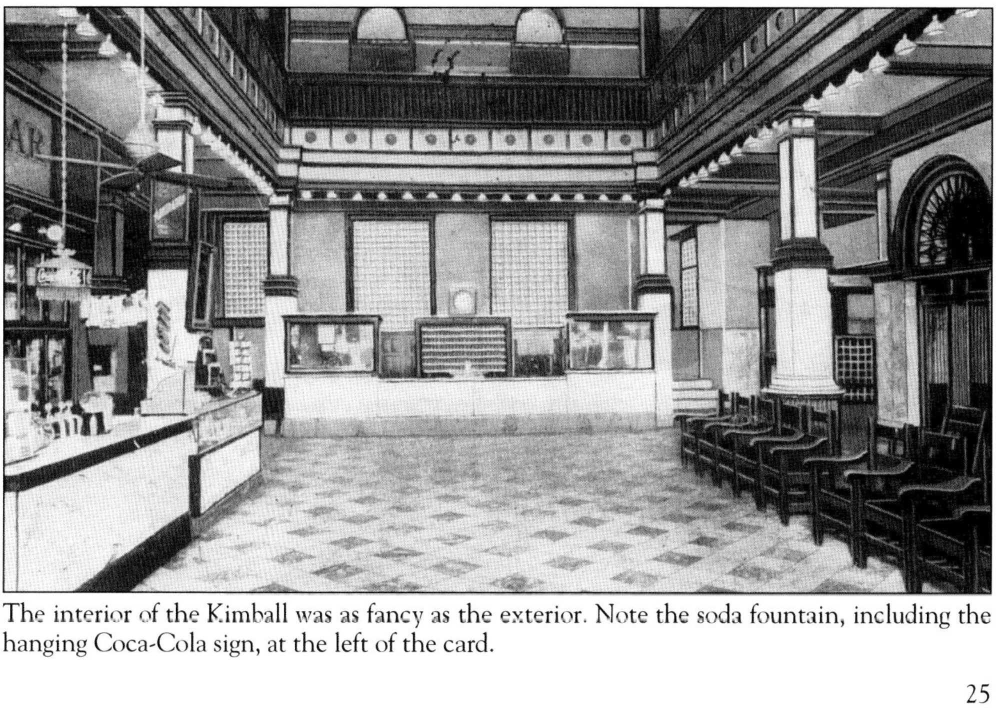

The interior of the Kimball was as fancy as the exterior. Note the soda fountain, including the hanging Coca-Cola sign, at the left of the card.

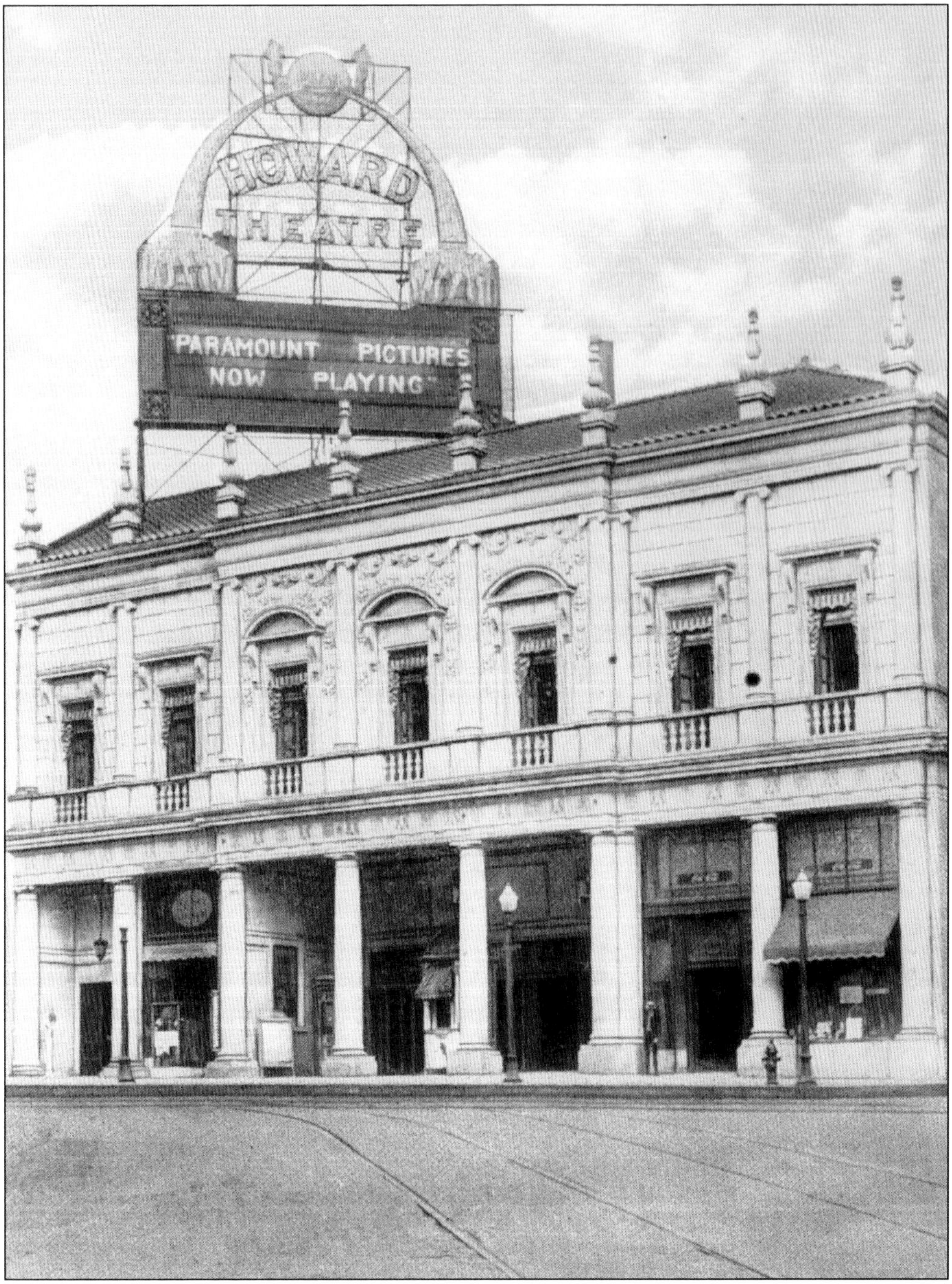

A printed message on the other side reads: "The Howard Theater, operated by the Atlanta Enterprises, considered by many to be the most beautiful theater in America. Constructed by Heintz, Reed & Adler, a local concern, at a cost exceeding one million dollars. The most modernly equipped motion picture theater in the South, the feature of which is a thirty piece orchestra." The Howard Theater was built in 1920 by George Troup Howard (1869–1924), a cotton merchant, just north of Loew's Grand Theater. The Howard later became the Paramount Theater.

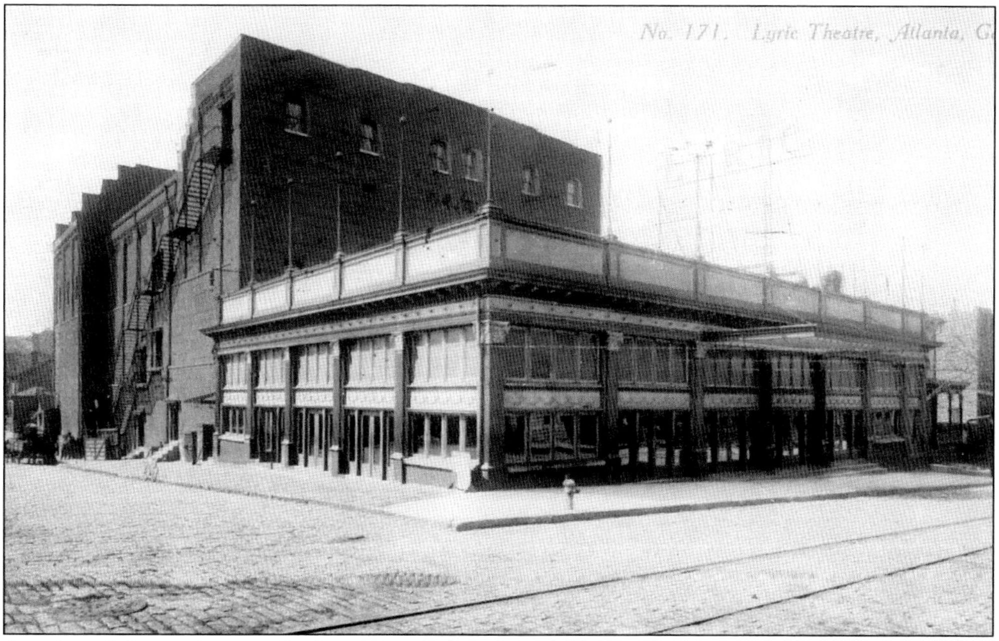

Another Atlanta theater, the Lyric, located at Carnegie Way and Cone Street, was demolished in 1925 and the New Atlanta Athletic Club building was erected on the site.

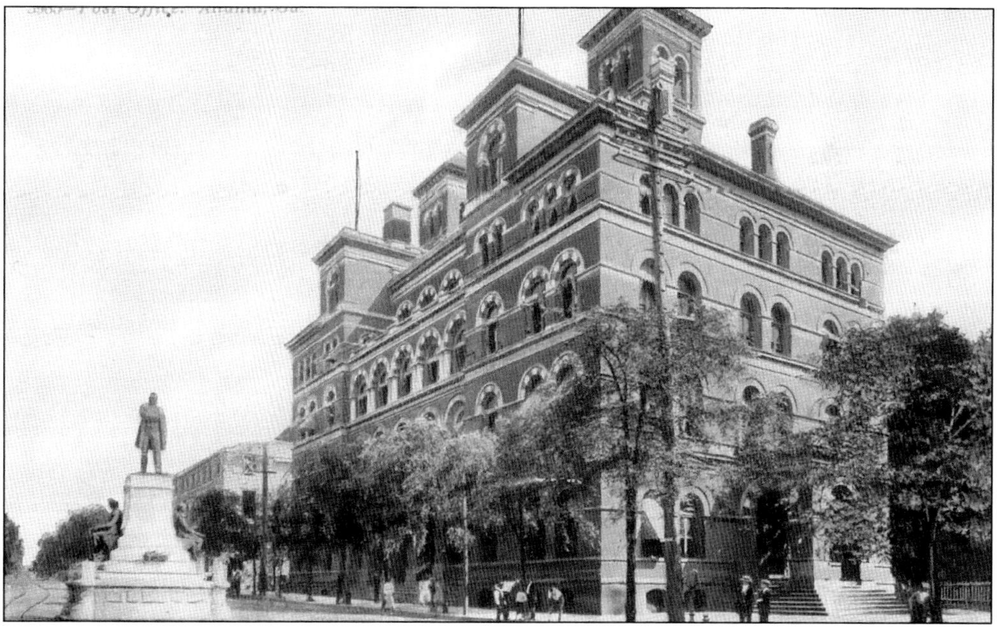

A new Atlanta Post Office, built in 1911 at Forsyth, Walton, and Fairlie Streets, was used until 1933, when it was replaced by a new $3 million building on Forsyth, Hunter, and Spring Streets.

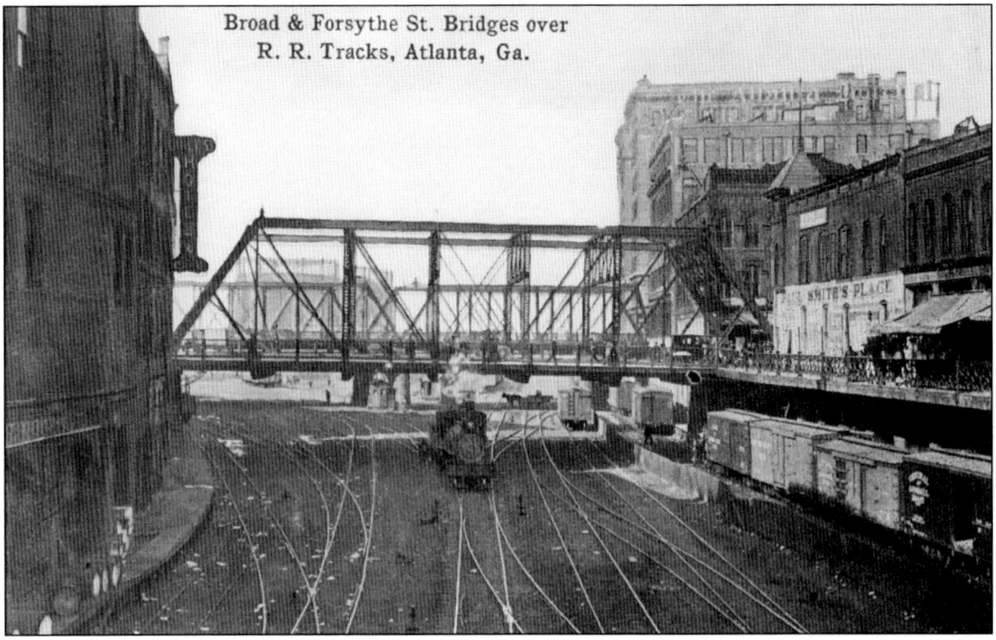

Signs for the Childs Hotel and Paul Smith's Place, as well as boxcars from the Central of Georgia Railroad, are visible in this view of the Broad and Forsyth Street bridges.

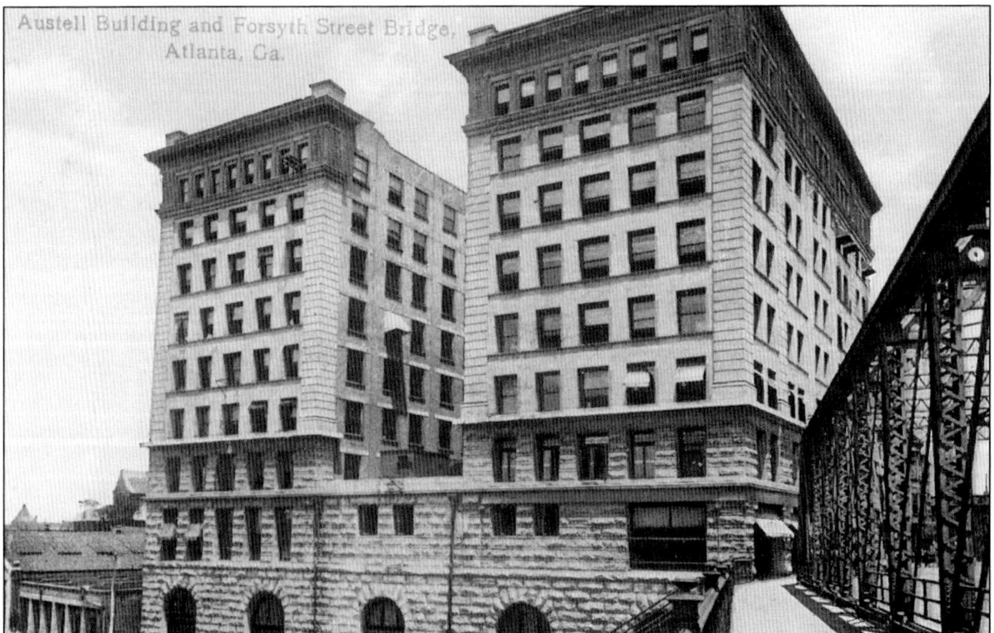

The Austell Building was demolished in 1930 and the Ten Pryor Street Building, an insurance office building, went up on the site.

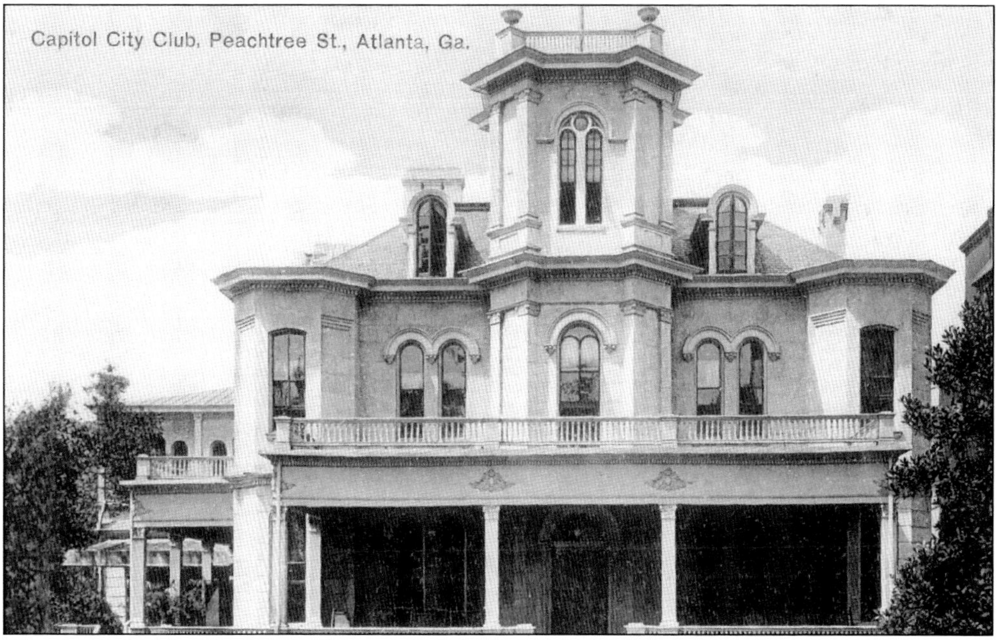

The Capitol City Club at Peachtree and Harris Streets was built in 1911.

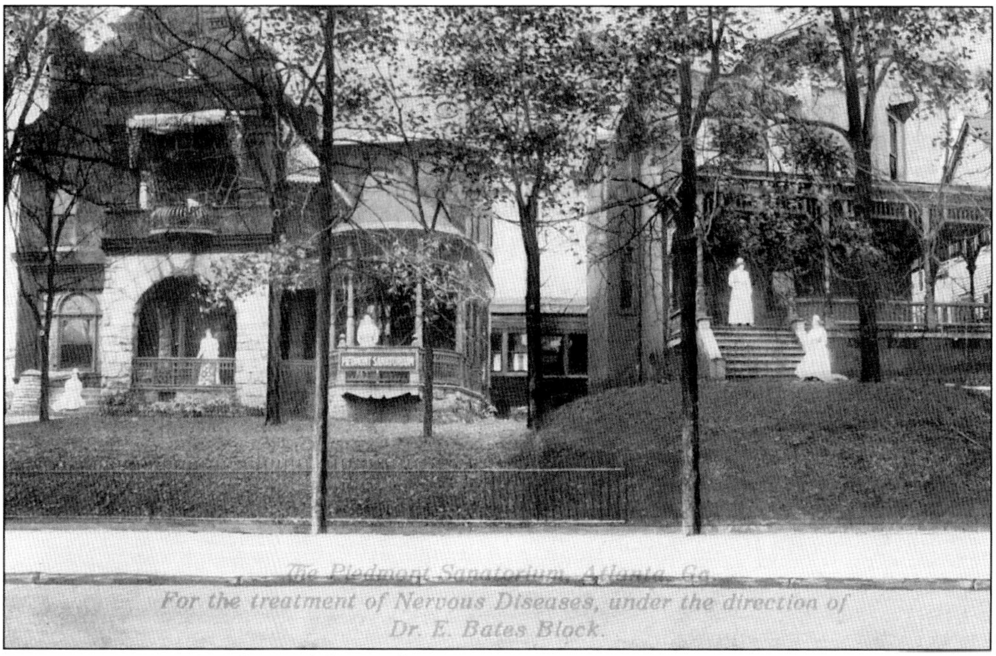

Nurses are pictured in front of the Piedmont Sanatorium, operated under the direction of Dr. E. Bates Block for nervous disorders.

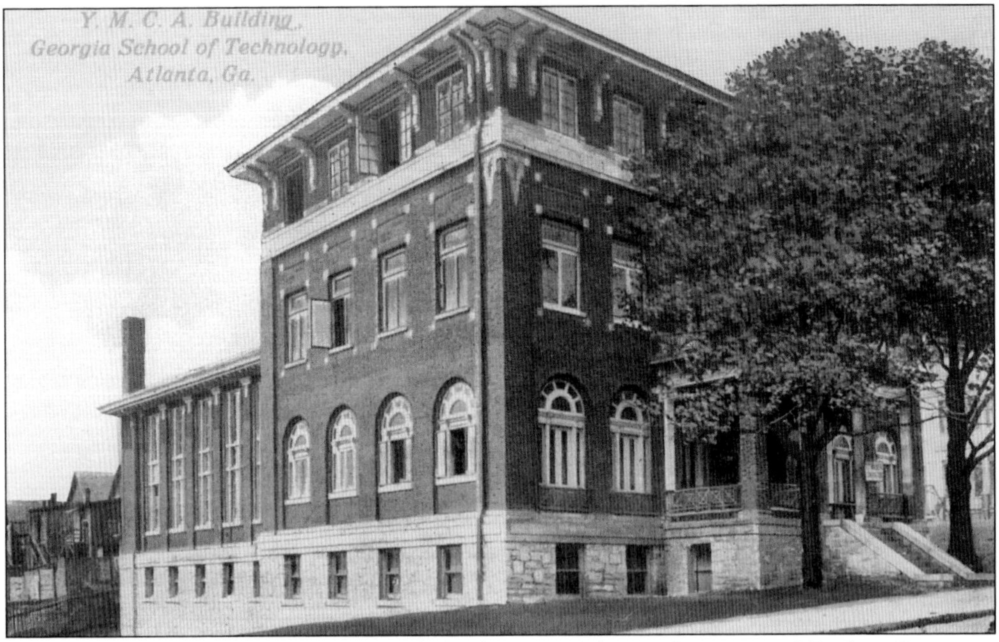

Witt Brothers, post card publishers with facilities in Atlanta, Georgia, and Berlin, Germany, produced this view of the YMCA building at Georgia Tech.

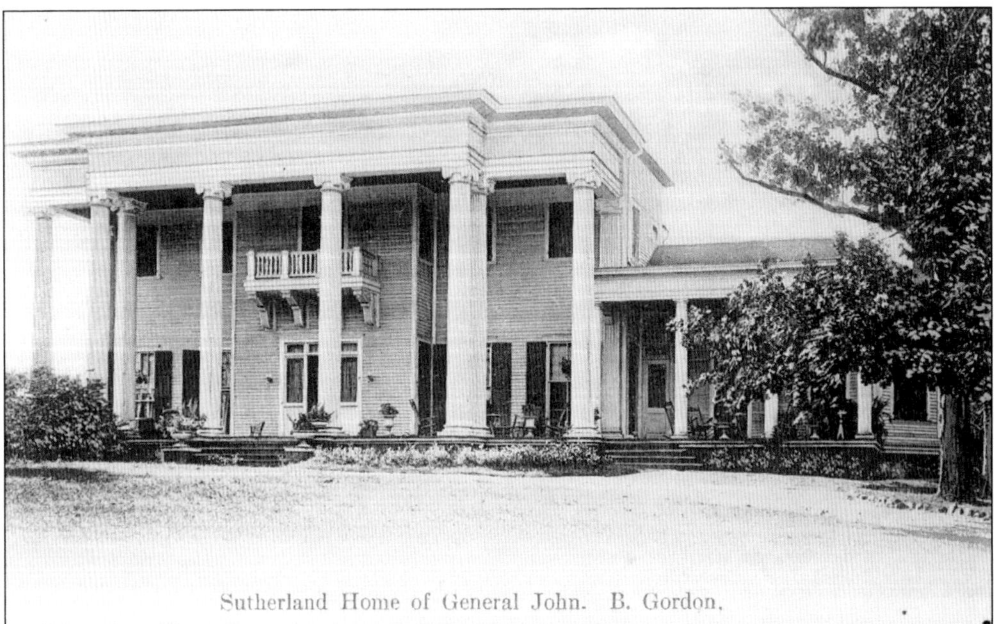

Sutherland, the home of Confederate General John B. Gordon, who served as governor of Georgia from 1886 to 1890, was built in 1899 to replace an earlier house at the site which had burned. Gordon died in 1904 and the house was demolished in 1942.

Two

Some Atlanta Environs

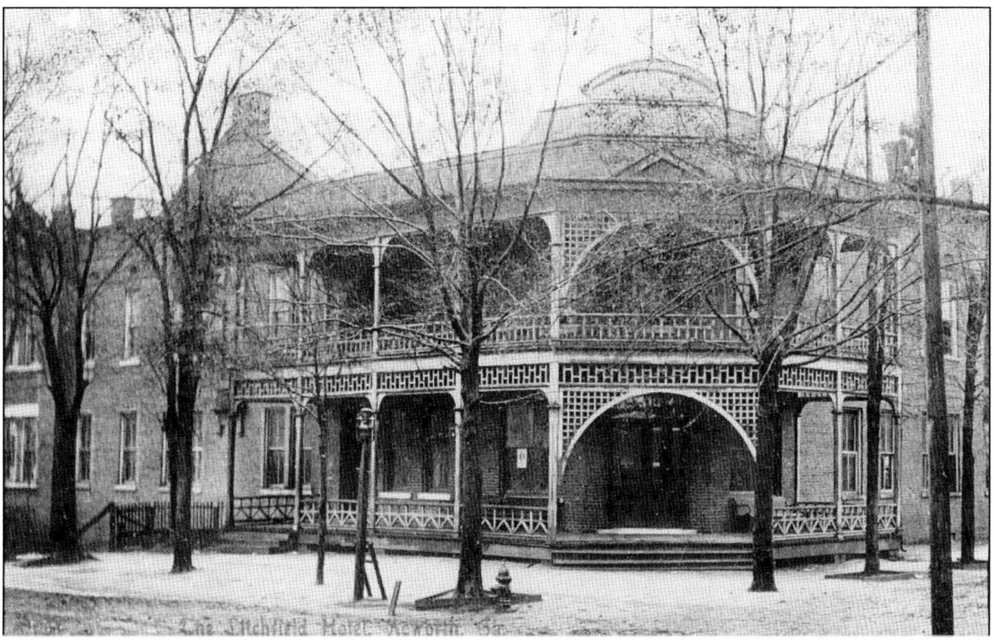

The Litchfield Hotel in Acworth was operated by J.J. Bentley. Note the old-fashioned streetlight in front of the hotel.

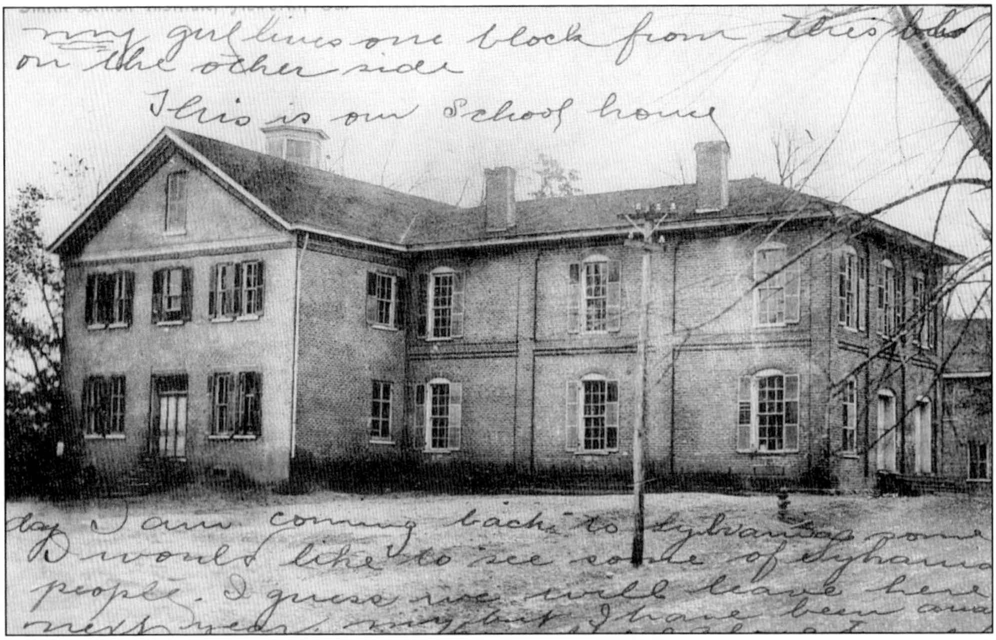

A student at the Smith-Lemon Institute in Acworth was evidently so homesick that it took both sides of this post card to express all he wanted to say.

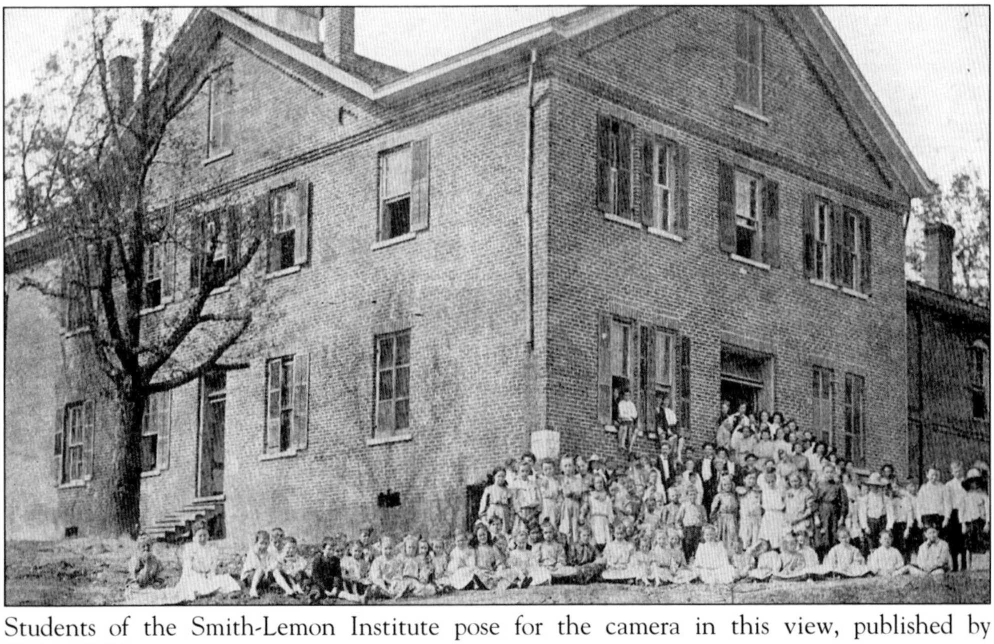

Students of the Smith-Lemon Institute pose for the camera in this view, published by W.M. Webb.

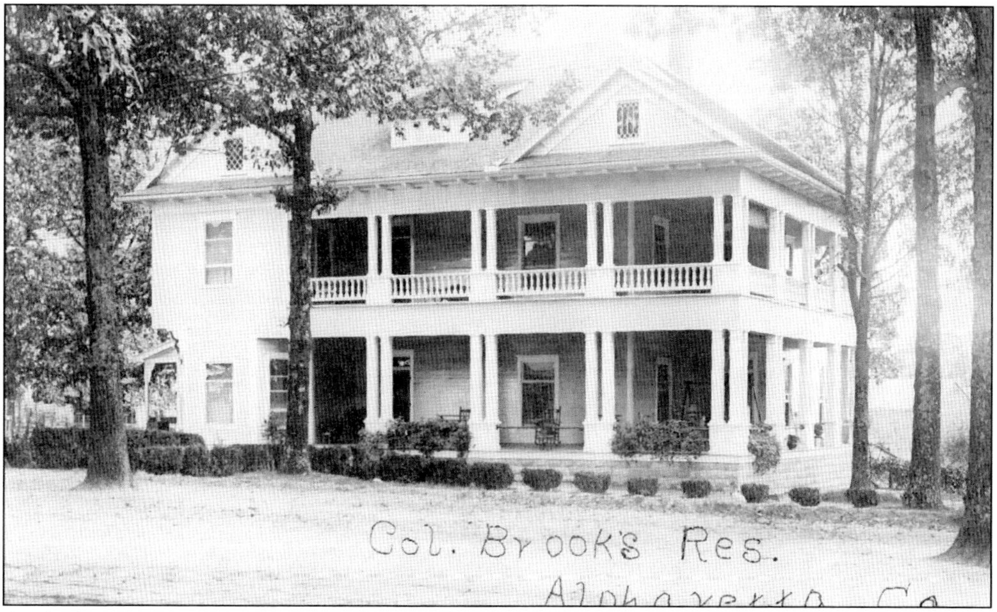

As the hand-written inscription indicates, this was the Colonel Brooks residence in Alpharetta.

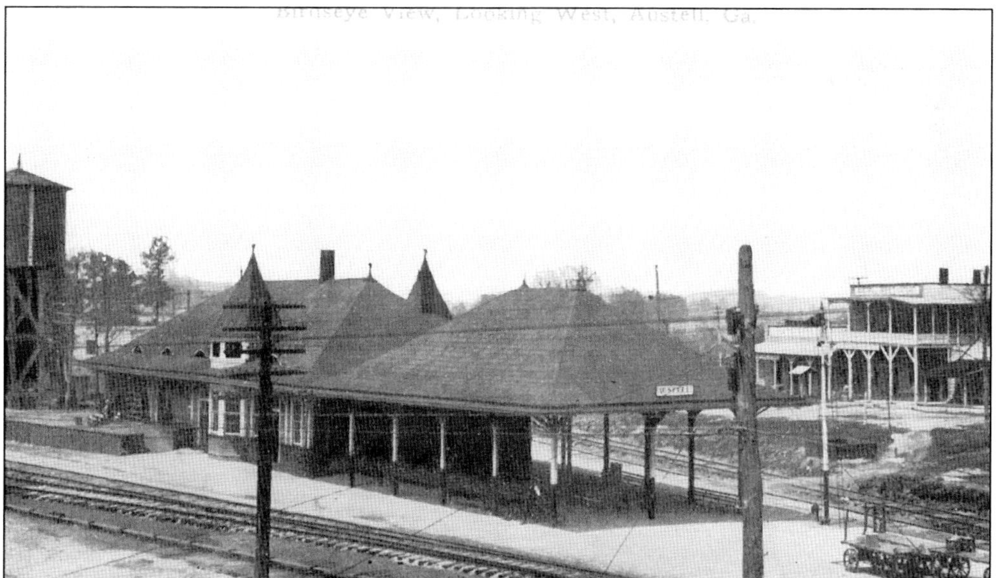

The Austell Railroad Depot is the focus of this view. The Austell Variety Store is visible in the background.

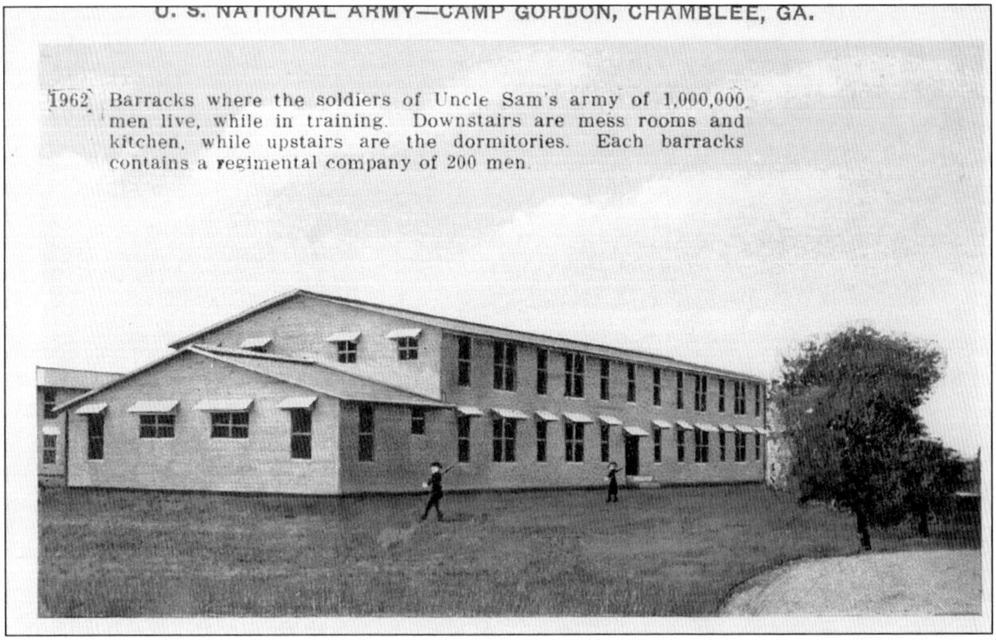

Camp Gordon, named for former Confederate General and Georgia Governor John B. Gordon, was developed in 1917 to provide a training facility for much needed troops during World War I. The government constructed 1,400 buildings to house officers and enlisted men.

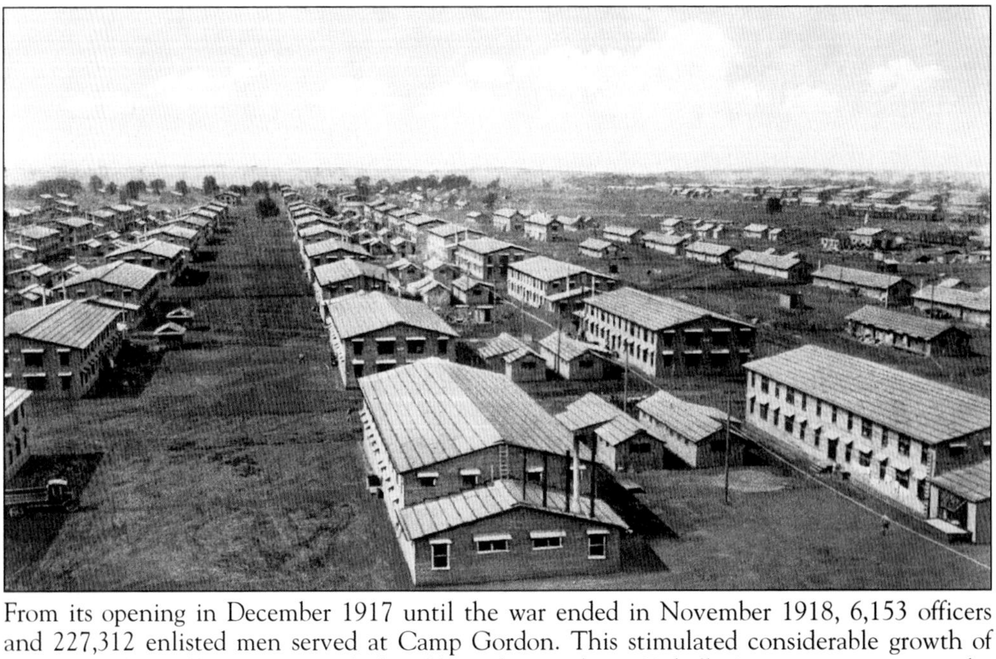

From its opening in December 1917 until the war ended in November 1918, 6,153 officers and 227,312 enlisted men served at Camp Gordon. This stimulated considerable growth of the relatively small community of Chamblee. The Peachtree-Dekalb Airport now occupies the site.

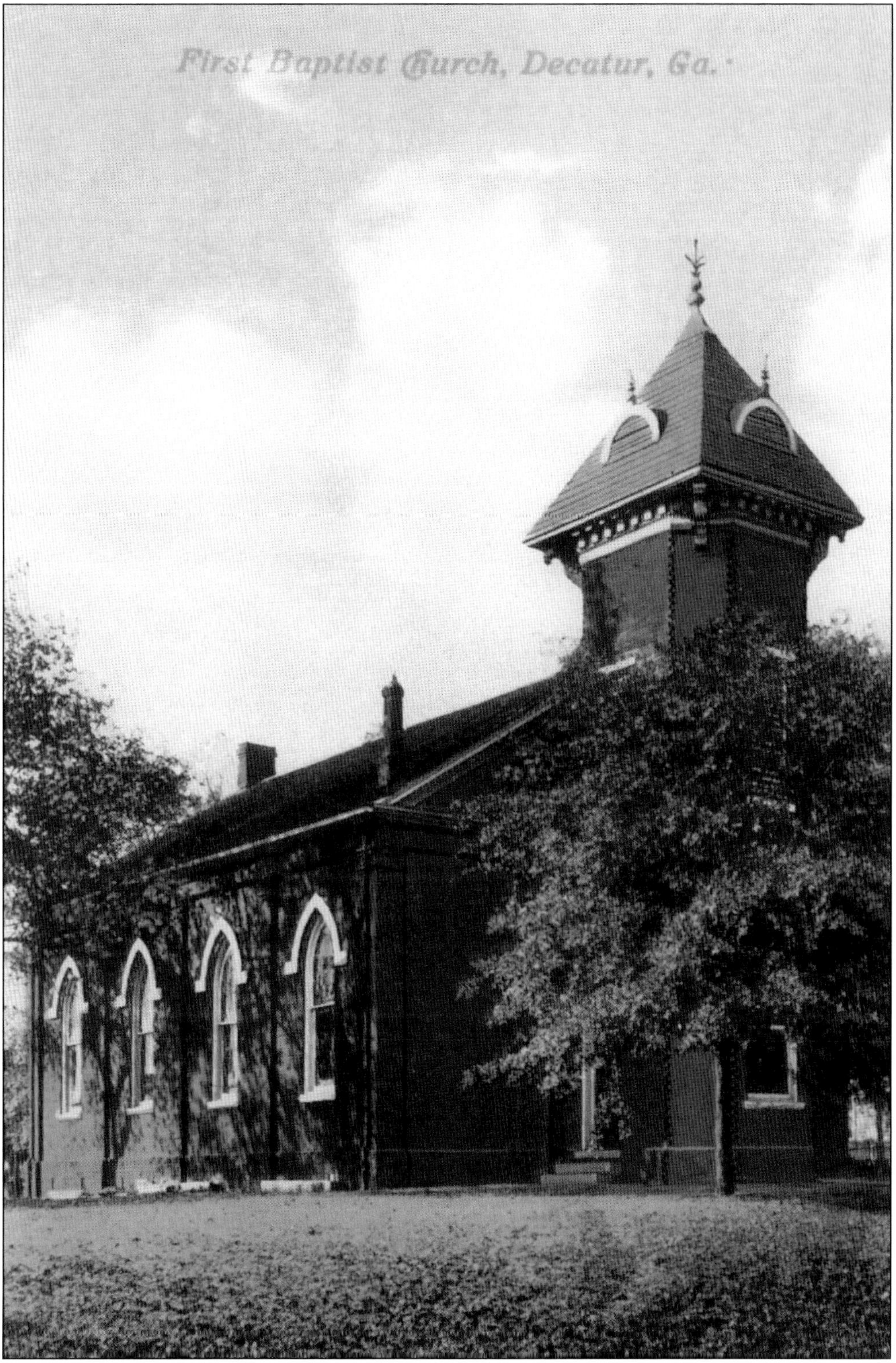

J.O. Bell of Decatur published this view of the First Baptist Church of Decatur.

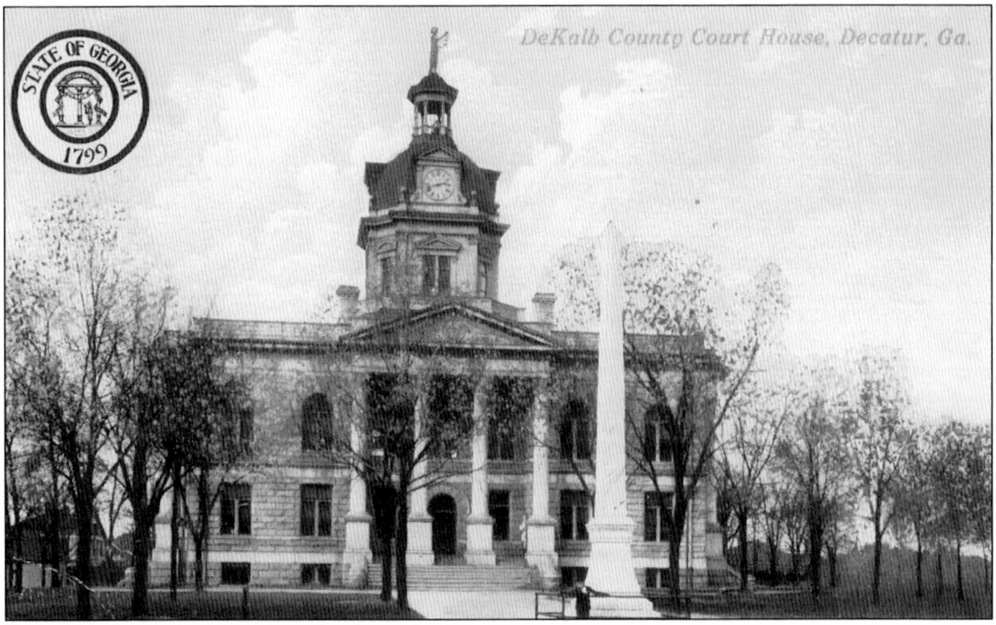

The DeKalb County Courthouse in Decatur was built in 1916 and was replaced by the present courthouse built in 1967. The old building houses the DeKalb Historical Society. On the back of the card, the sender wrote: "I haven't time to write a letter but just want to tell you I am certainly expecting you Fri. or Sat. I am so glad you can come. Write me exactly on what train you will leave so we can meet you. W.B. and I are wild over the thoughts of you and Mildred coming. Hope we can give you a big time. Clara."

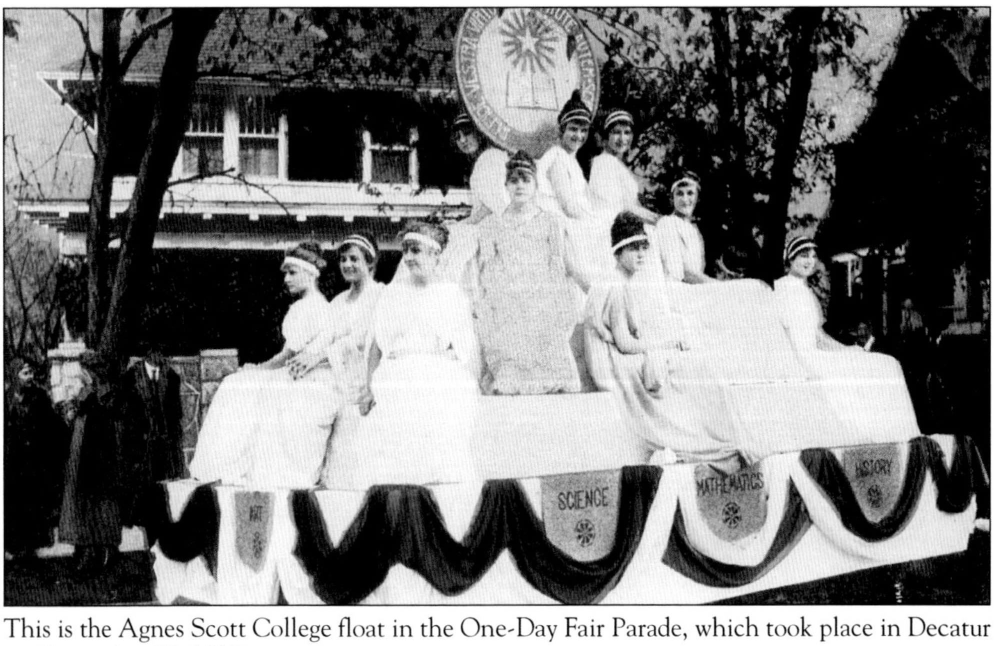

This is the Agnes Scott College float in the One-Day Fair Parade, which took place in Decatur on November 10, 1915.

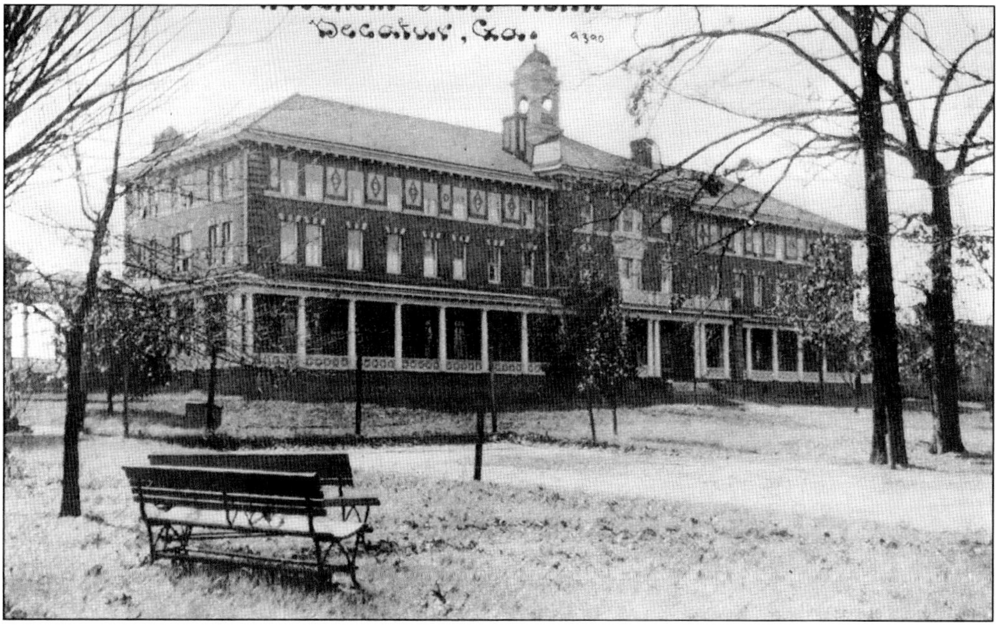

On the back of this post card of Rebekah Scott Hall in Decatur, the sender wrote: "Nov. 7, 1910. Dear Alvie-We haven't much longer to write '1910'-we all have one year less to live."

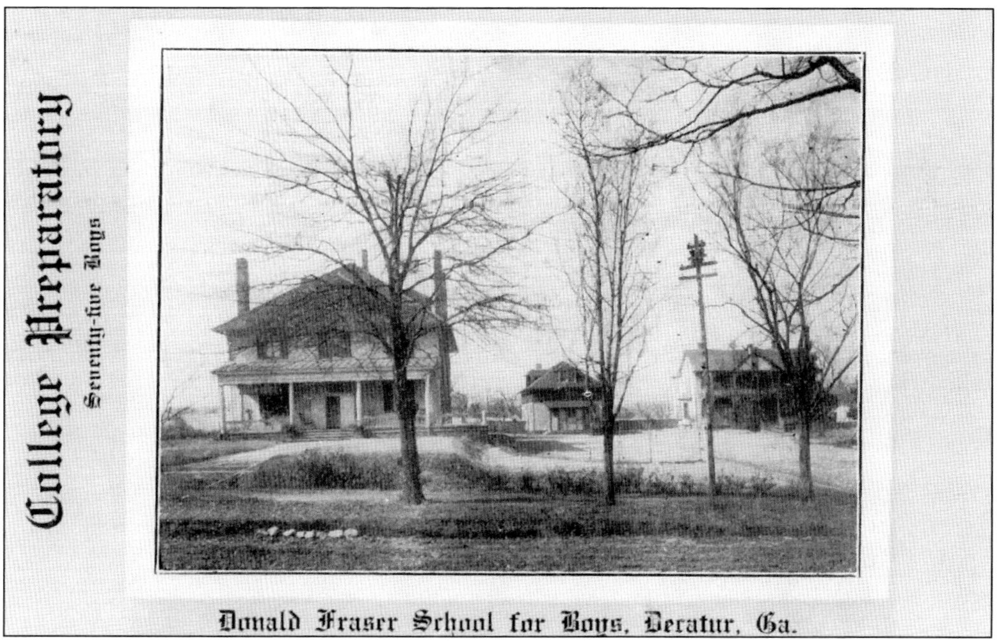

The Donald Fraser School for Boys, a college preparatory school in Decatur, was begun in the early 1870s. Fraser was a native of Liberty County, Georgia, and had served as a chaplain in the Confederate Army. He graduated from the old Oglethorpe University at Midway, Georgia.

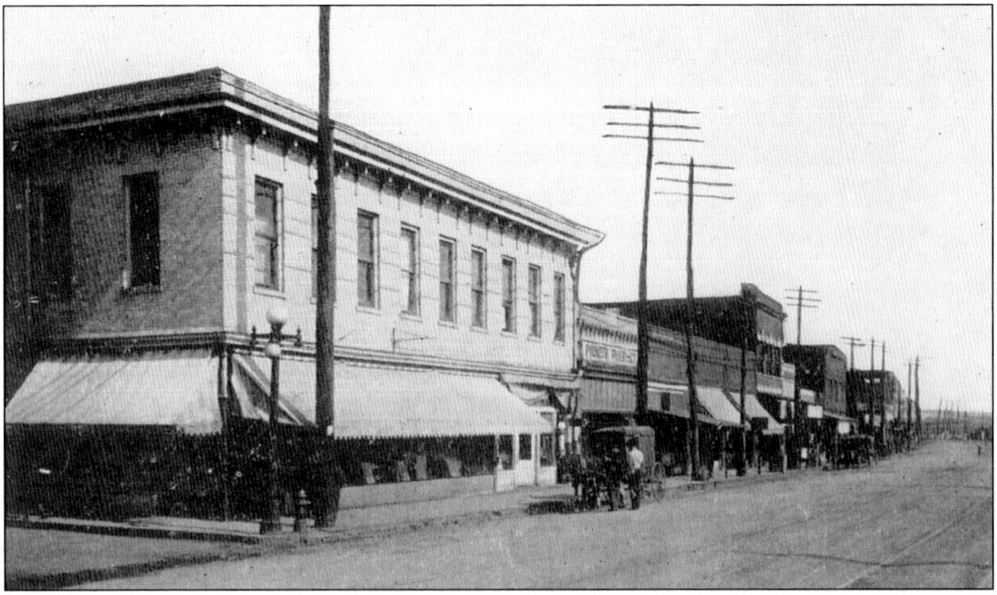

In this view of East Point's Main Street, both horse-drawn carriages and automobiles are visible.

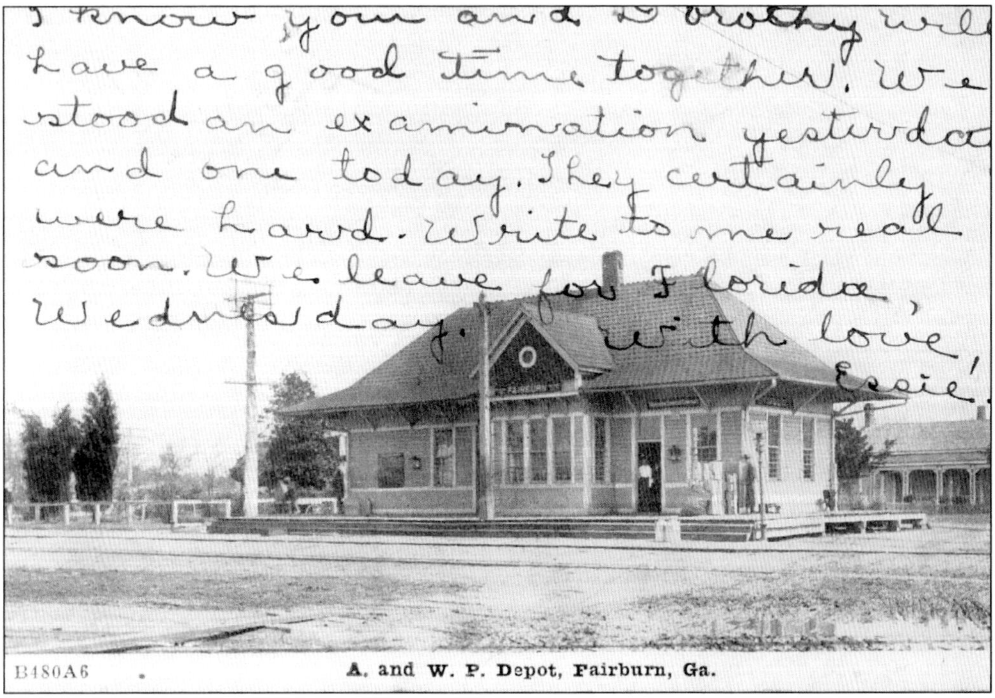

When this view of the Atlanta and West Point Depot at Fairburn was made about 1907, Fairburn was the county seat of Campbell County. Campbell County was merged into Fulton County in 1932.

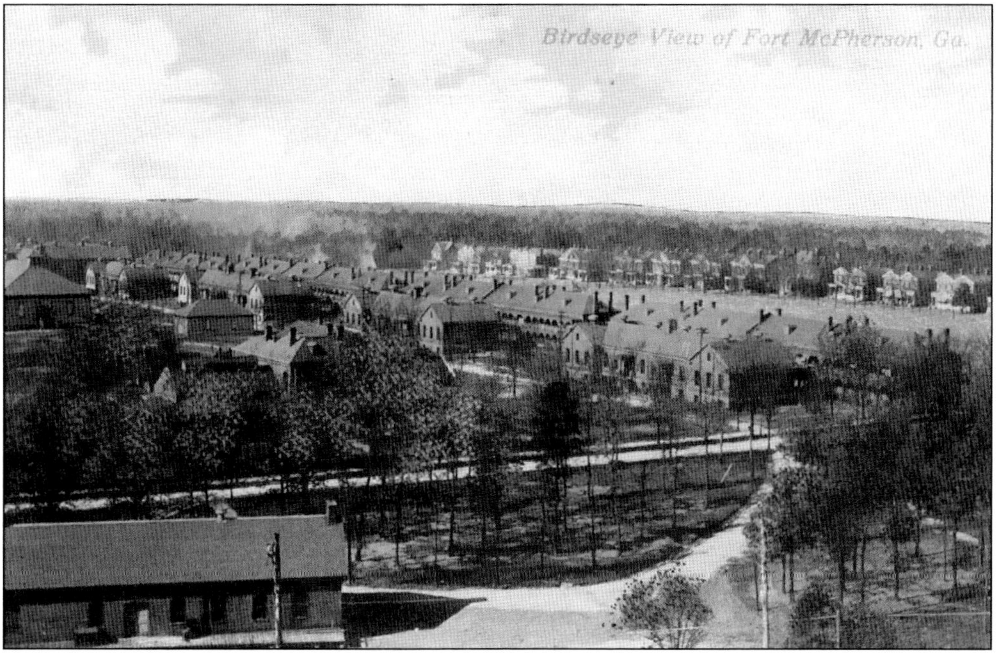

The sprawling grounds of Fort McPherson covered 250 acres when it was completed in 1889. It was eventually expanded to its present size of 504 acres. The fort was named for Confederate General James B. McPherson, who was killed at the Battle of Atlanta in 1864.

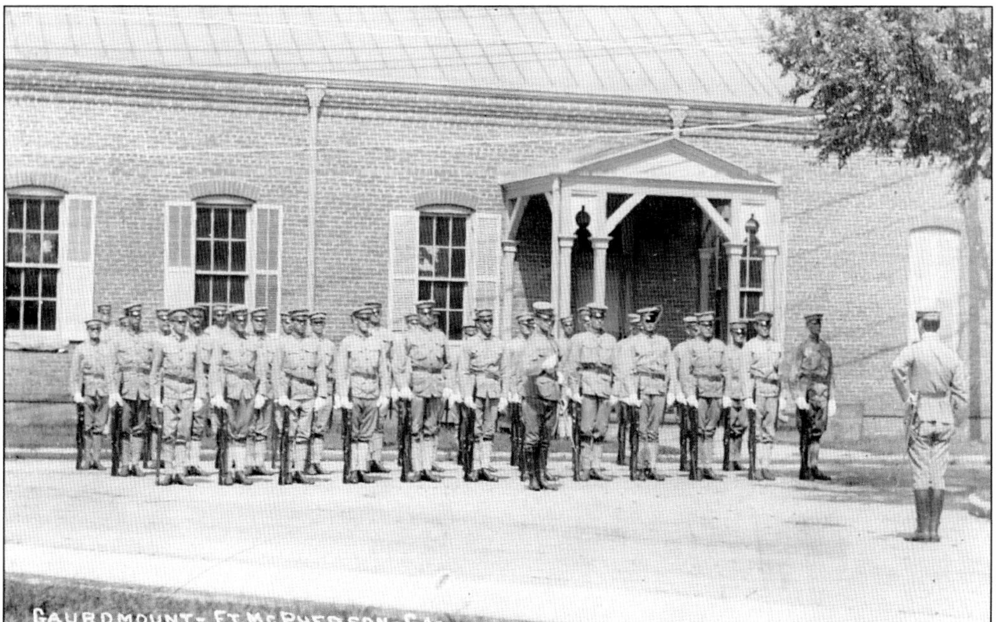

White gloved soldiers in their dress uniforms stand at attention in this post card of Ft. McPherson.

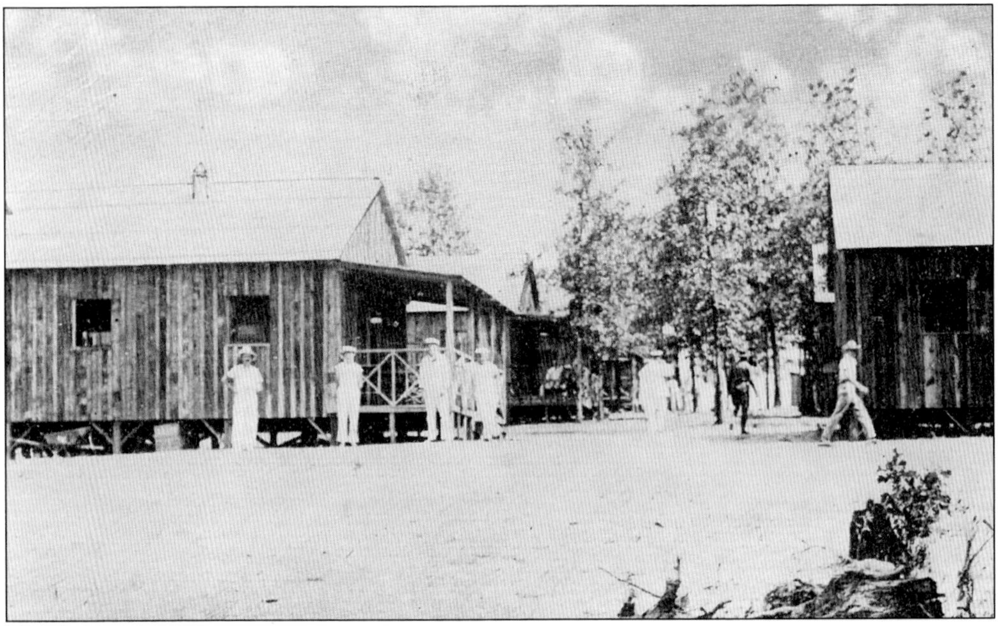

Not only U.S. soldiers populated Ft. McPherson. German prisoners of war were incarcerated here during World War I.

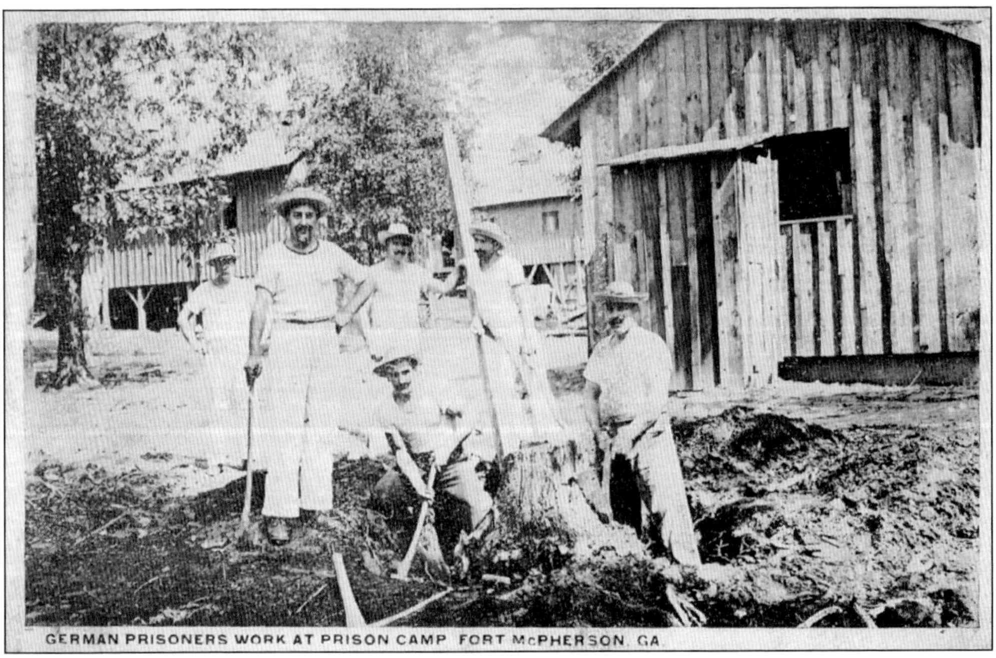

The German prisoners at Ft. McPherson were made to work, also. Here, some prisoners appear to be removing a tree stump.

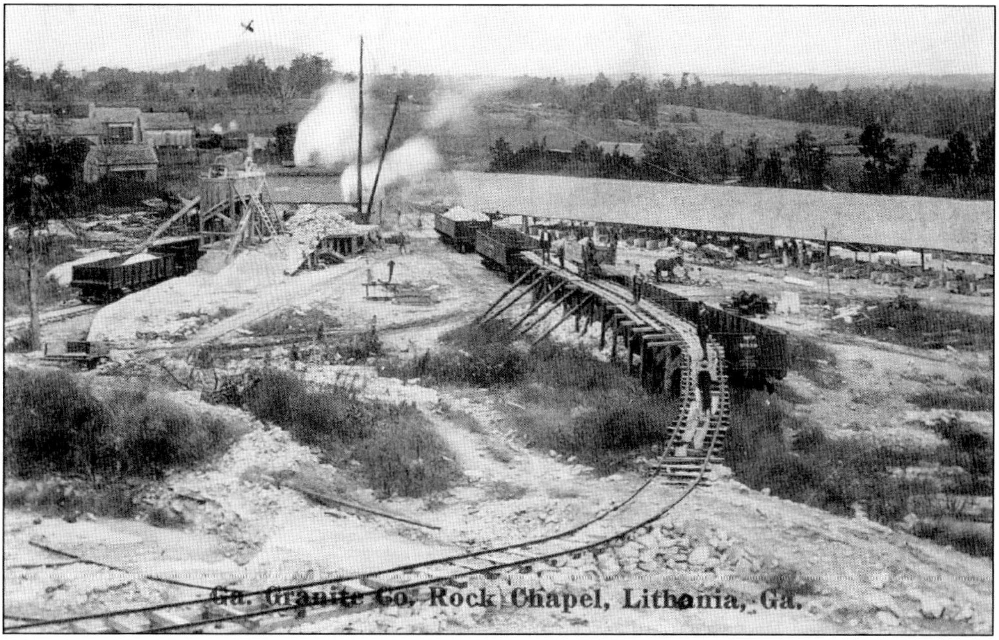

This is a view of the Georgia Granite Company's stone-cutting shed at Lithonia.

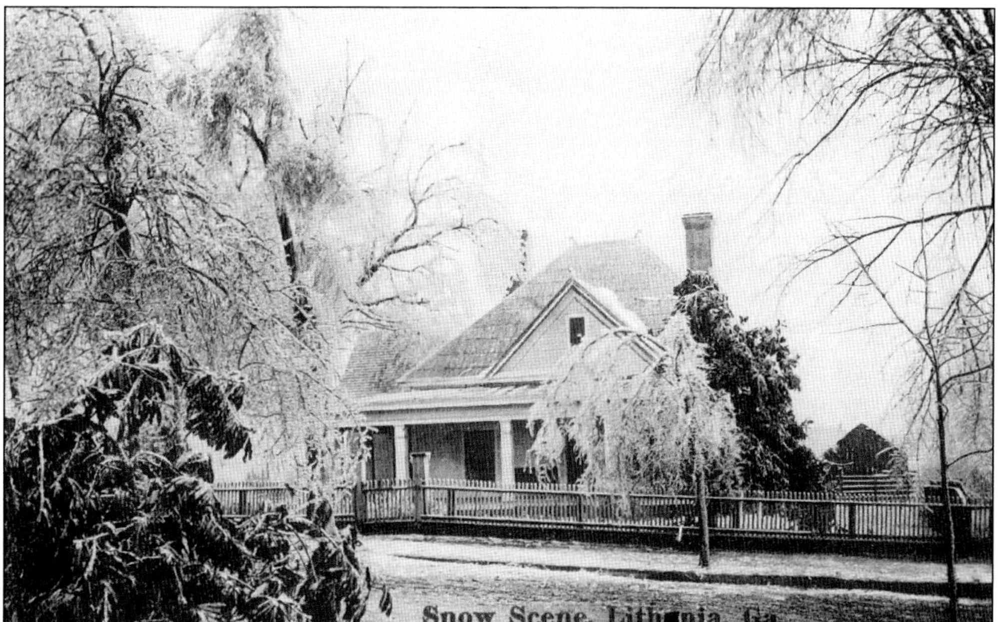

A covering of snow, an occasion rare for Georgia, blankets the landscape in this post card of Lithonia.

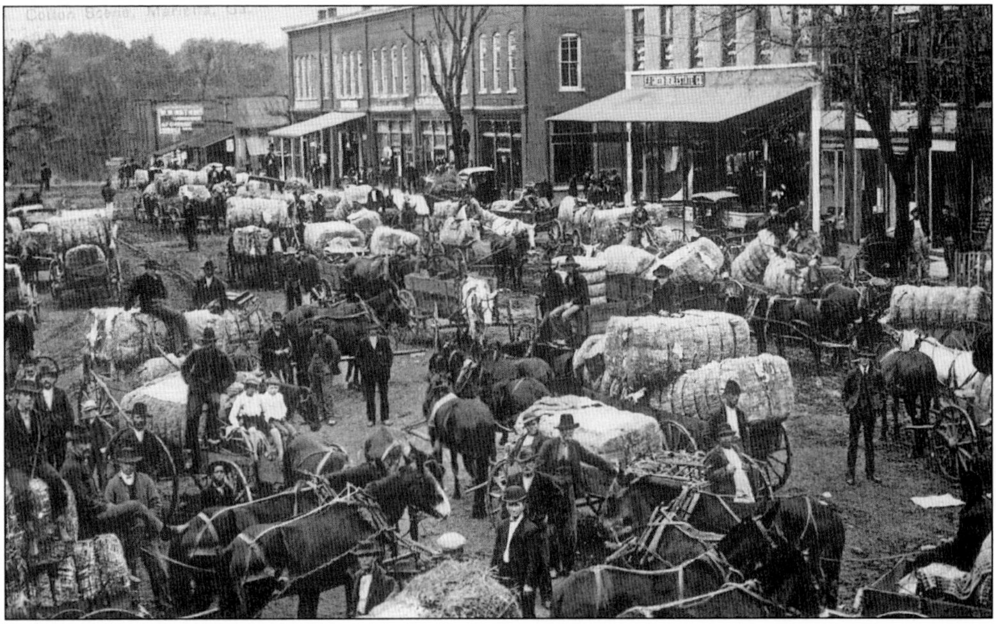

Cotton farmers bring their crop to market in this scene from Marietta. In the days before high-tech farming and extensive fertilizing, farmers were fortunate to pick a bale of cotton per acre. It took 1,500 pounds of unginned cotton to produce a 500-pound bale of ginned cotton. Farmers usually brought their cotton to market on Sunday, and often had to spend all day waiting in line for their cotton to be ginned.

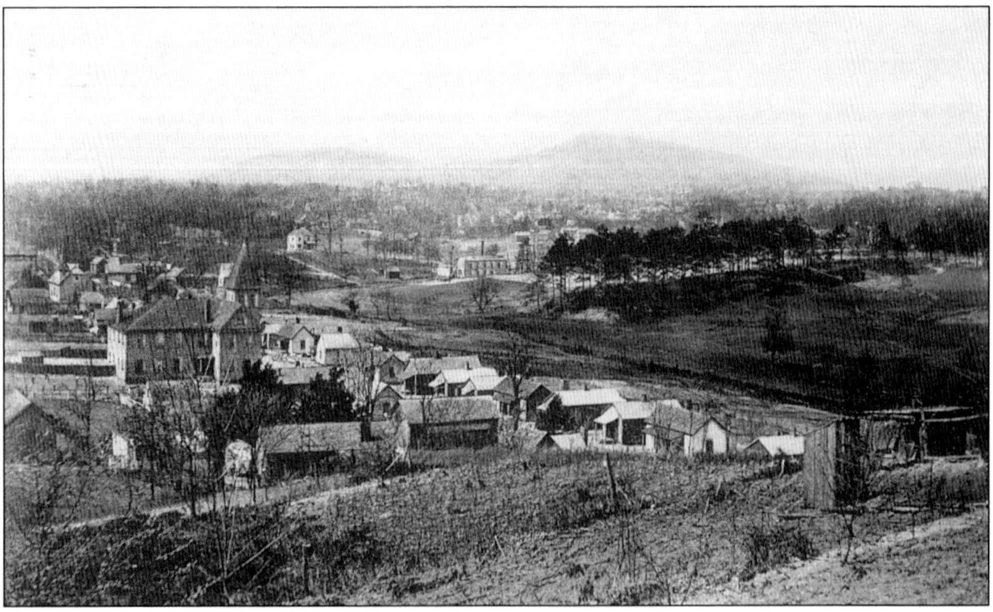

In this bird's-eye view of Marietta, Kennesaw Mountain can be seen in the distance.

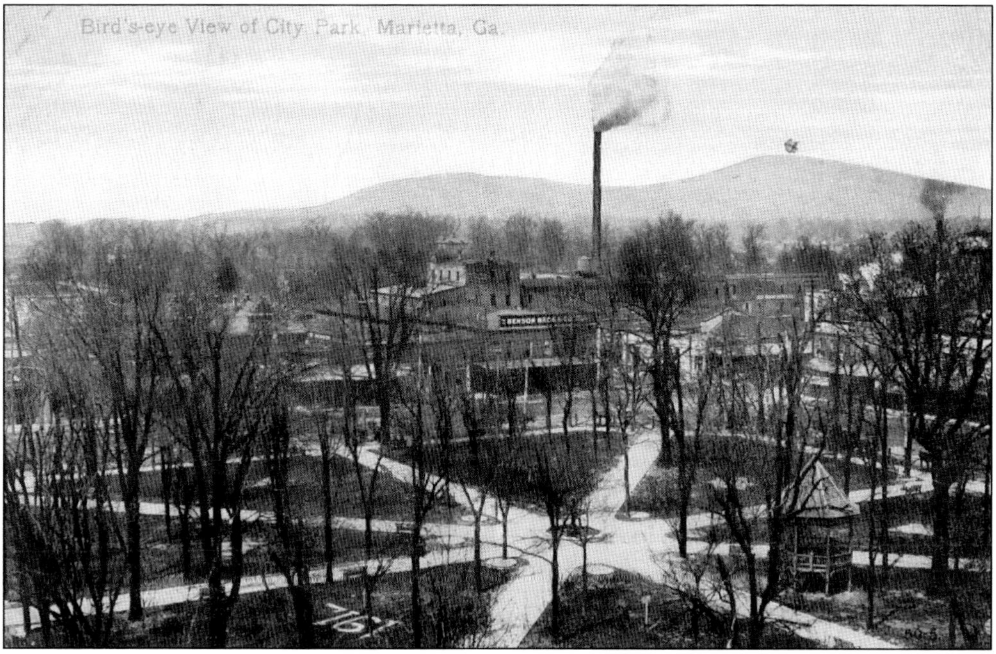

The Benson Brothers and Company is visible in the center of this post card of the City Park in Marietta. On the back, the sender wrote: "5-26-13. Greetings from Marietta. The cross will show you Kennesaw Mt. where we are this morning. Will go to Stone Mt. tomorrow. Having fine time indeed. Wish you were along. Sincerely, D.W. Laughlin."

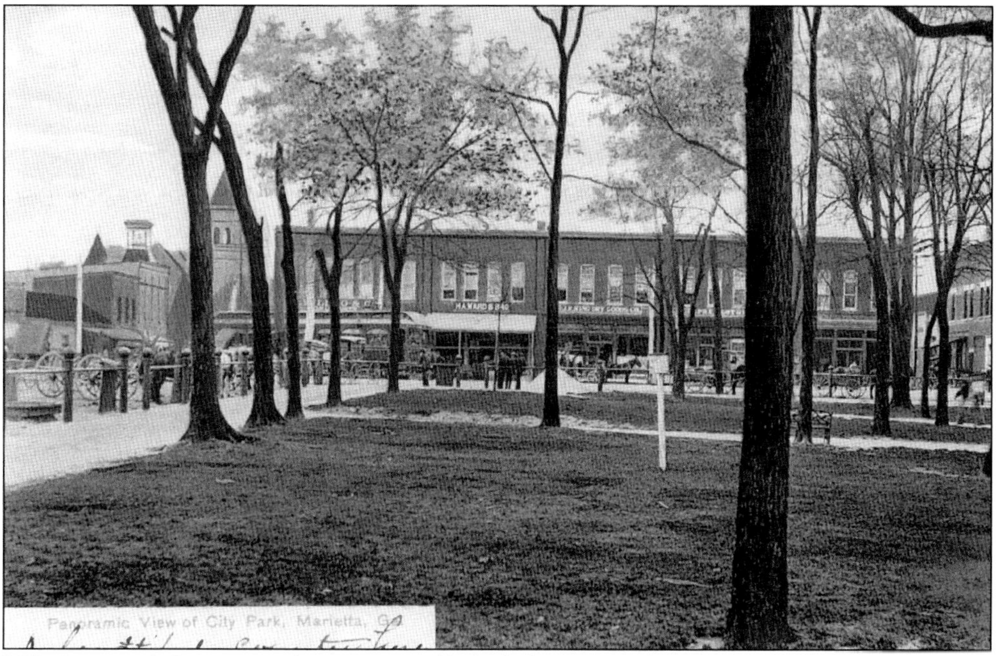

J.W. Legg and Company of Marietta published this view of City Park in Marietta which is postmarked December 4, 1909.

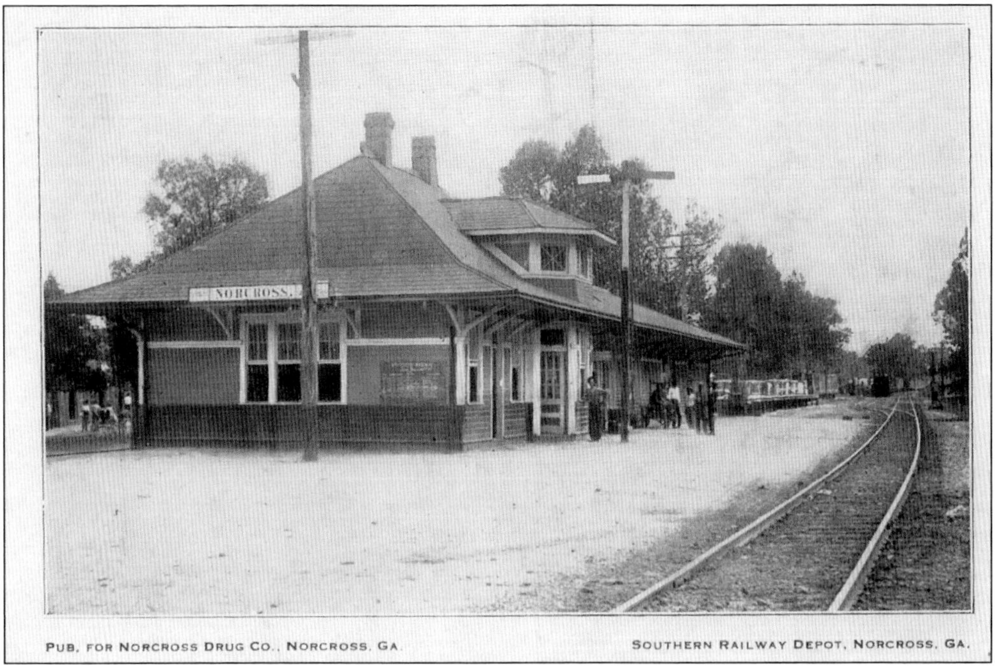

The Southern Railway Depot in Norcross is the focus of this post card, which was published for the Norcross Drug Company.

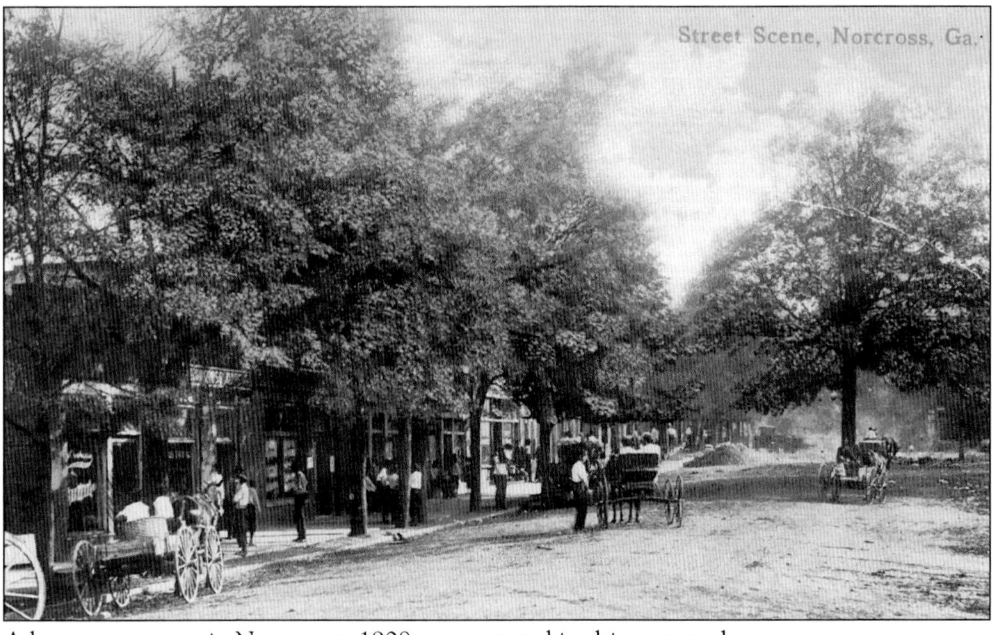

A busy street scene in Norcross *c.* 1908 was captured in this post card.

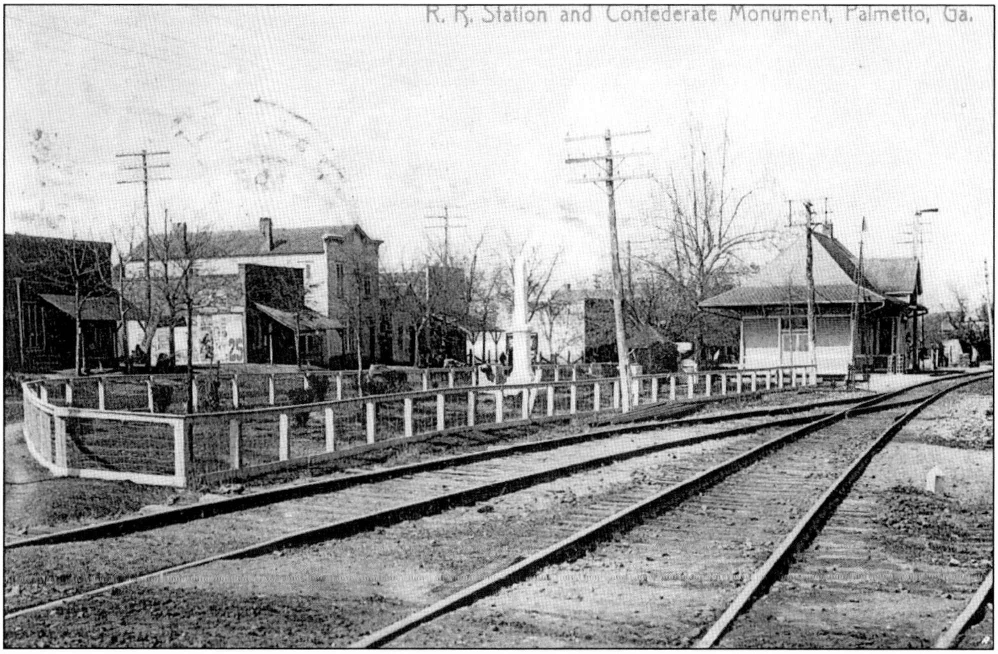

The Holt and Cates Company of Newnan, Georgia, published this early view of the railroad station and Confederate Monument in Palmetto. Palmetto was another small town in Campbell County which was merged with Fulton County in 1932. The Confederate Monument was erected in 1906 by the United Daughters of the Confederacy.

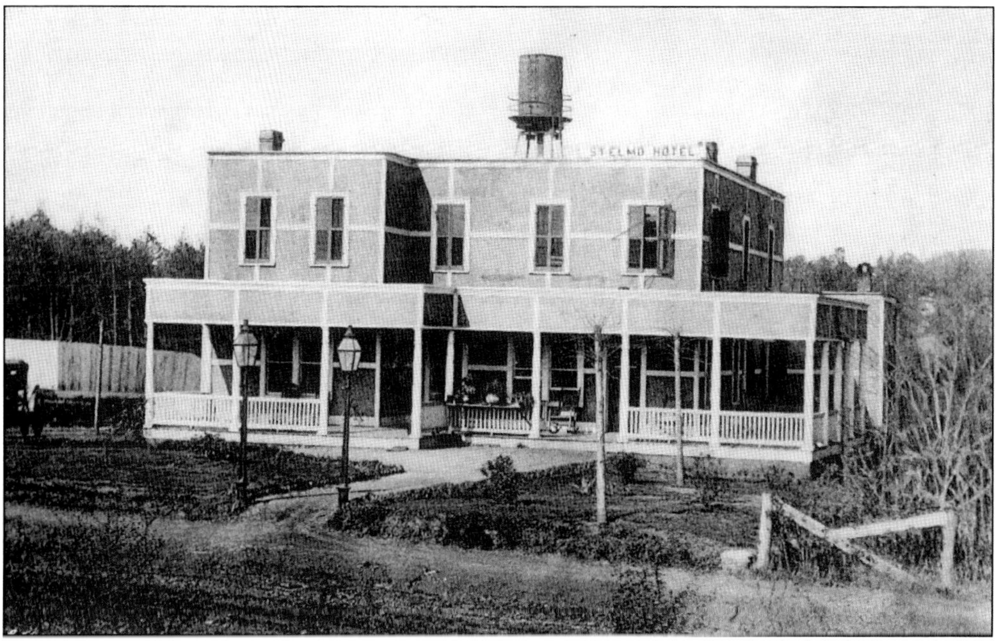

This is the St. Elmo Hotel in Palmetto *c.* 1909. The hotel was owned by a Mrs. Abrahams.

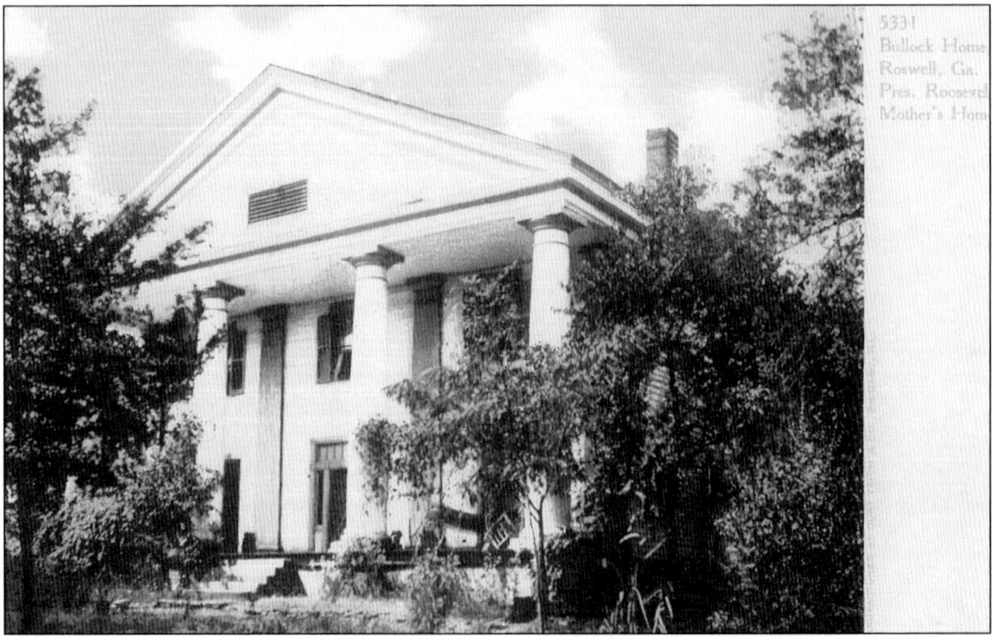

This pre-1907 undivided-back post card shows the Bullock residence in Roswell, the home of Teddy Roosevelt's mother.

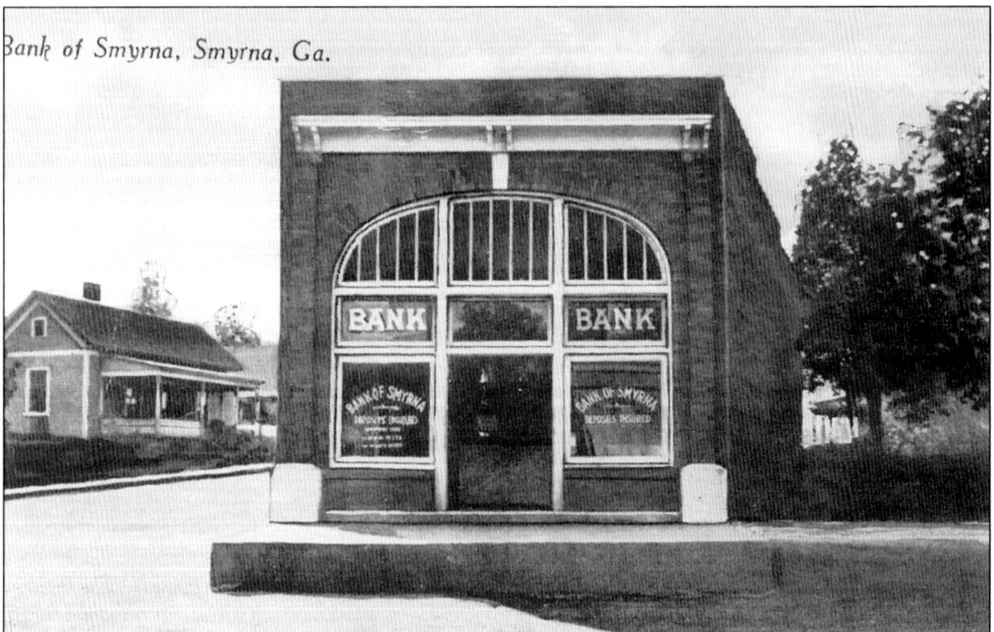

The Bank of Smyrna is featured in this post card, published by G.C. Green of Smyrna.

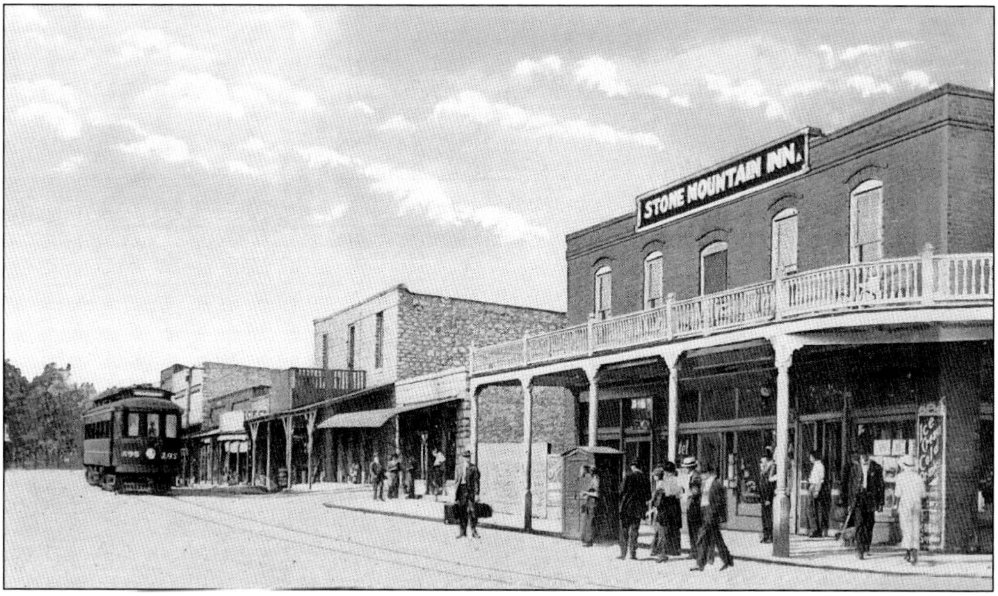

The Stone Mountain Drug Company published this view of Main Street in Stone Mountain. The back copy reads, in part: "Stone Mountain, near Atlanta, GA. This mass of solid granite, 700 feet high, relic of the glacial period, is the biggest monolith in the world. Stone Mountain can be reached by trolley, automobile road or train. It is one of the natural curiosities of America. Stone quarried from it goes to pave the streets of Chicago, Cincinnati and several other cities. It is an inexhaustible store of granite. Man has been pecking at its base for generations and hasn't left a mark. The mountain was a landmark for the Indians in aboriginal days, and is visible for many miles in all directions."

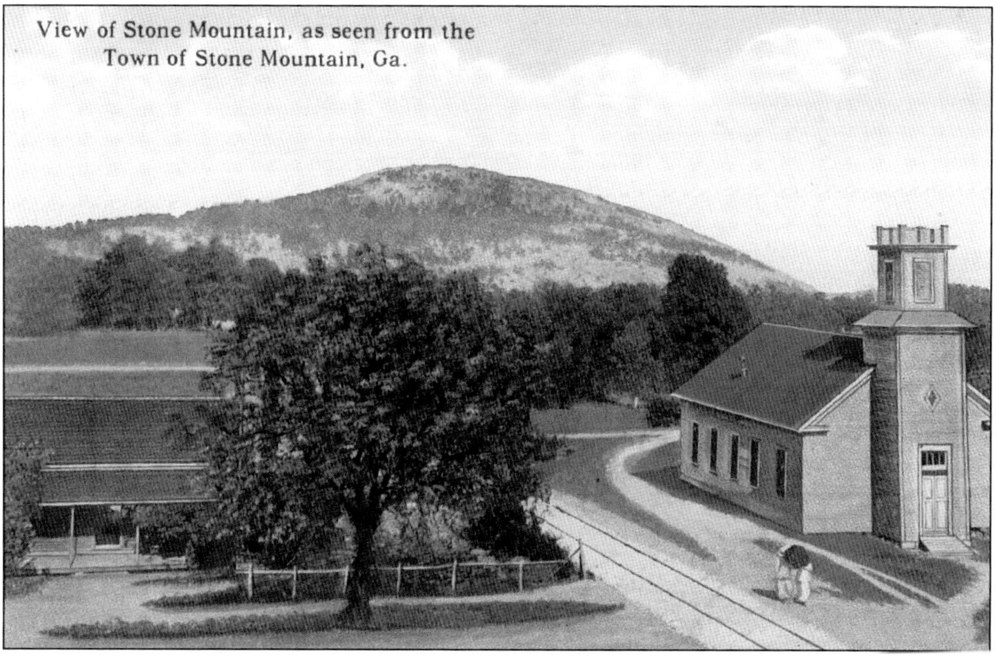

Stone Mountain towers in the distance in this view. The card has the same back copy as the previous card.

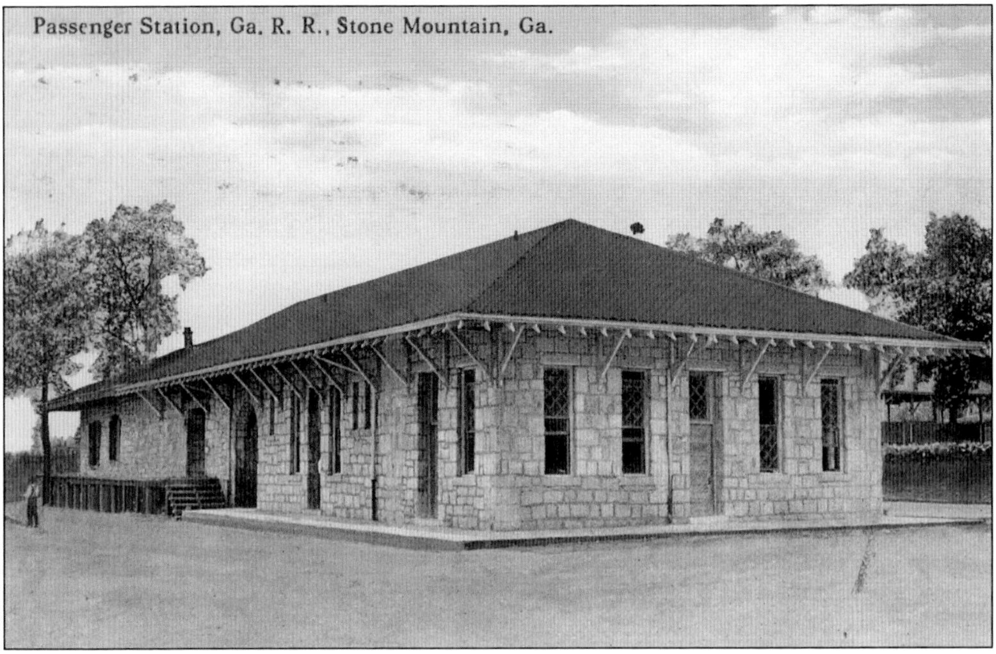

Another card published by the Stone Mountain Drug Company shows the passenger station of the Georgia Railroad in Stone Mountain, no doubt built of granite quarried from the base of the mountain.

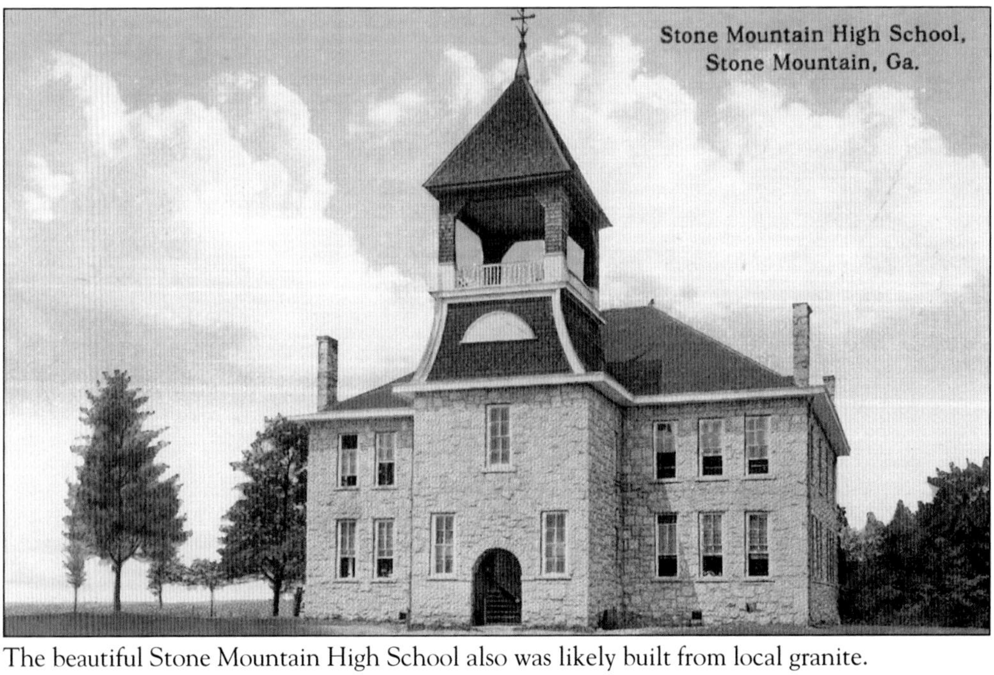

The beautiful Stone Mountain High School also was likely built from local granite.

Three

Bartow, Cherokee, and Gordon Counties

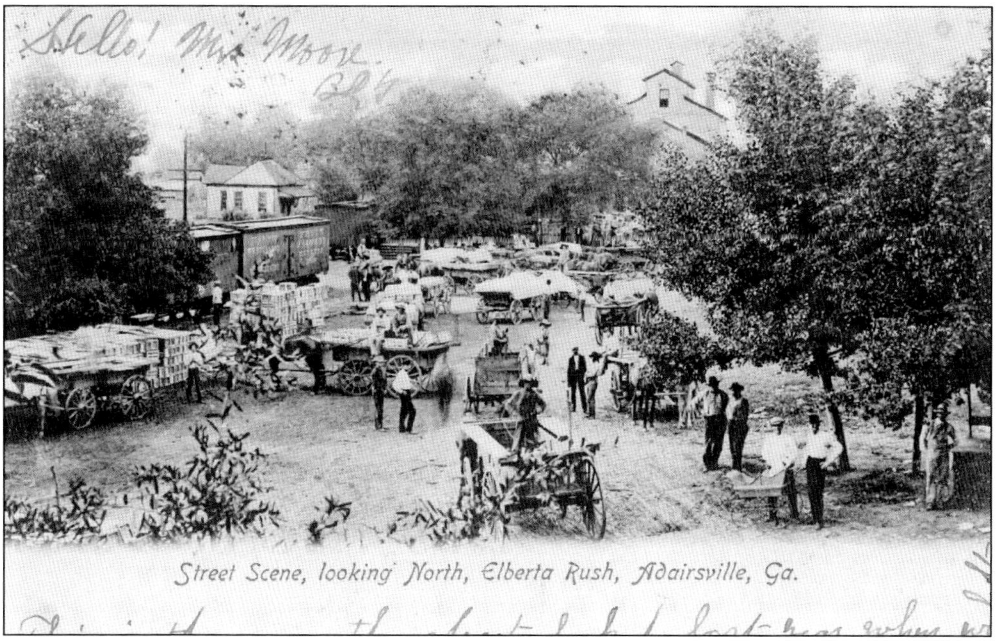

The "Elberta Rush," or peach picking season, is in full swing in this post card of Adairsville. This post card was mailed to Bolton, Georgia, on September 2, 1907, with this message: "Dear Friends, Brax is so much better today. Fever is broken and I think he will improve rapidly. This is the way the street looked last year when we left. Bill G."

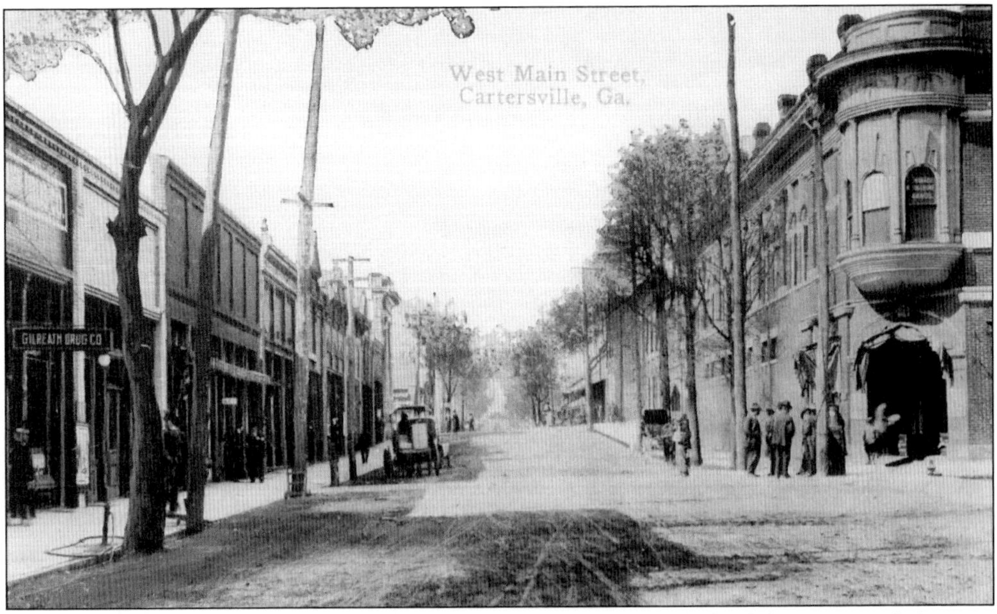

A sign advertising the Gilreath Drug Company is visible to the left of this post card showing West Main Street in Cartersville.

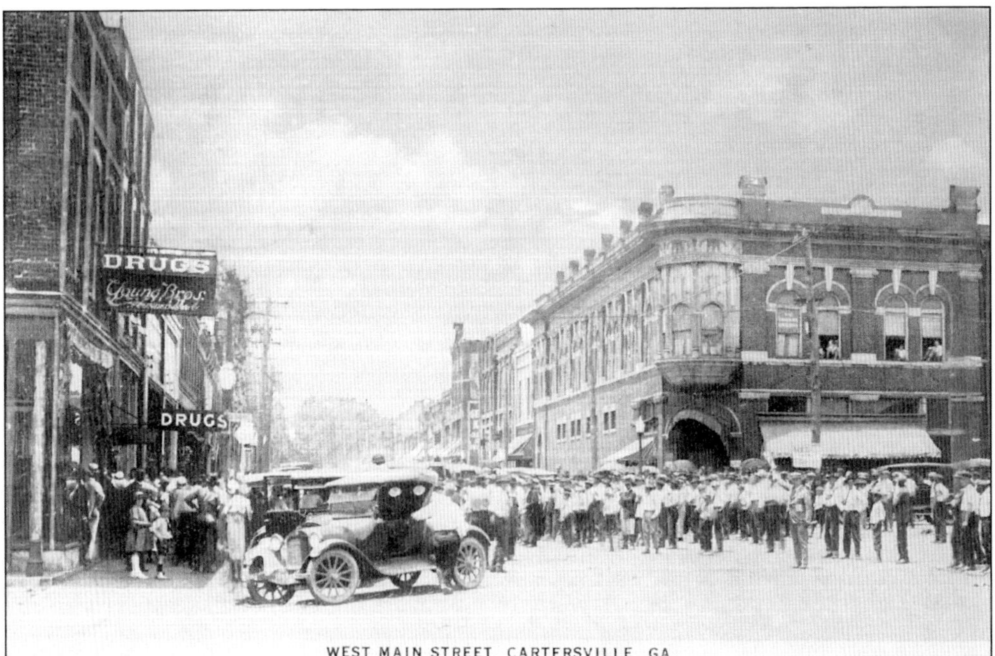

The Cartersville Book Store published this view of a busy scene on Cartersville's Main Street. A sign tacked to a pole advertises "Baseball Exhibition Today."

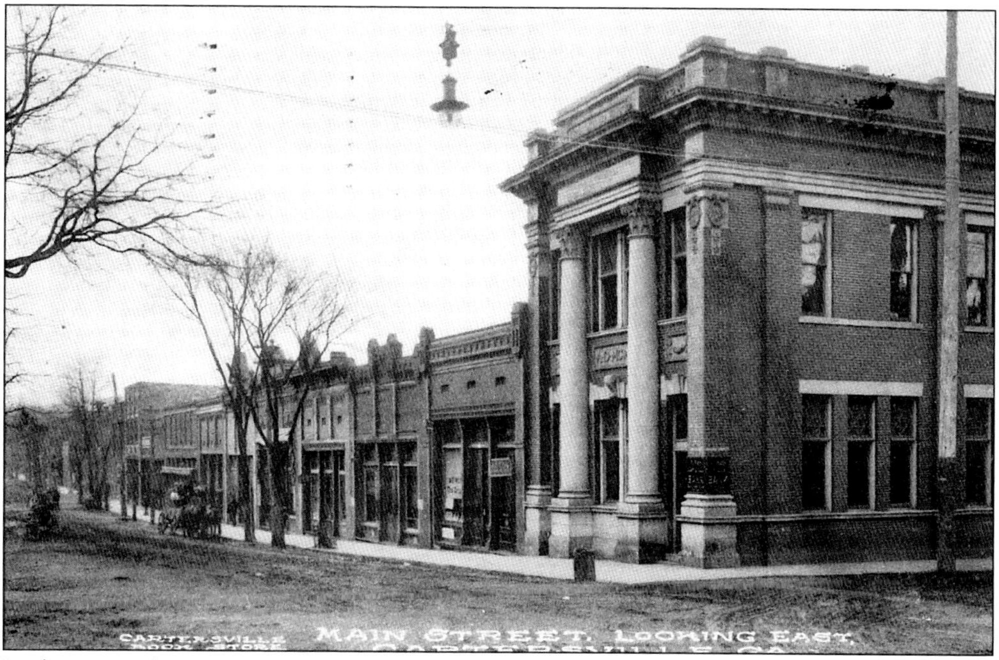

In this view of Main Street in Cartersville, notice the old-fashioned streetlight in the center of the post card.

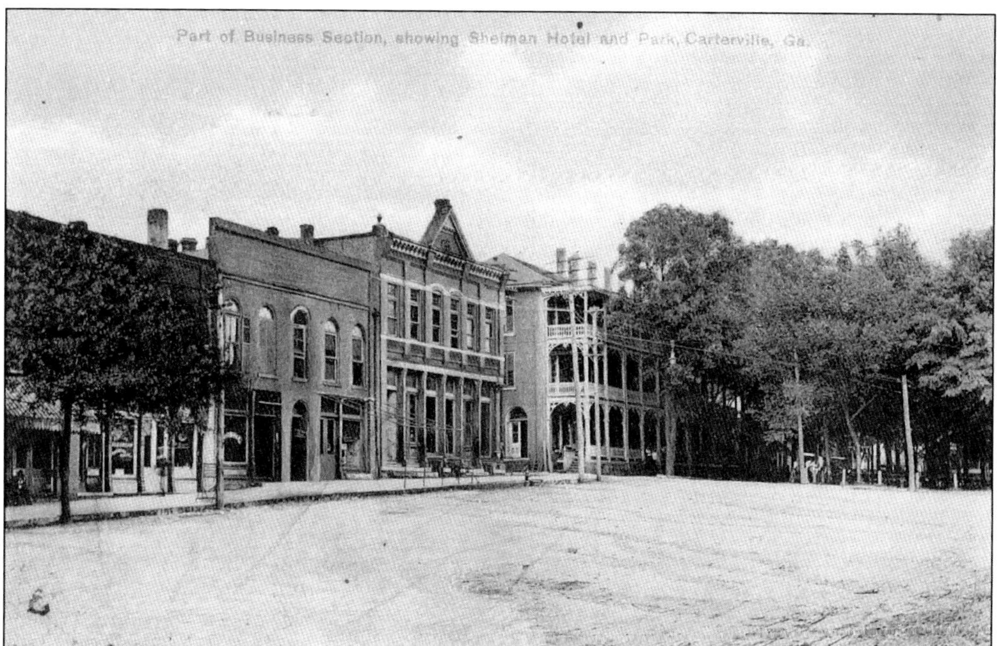

The Shelman Hotel and Park are visible in this view of Cartersville.

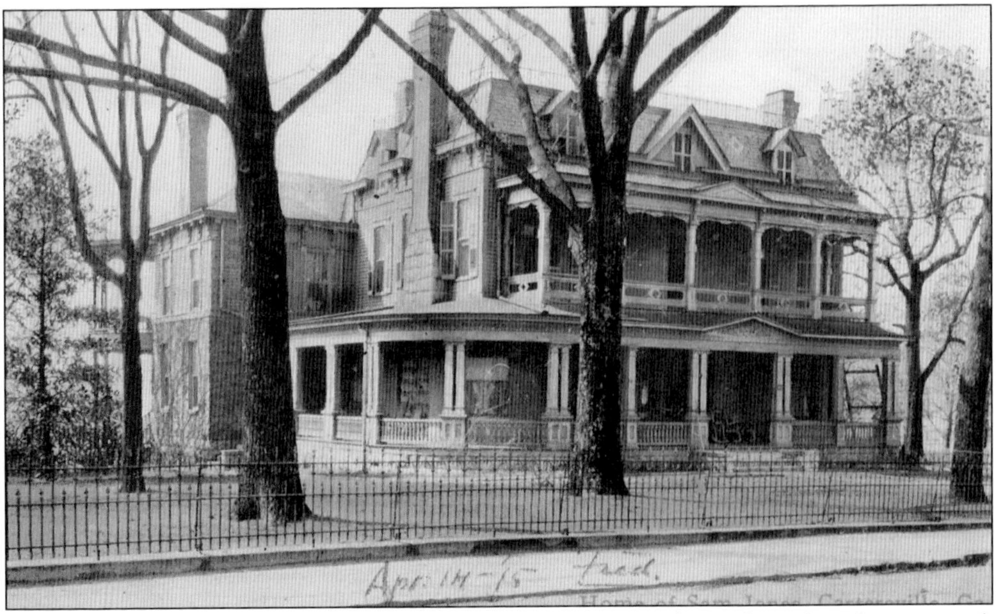

The beautiful Cartersville home of evangelist Sam Jones was deemed worthy of a post card. Note the rocking chairs on the wrap-around porch.

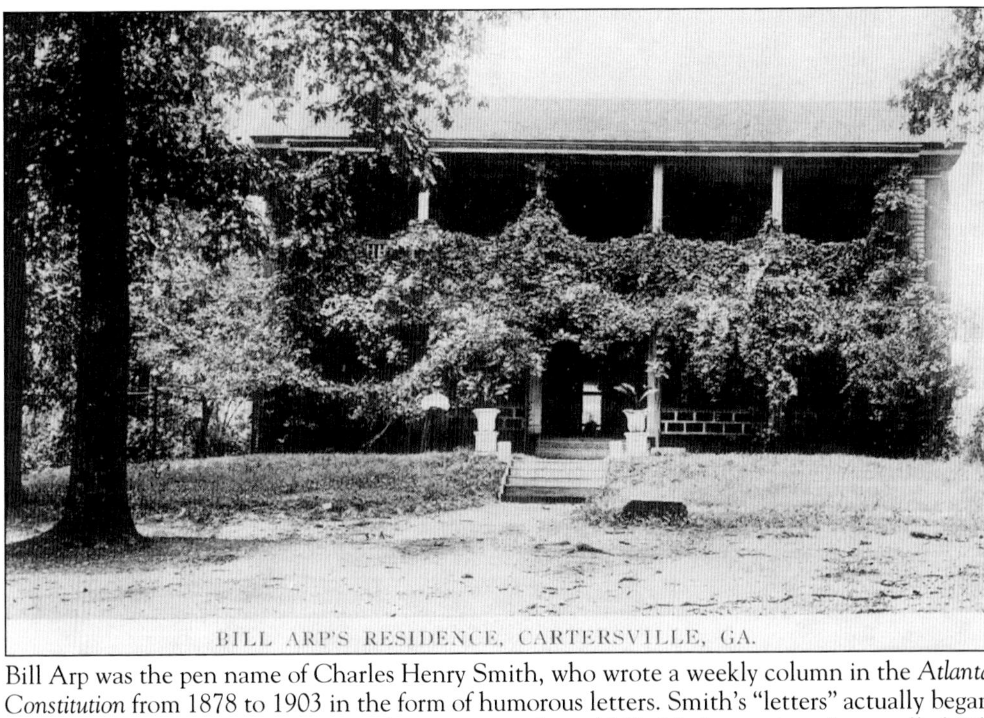

Bill Arp was the pen name of Charles Henry Smith, who wrote a weekly column in the *Atlanta Constitution* from 1878 to 1903 in the form of humorous letters. Smith's "letters" actually began appearing in various newspapers in the state as early as 1861. Modern writers have called Bill Arp a "political satirist" and "country sage."

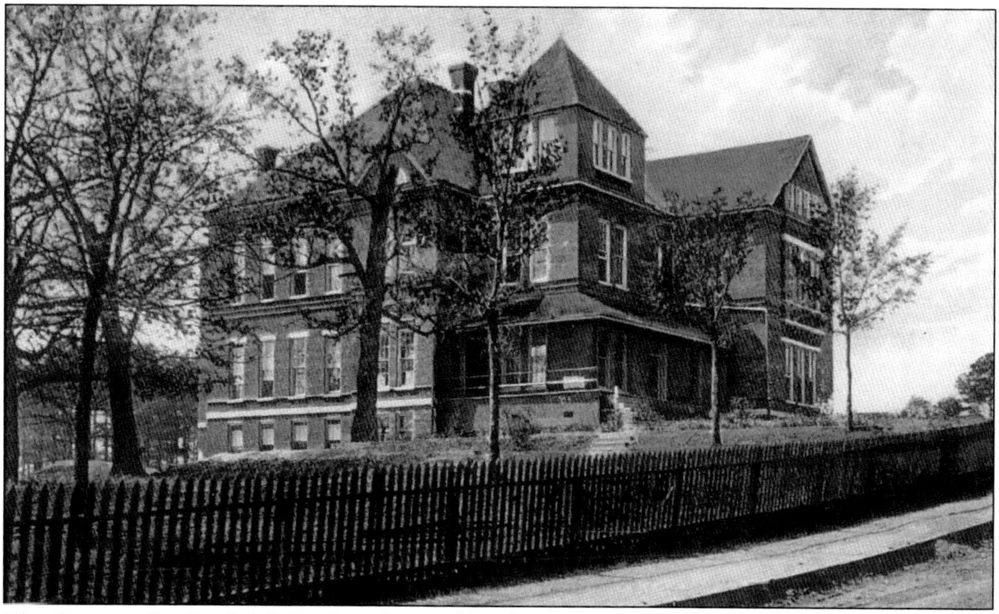

The Cartersville Graded School, with its picket fence, was the subject of this card published by the American News Company.

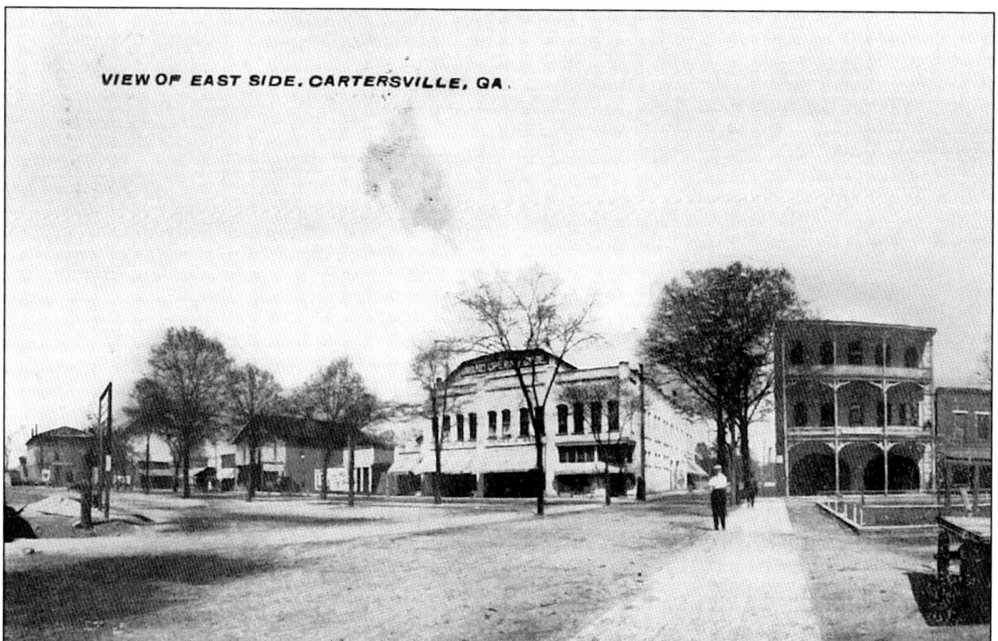

On the back of this view of Cartersville's east side, an evidently impatient sender wrote: "I'm still here and looking for that letter."

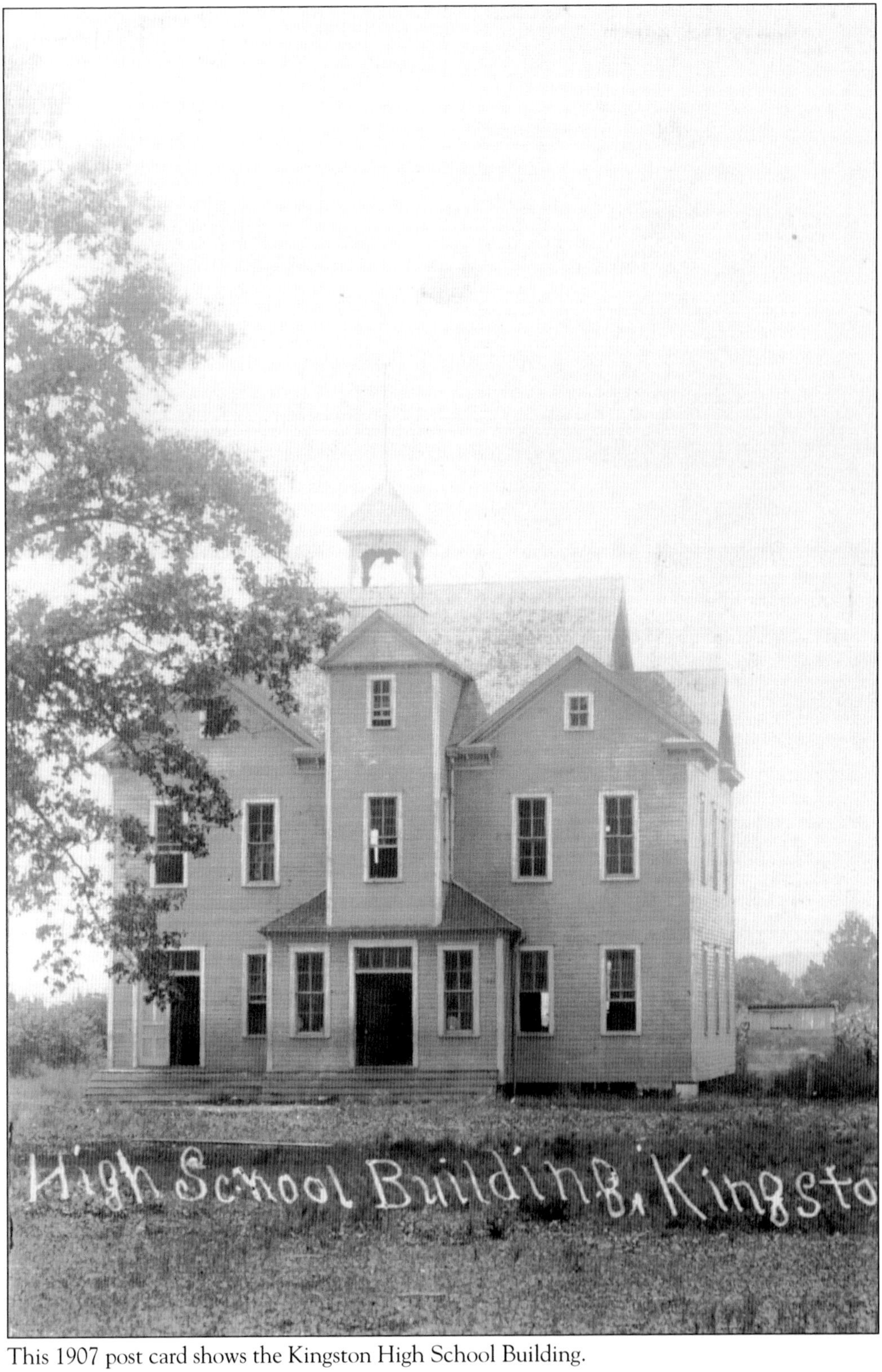

This 1907 post card shows the Kingston High School Building.

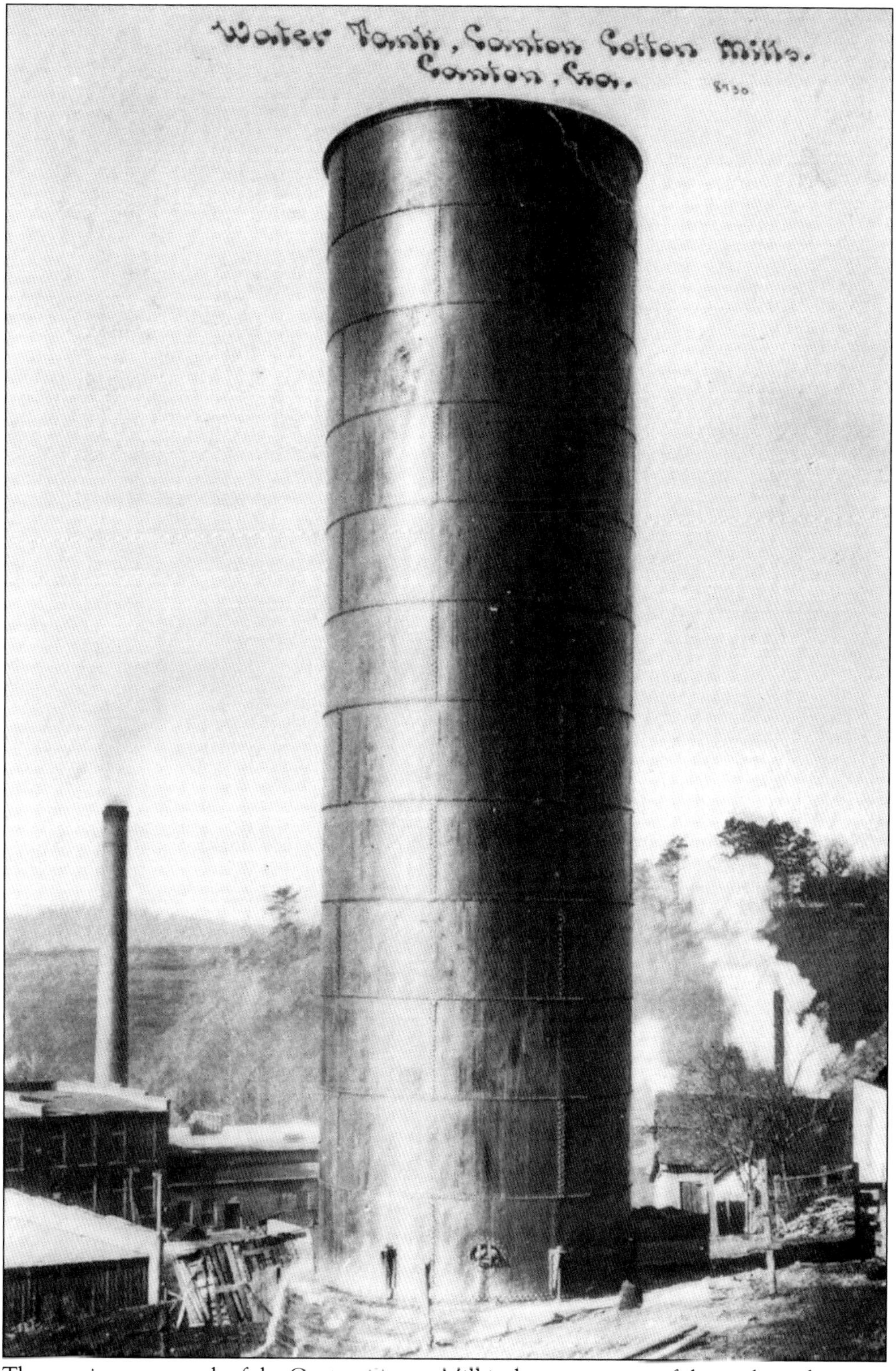

The massive water tank of the Canton Cotton Mill is the centerpiece of this early card.

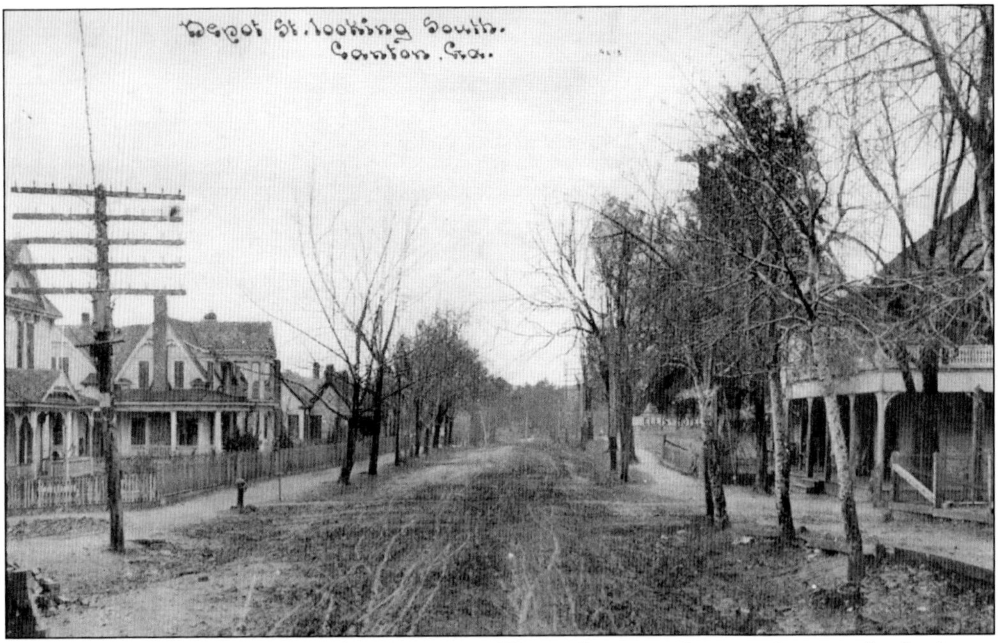

Although the streets are unpaved in this view of Depot Street in Canton, there are fire hydrants visible. The Ellis Hotel is seen on the right side of the photograph.

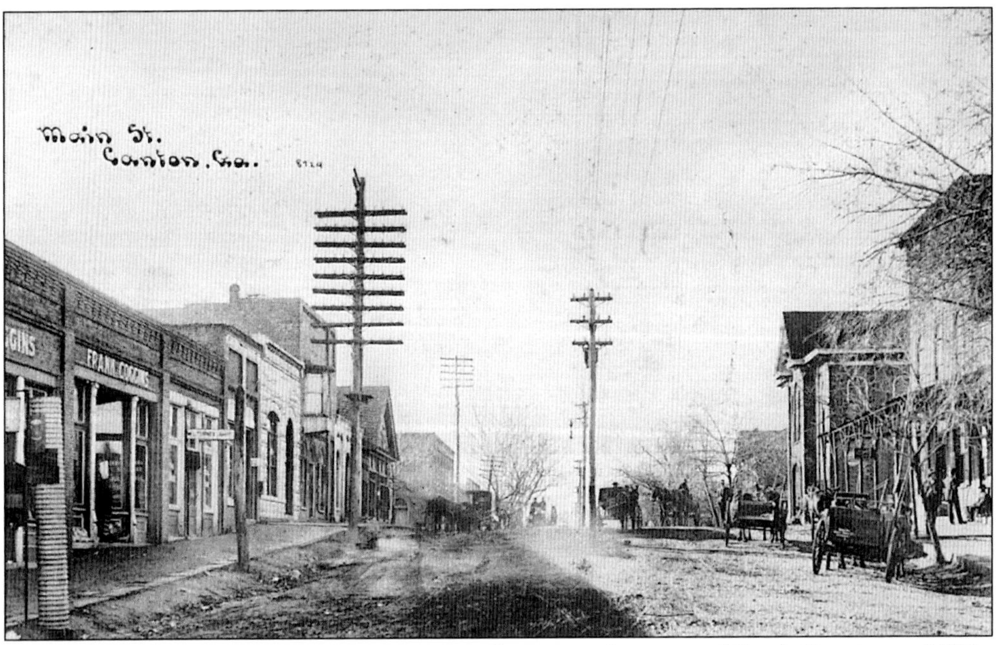

In this view of Main Street in Canton, signs advertising the stores of Frank Coggins and W.L. Turner are visible. Note that utility poles are located in the center of the street.

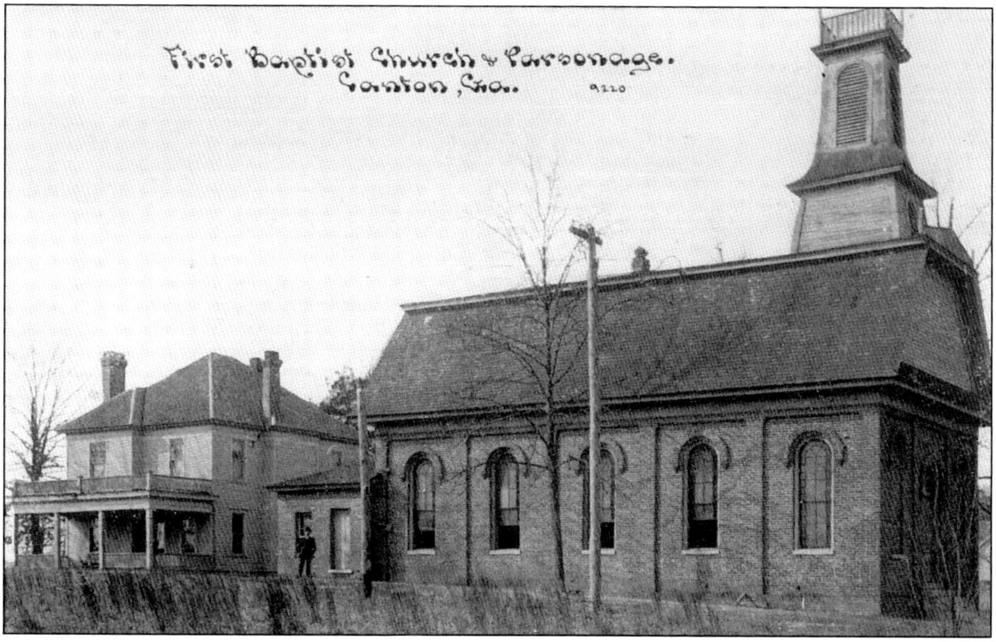

Canton's First Baptist Church and Parsonage, along with a lone bystander, are shown in this c. 1908 post card.

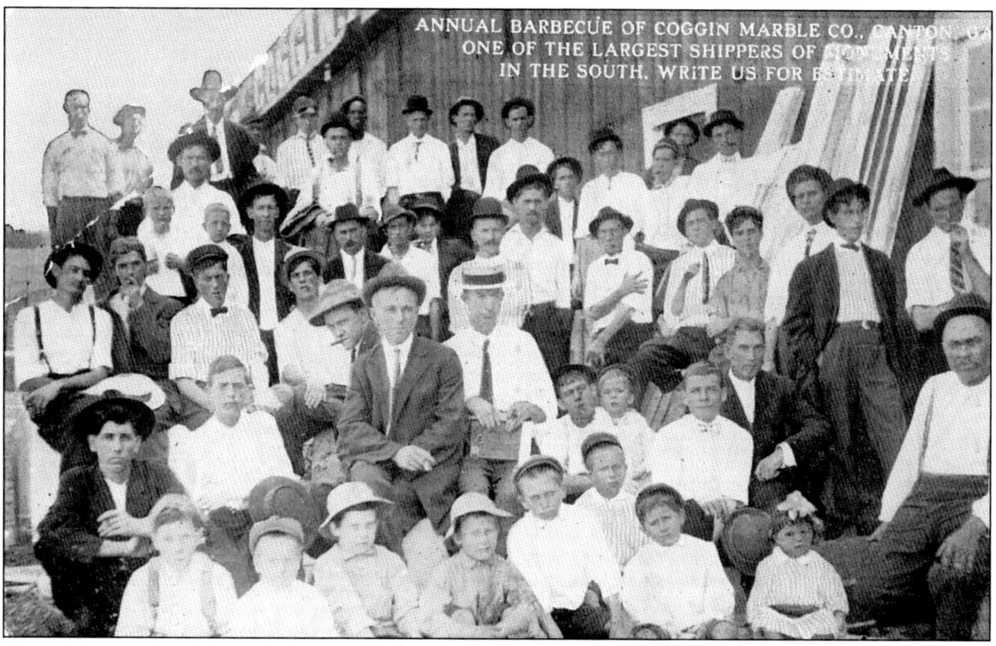

According to the front of this card, the gathering shown here was the "Annual Barbecue Of Coggin Marble Co., Canton, GA. One Of The Largest Shippers of Monuments In The South." The card goes on to say, "Write Us For Estimate."

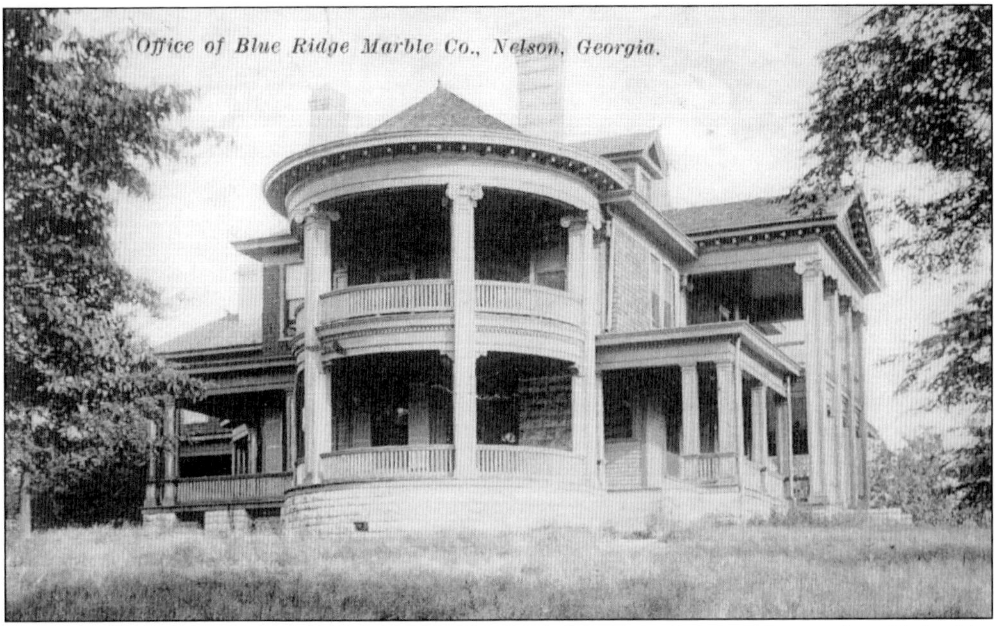

The ornate office of the Blue Ridge Marble Company was the subject of this card, published by the Nelson Mercantile Corporation of Nelson, Georgia.

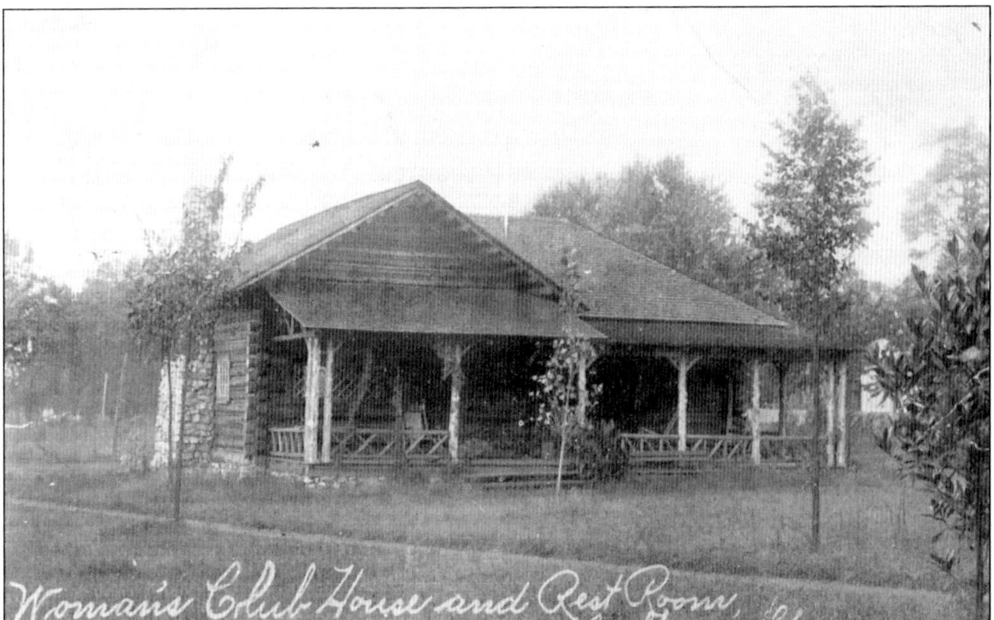

Public rest rooms were rare enough to constitute a bragging point for the Woman's Club House in Calhoun, Georgia, in 1907.

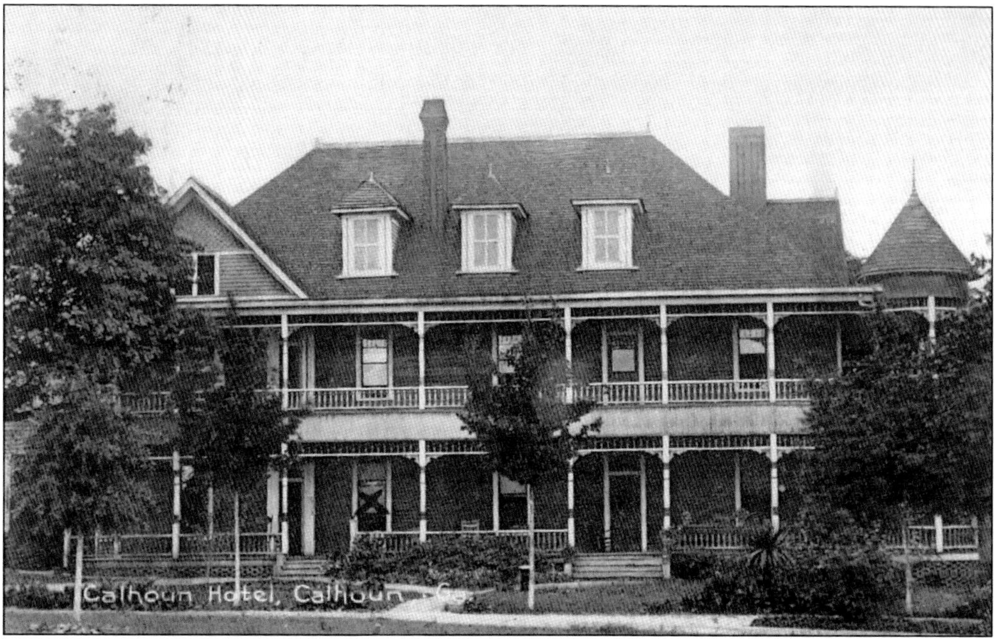

Rankins Book Store in Calhoun published this view of the magnificent Calhoun Hotel.

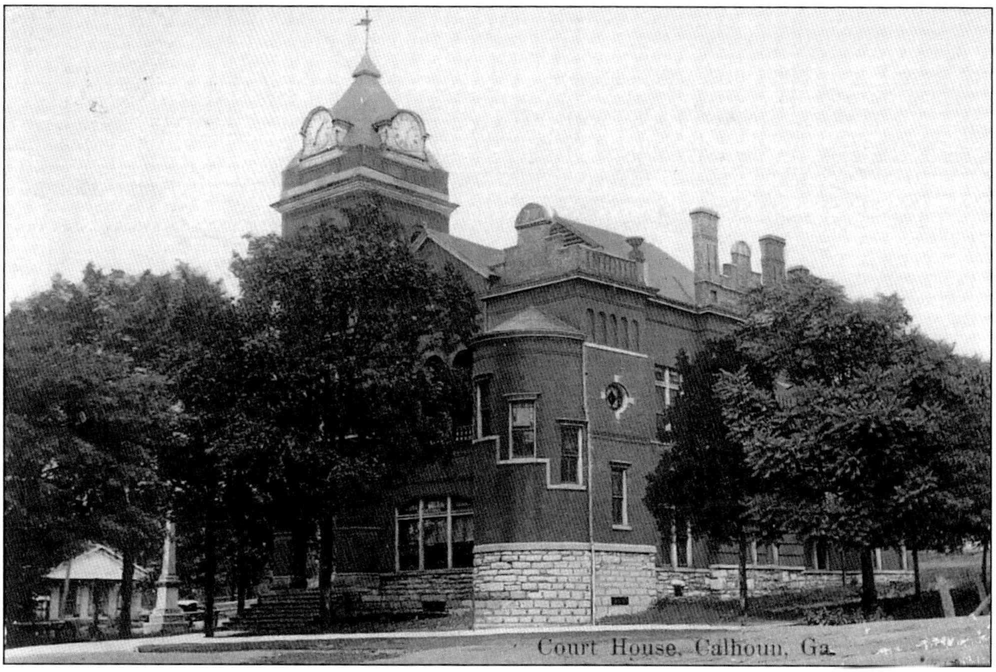

The Gordon County Court House in Calhoun was built in 1889 at a cost of $14,000. It served until the present facility was completed in 1961.

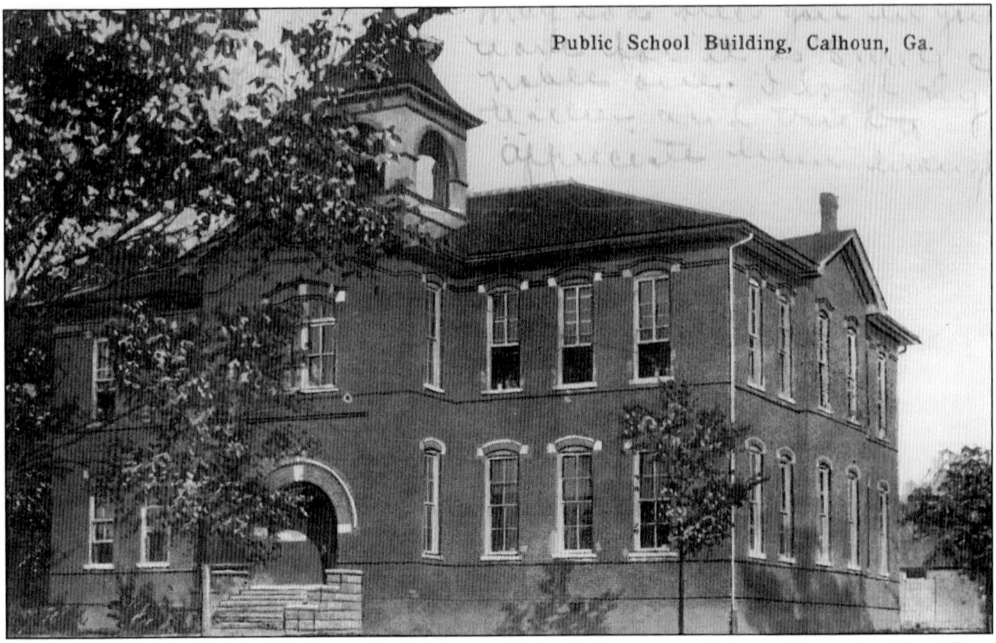

The Gilbert Post Card Company of Chicago published this view of the public school building in Calhoun.

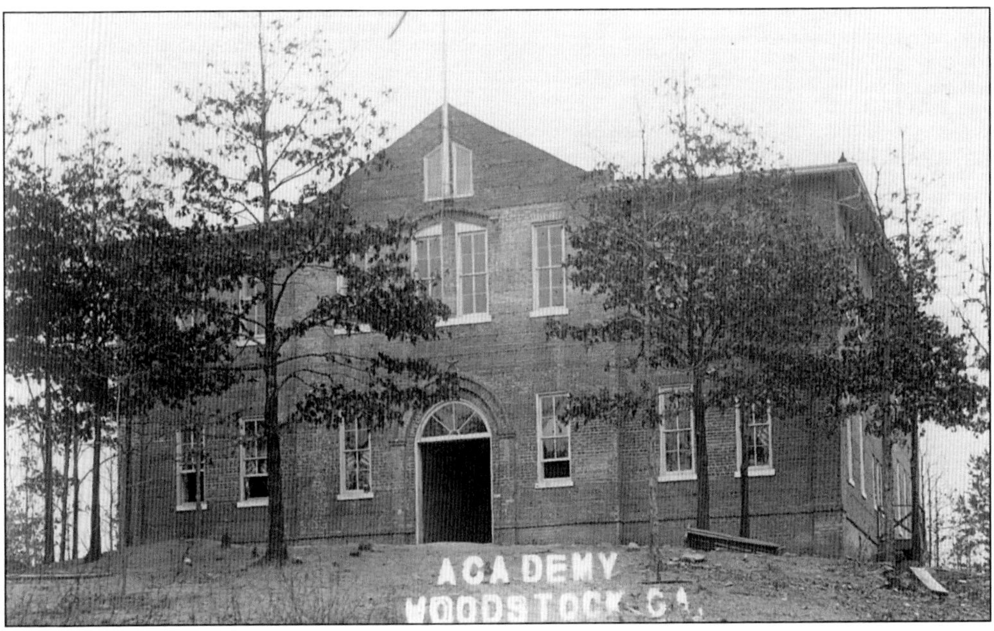

Woodstock Academy in Woodstock was captured in this real-photograph post card about 1908.

Four

Carroll and Douglas Counties

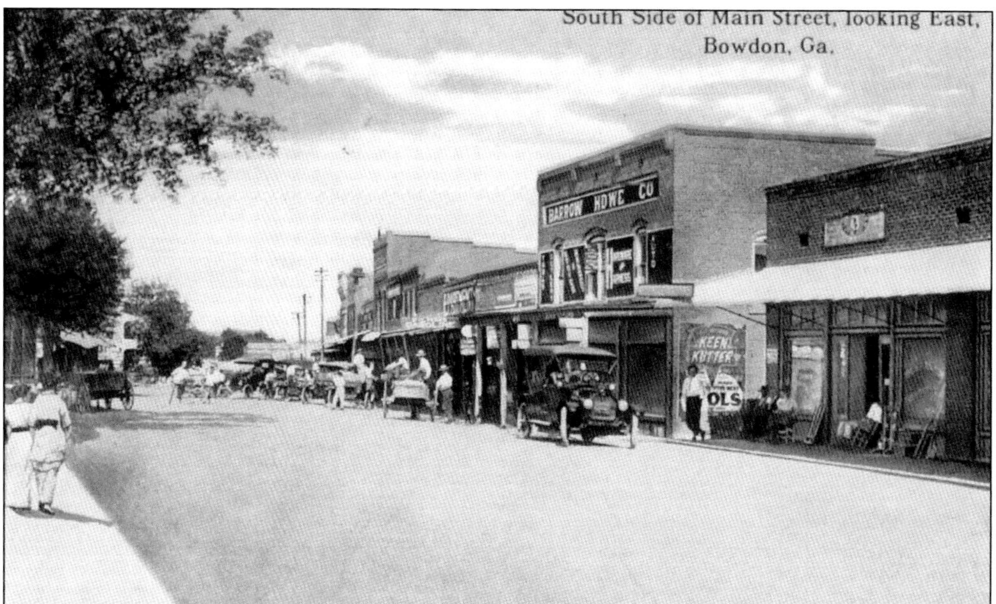

In this view of Bowdon's Main Street in the early 'teens, signs advertising the Barrow Hardware Company, Keen-Kutter Oils, filtered gasoline, and Coca-Cola are present.

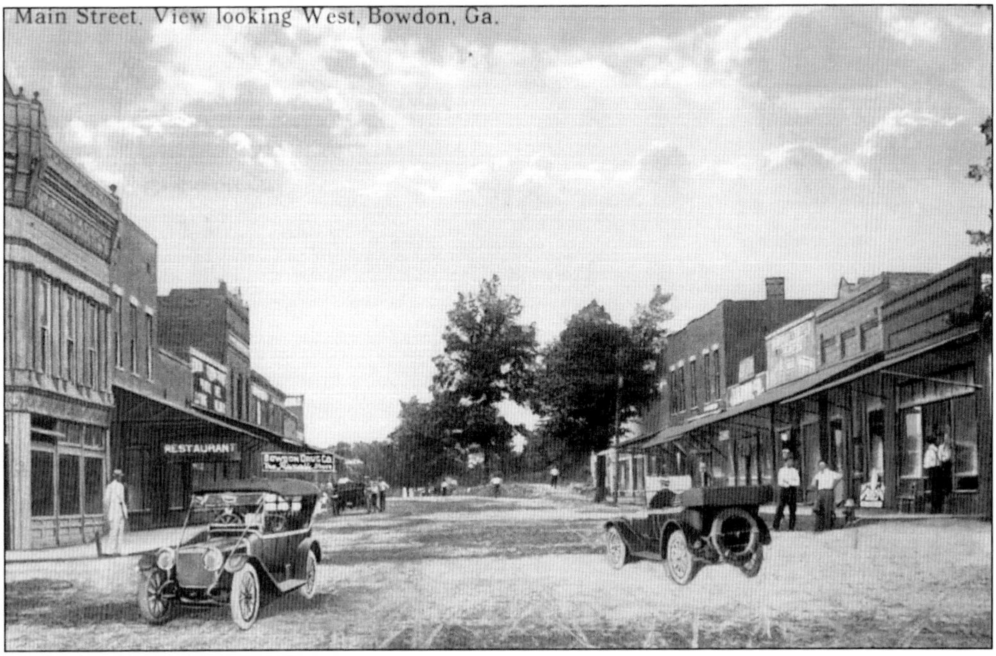

In this view of Main Street, the Bowdon Drug Company, the publisher of the card, managed to include themselves in the picture. The phony automobiles were the product of "artistic license" and were added to the picture by the printer.

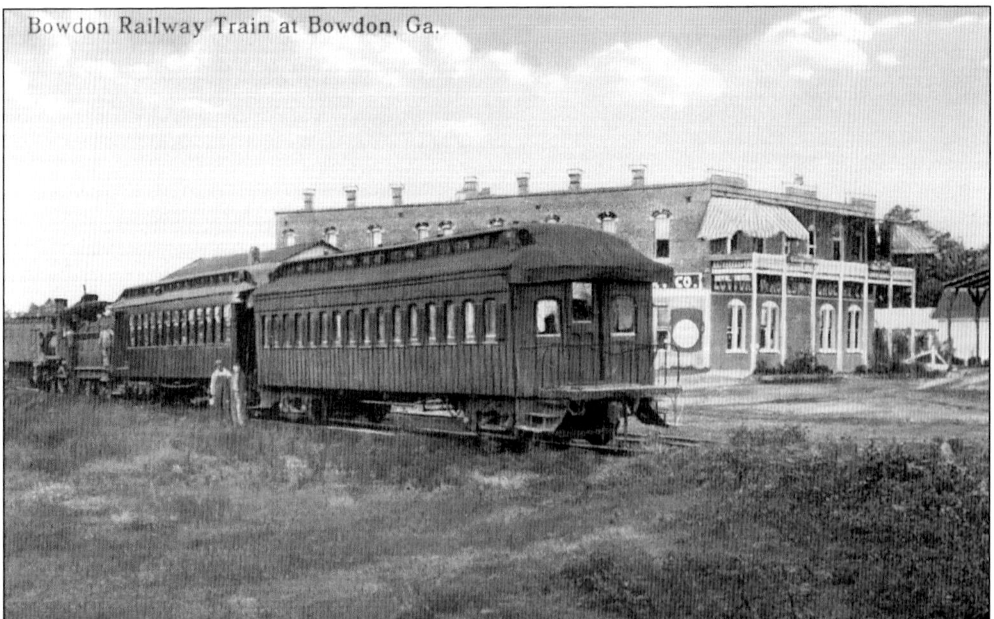

A Bowdon Railway train stands at the depot, the top of which can be seen over the passenger cars.

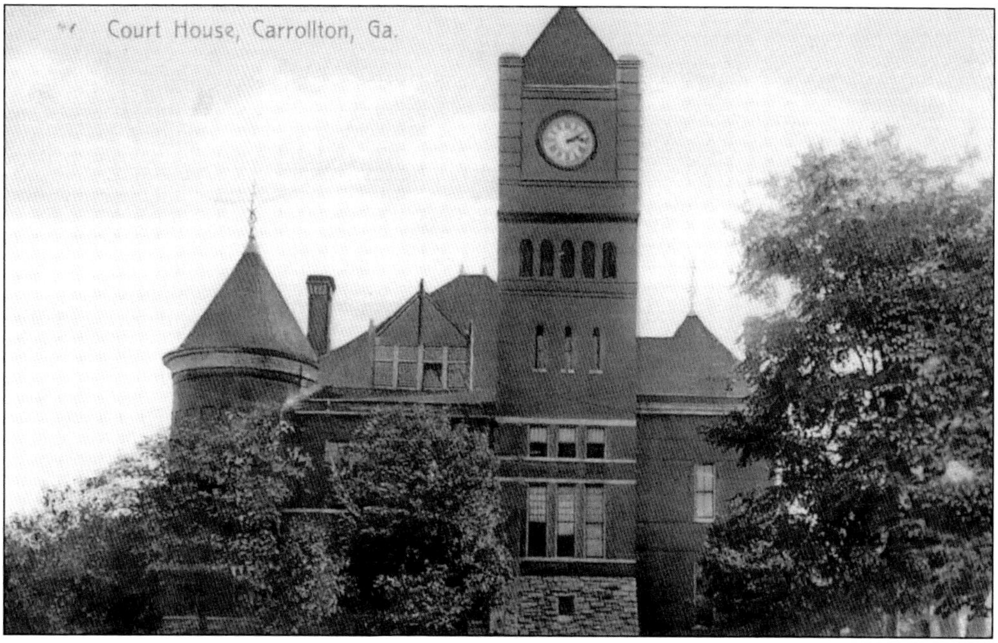

This courthouse building in Carrollton was built in the 1880s, and burned down in 1927.

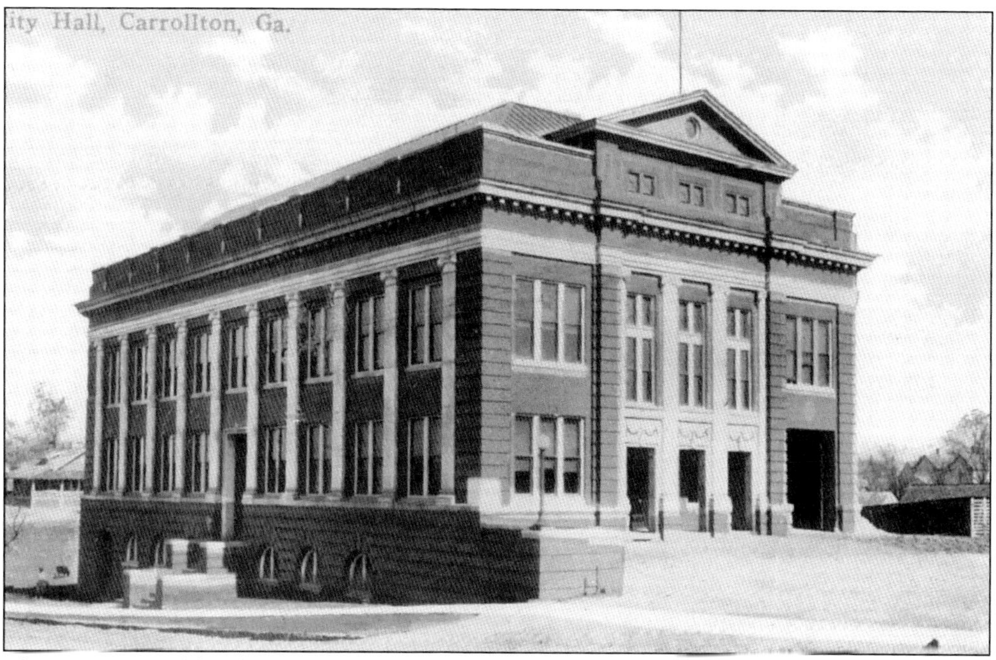

The imposing red-brick structure of the Carrollton City Hall is the focus of this post card.

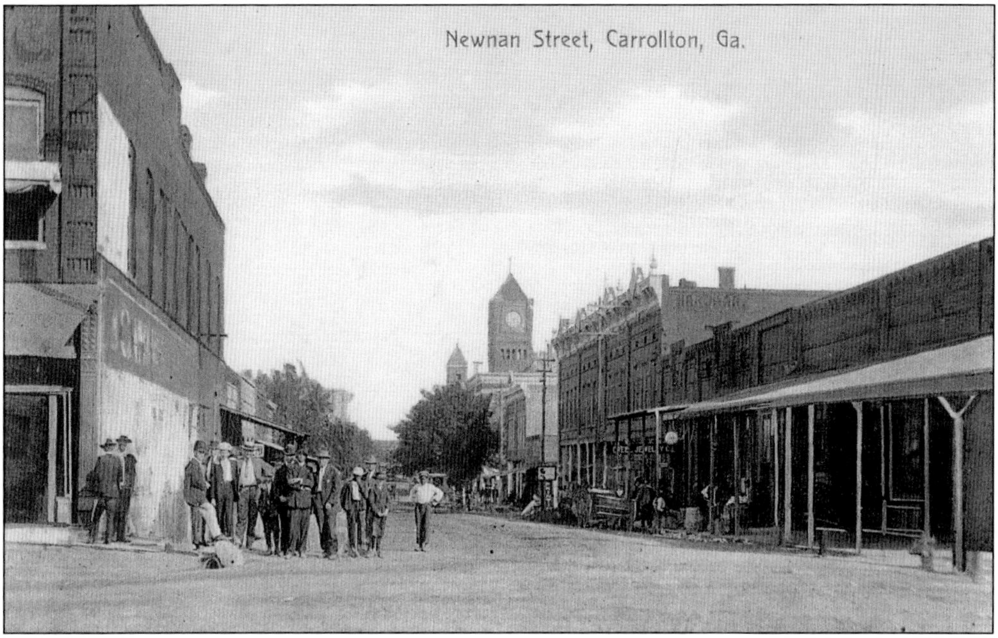

N.A. Horton of Carrollton published this view of Newnan Street in Carrollton.

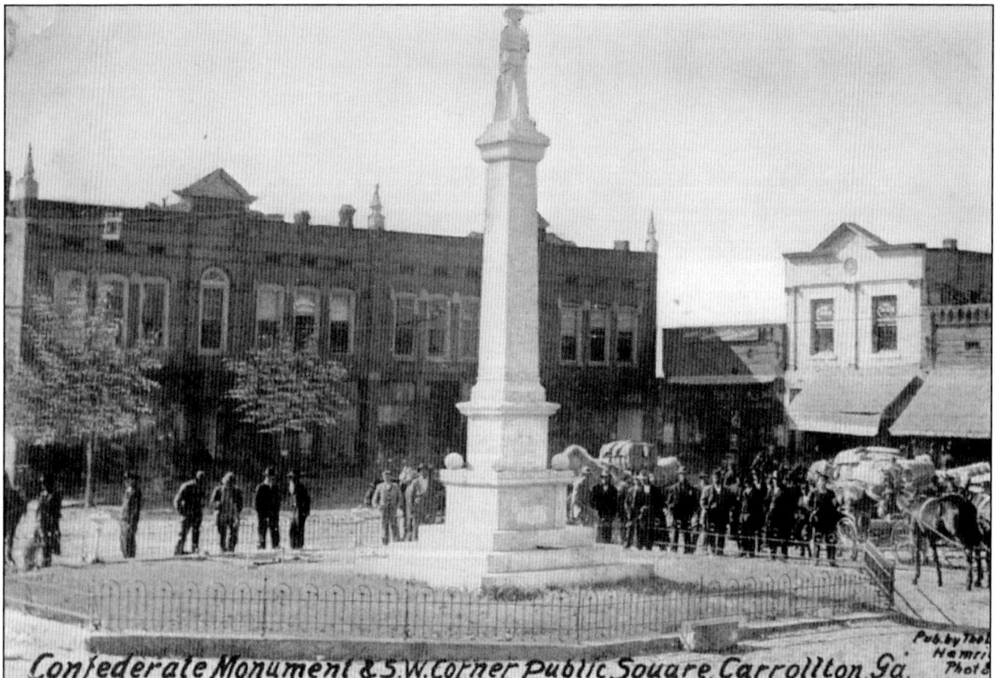

Farmers with their wagon loads of cotton surround the Confederate Monument in Carrollton. The monument was dedicated on May 28, 1910. When the town square was eliminated in the 1950s, the monument was moved to the grounds of the hospital and later to the courthouse lawn.

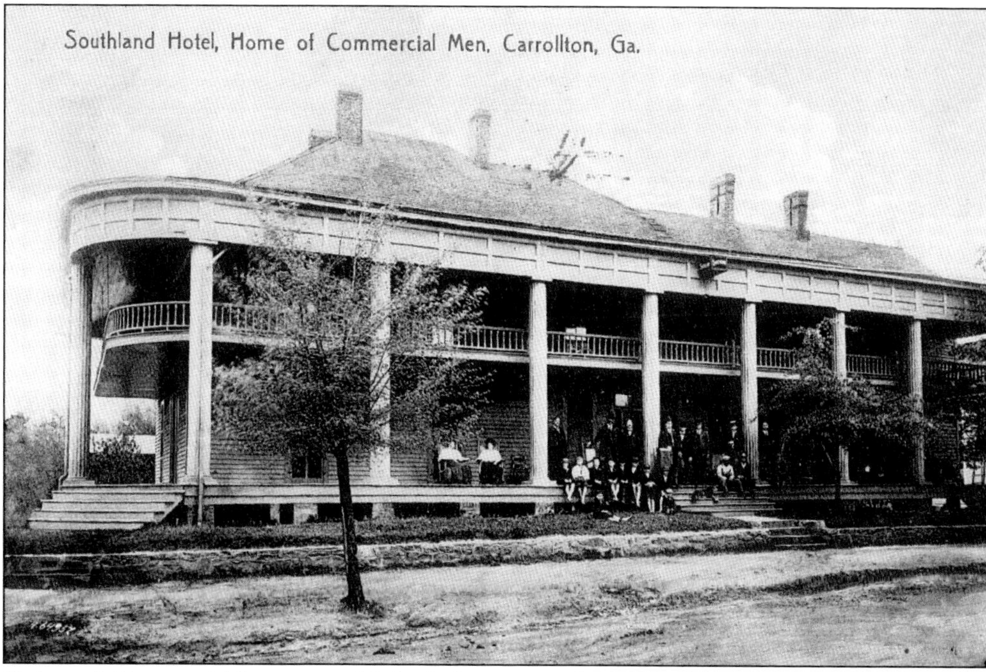

Holt and Cates, of Newnan, published this view of the Southland Hotel, the "Home of Commercial Men," in Carrollton.

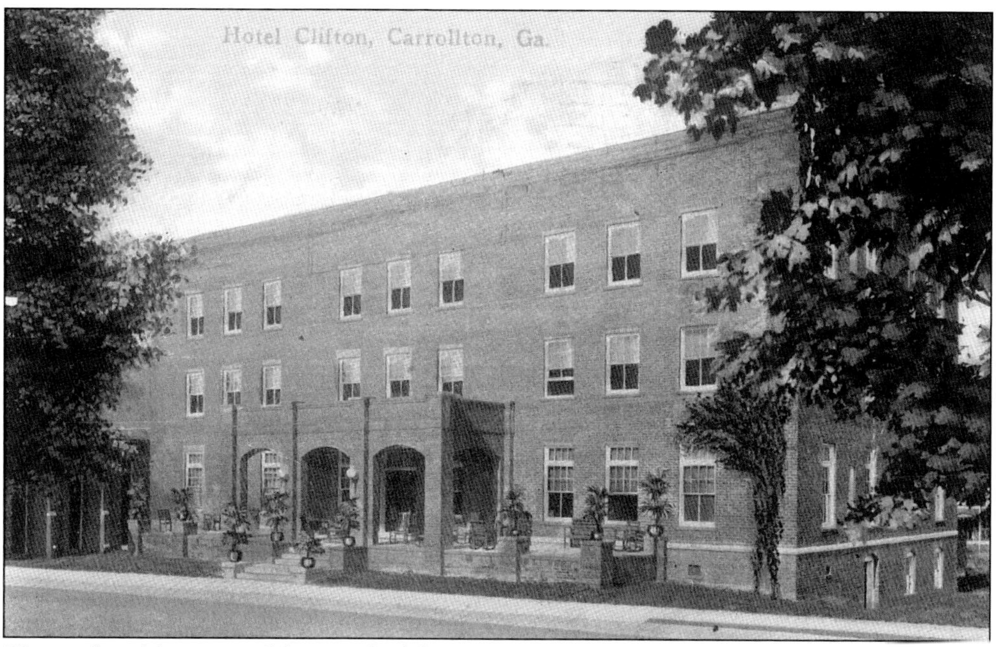

The sender of this view of the Hotel Clifton in Carrollton was very concise. On the back of this card, he wrote: "A very nice day. J.T.O."

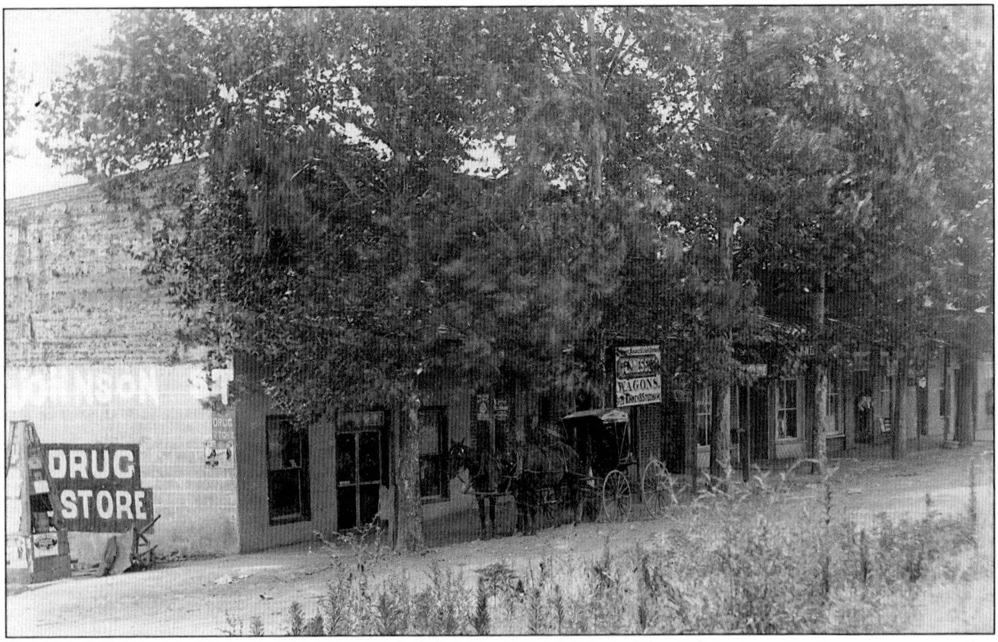

Visible in this real photo view of Johnson Street in Temple is an advertisement for Tennessee Wagons.

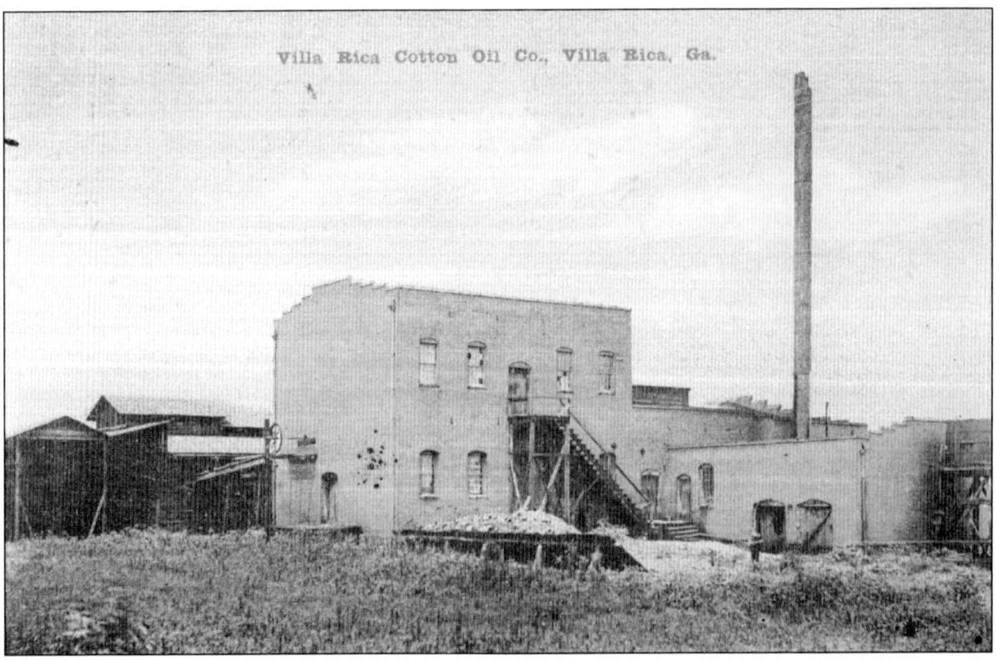

Like the sender of the Hotel Clifton card, the sender of this card featuring the Villa Rica Cotton Oil Company was concise in his correspondence. He wrote: "Villa Rica Ga. Sept. 26, 1913. Dear Bud: I saw lots of cotton here. Dad."

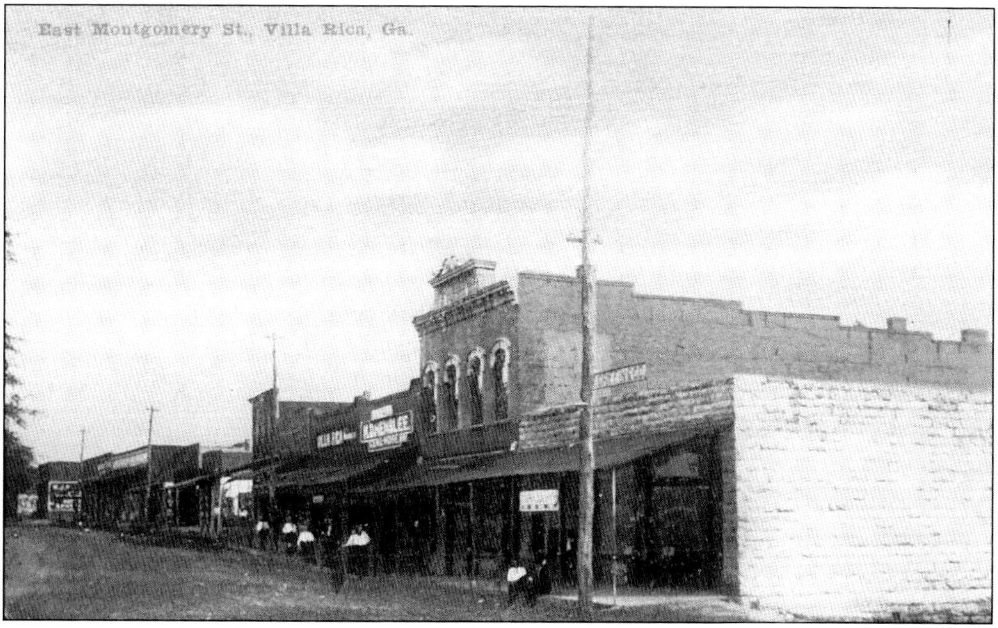

The Powell-Marchmann Pharmacy of Villa Rica published this view of East Montgomery Street in Villa Rica.

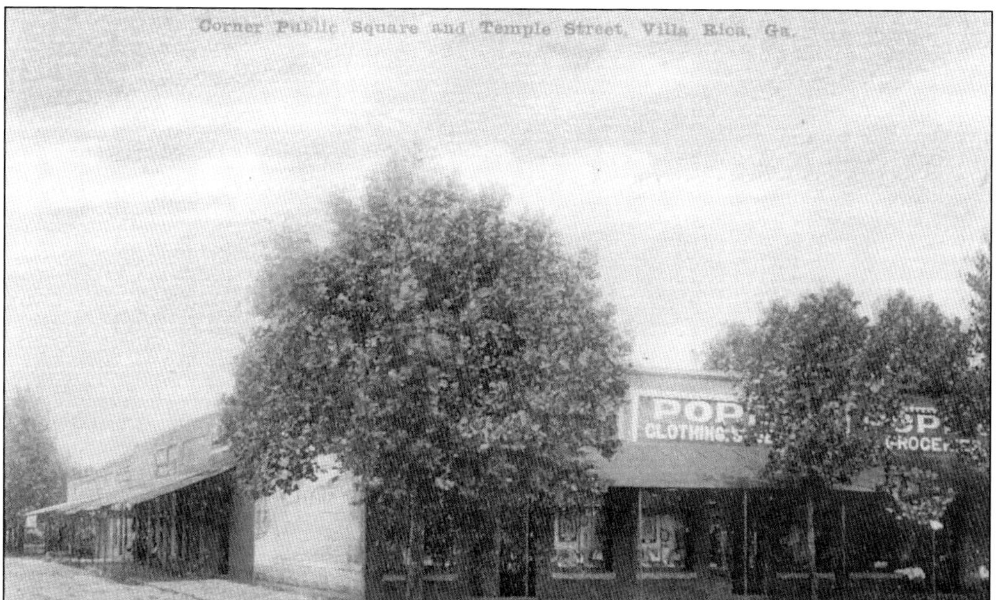

Business seems a little slow in this view of Temple Street in Villa Rica. The large store on the right was Pope Brothers, dealers in general merchandise.

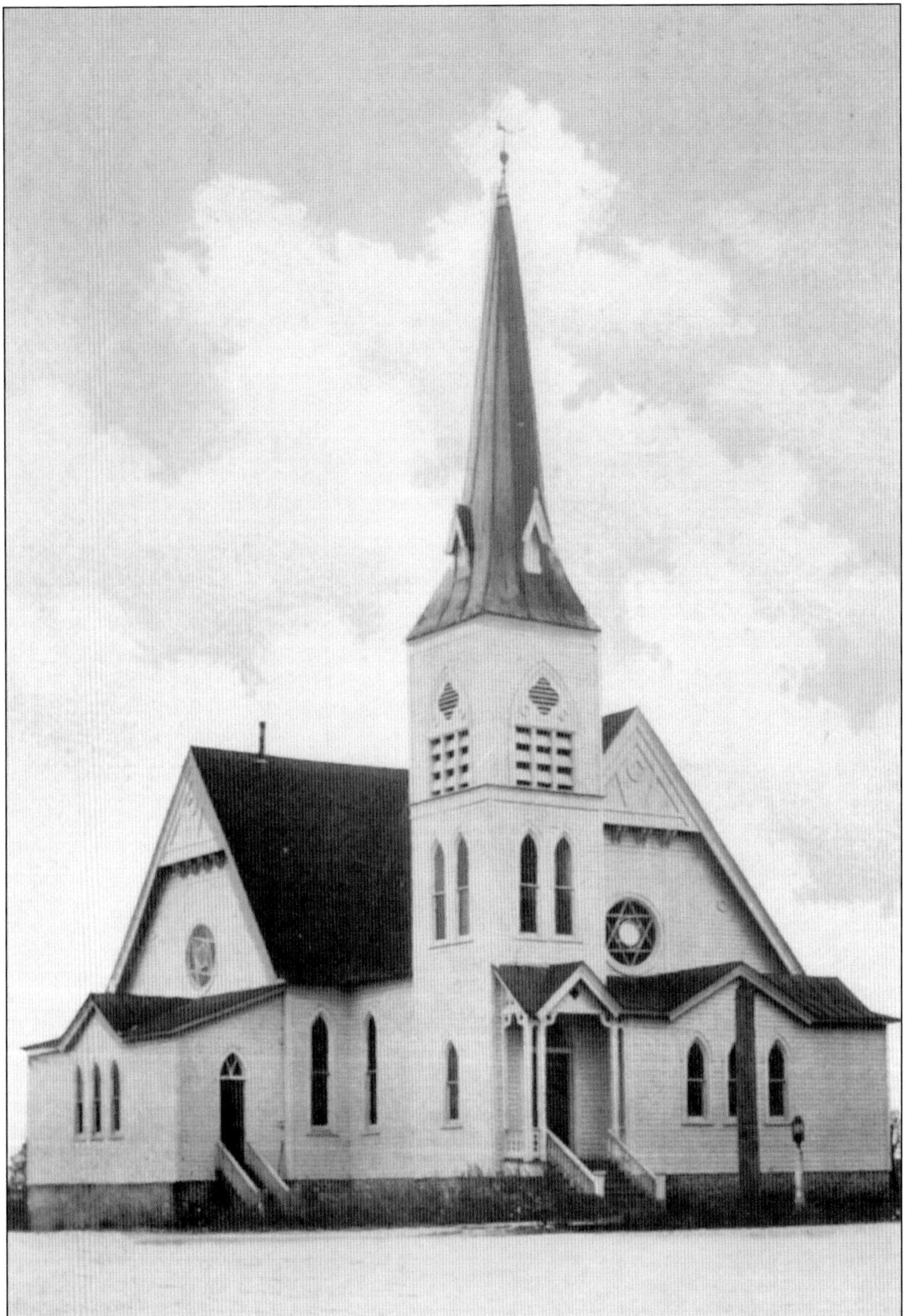

J.L. Selman and Son, of Douglasville, published this view of the Methodist church in Douglasville.

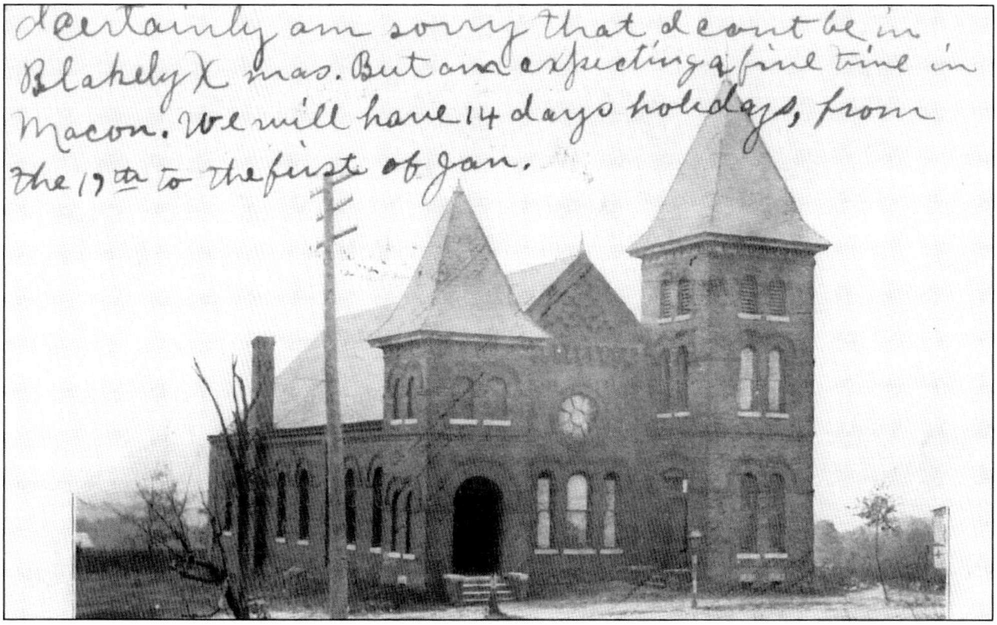

The Baptist church in Douglasville was the focus of this *c.* 1907 card.

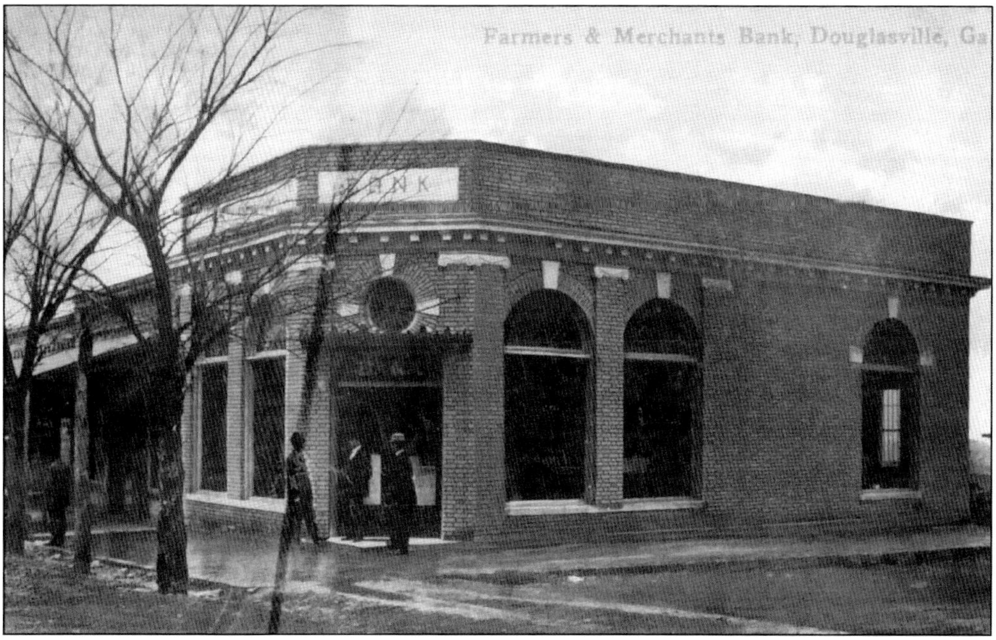

The Farmers and Merchants Bank of Douglasville, along with some gentlemen in front of the bank, were captured in this view, *c.* 1908. The bank president was W.C. Abercrombie, the vice president was R.M. Johnston, and the cashier was R.E. Edwards.

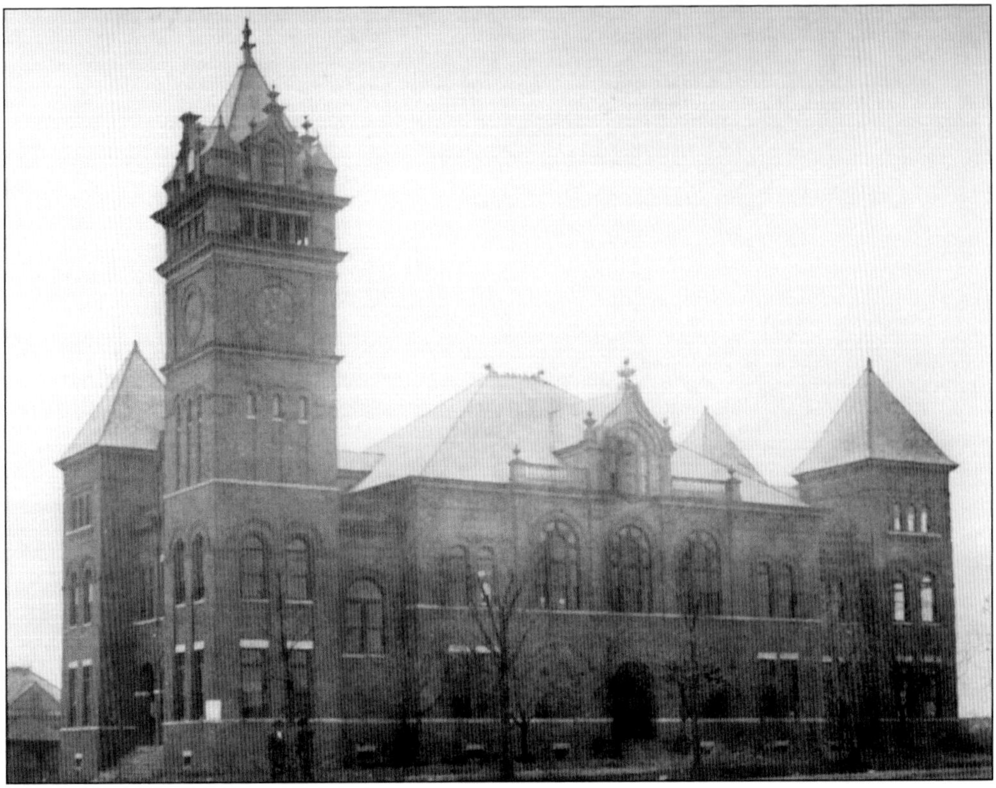

The old courthouse in Douglasville was destroyed by fire in the 1950s.

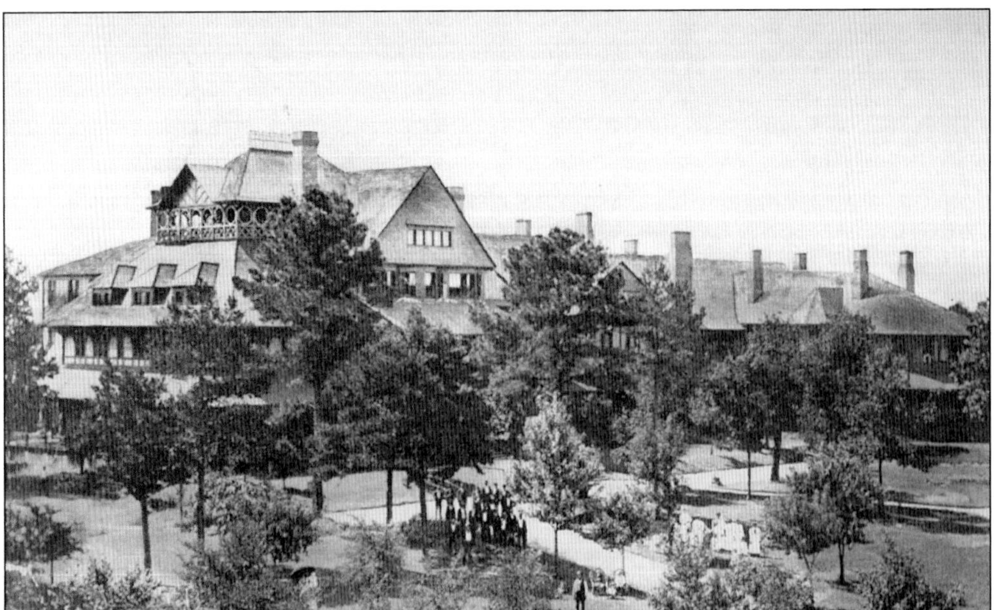

The Sweetwater Park Hotel in Lithia Springs provided a home away from home for the multitudes who came to partake of the mineral waters for their health's sake.

Five

Catoosa, Chattooga, Dade, and Walker Counties

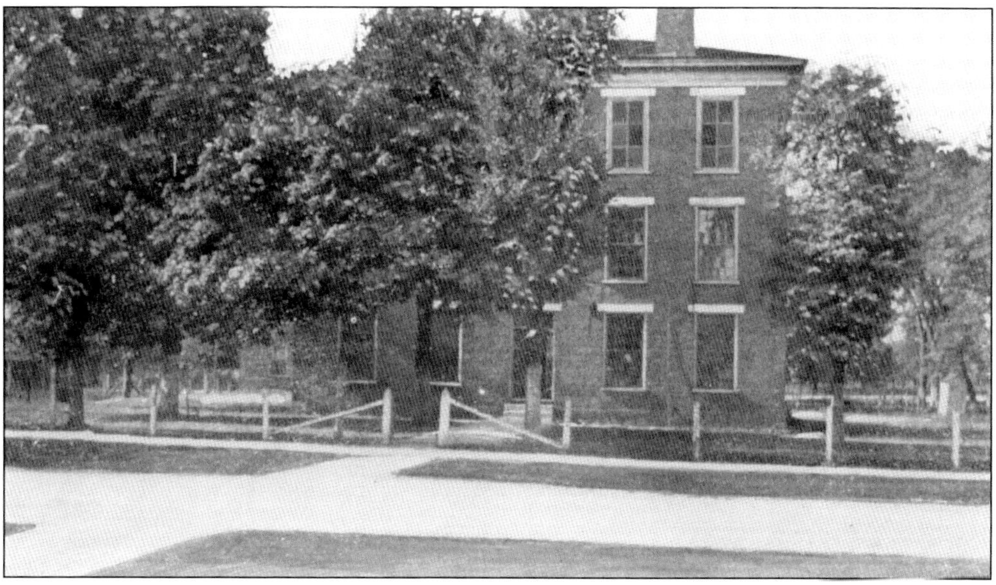

This courthouse building in Ringgold was built in 1856. The top floor was the Masonic Lodge. This courthouse was replaced with the present facility in 1939.

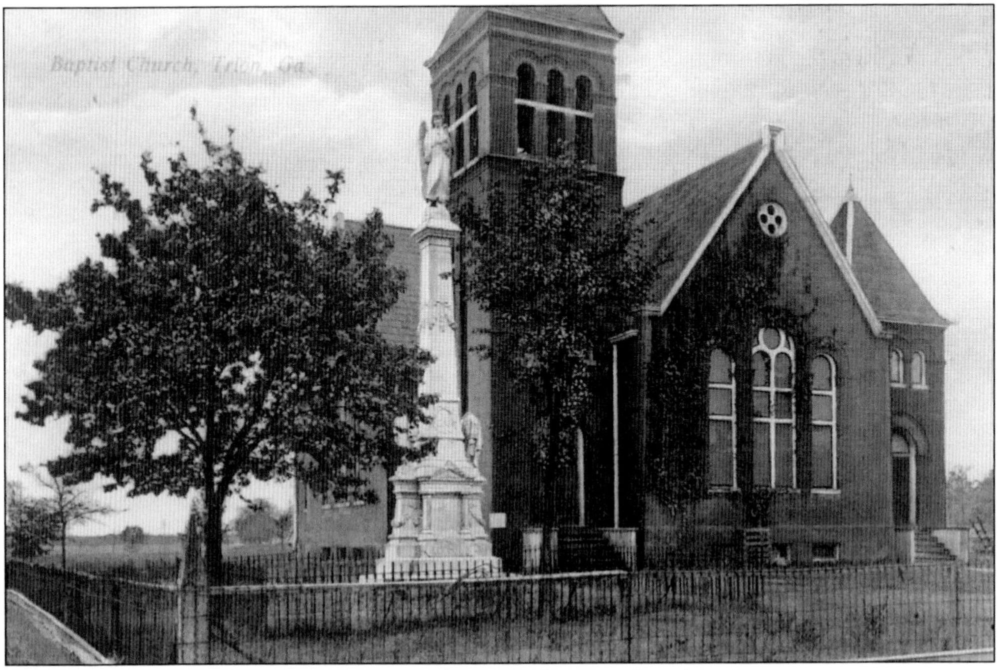

This hand-tinted card made in Germany shows the Baptist church in Trion.

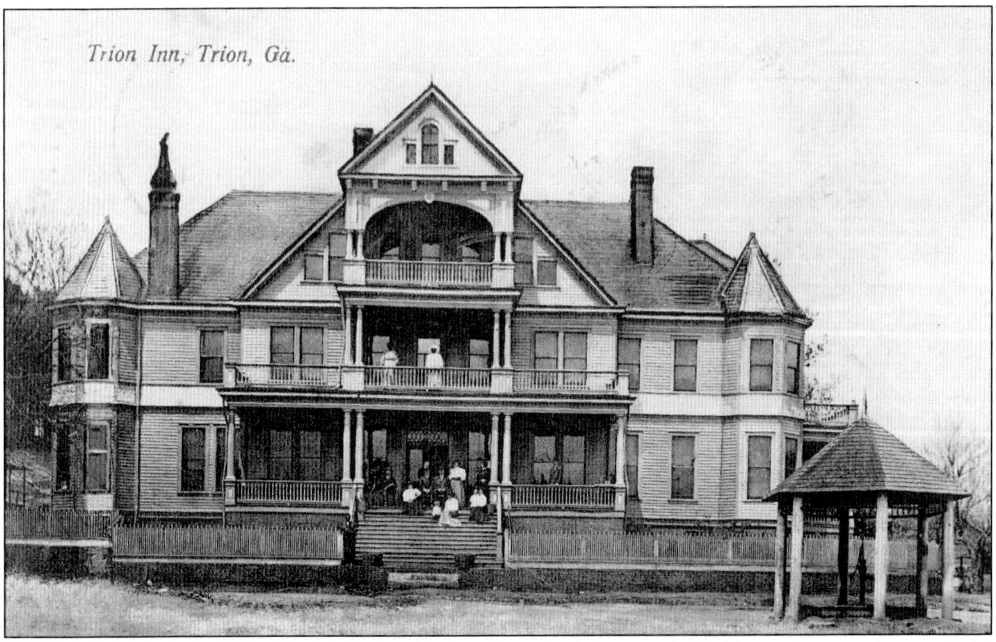

A crowd of people stands on both the first and second floors of the Trion Inn in this c. 1911 post card. Note the gazebo covering the well and hand pump on the right.

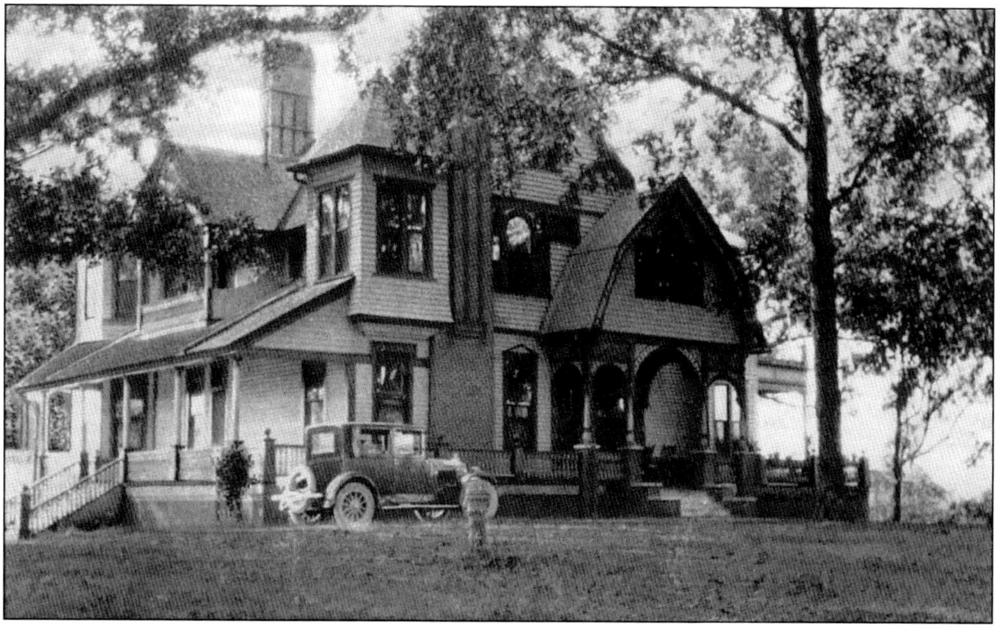

The home of the assistant treasurer of the Trion Company was an imposing structure.

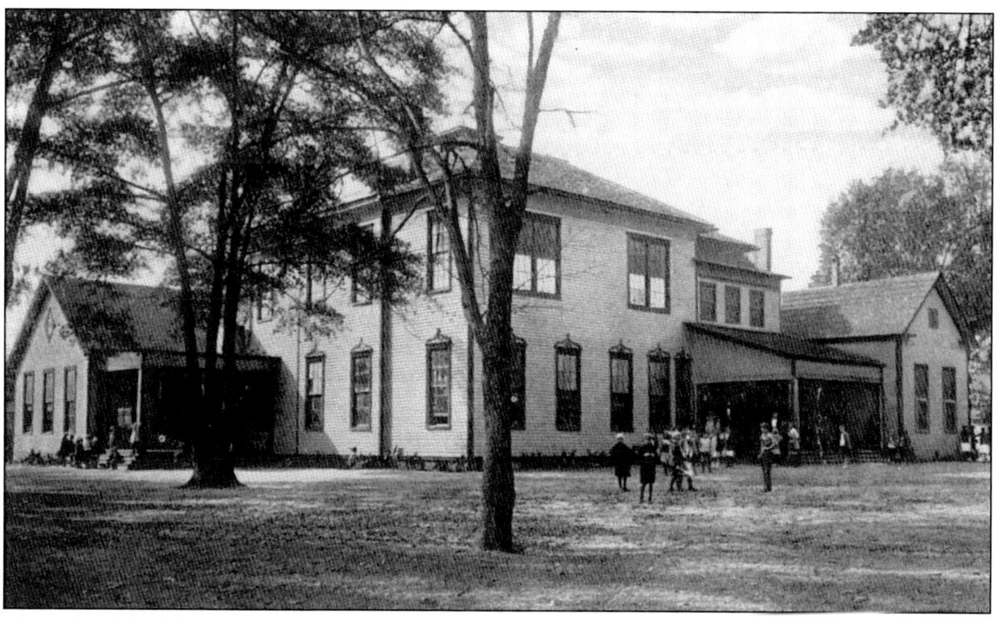

The school building in Trion was attended by the children of the workers at the huge Trion Company. Schoolchildren can be seen at play in front of the school.

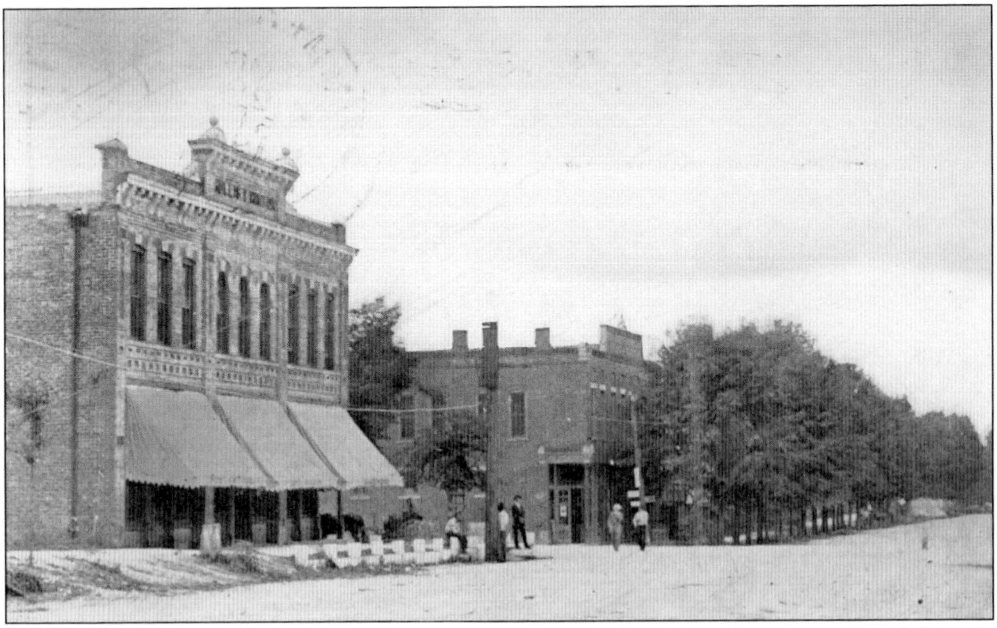

The sender of this *c*. 1911 card featuring a street scene in Summerville wrote a friend that, "a crowd from here are going to Chat. tomorrow. Wish you could go with us."

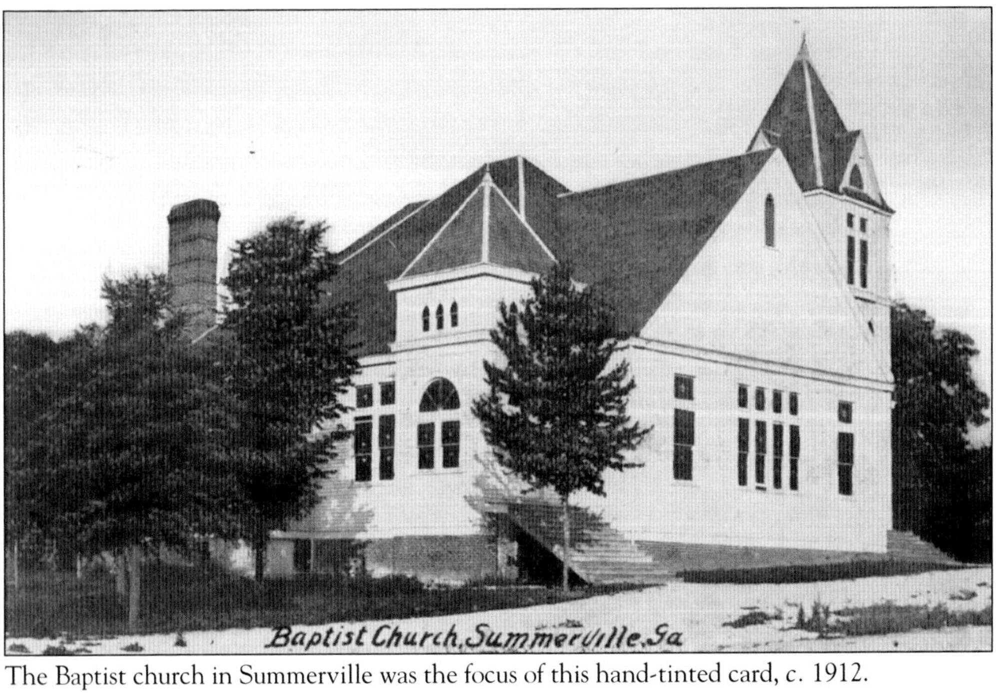

The Baptist church in Summerville was the focus of this hand-tinted card, *c*. 1912.

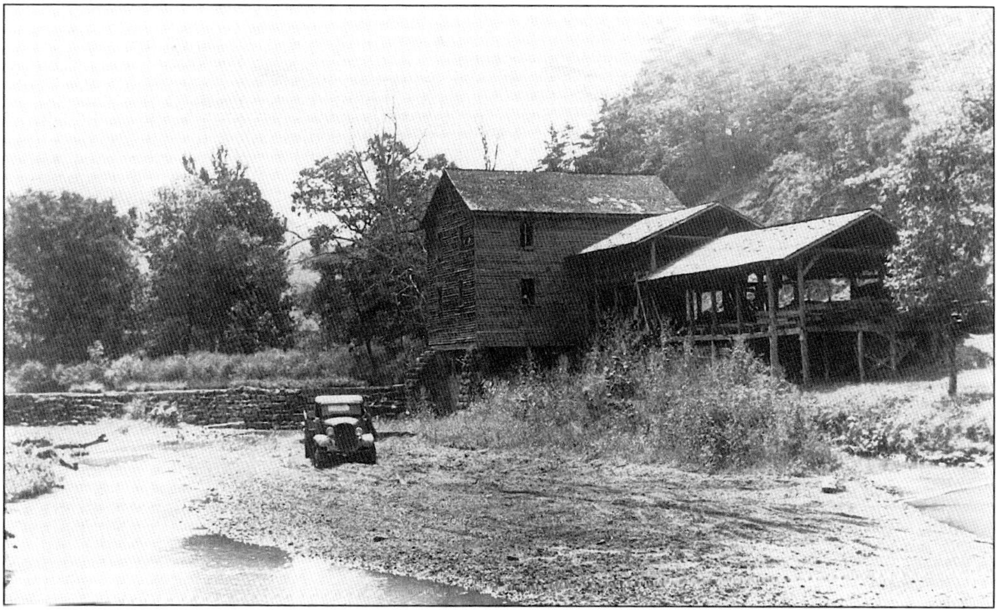

An early-model truck can be seen parked at the side of a stream in this c. 1917 post card of Sutton's Mill in Trenton.

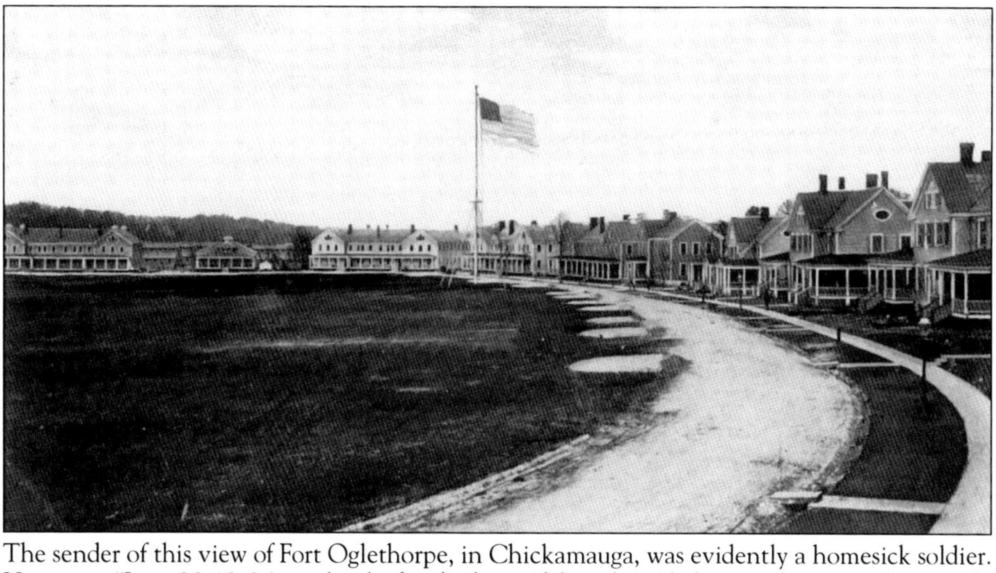

The sender of this view of Fort Oglethorpe, in Chickamauga, was evidently a homesick soldier. He wrote: "June 28-12. Many thanks for the beautiful card rec'd about an hour ago. I certainly would enjoy going with you to some of those picnics. This is a photo of the east side of the post. Write real soon. Very Sincerely, Roy."

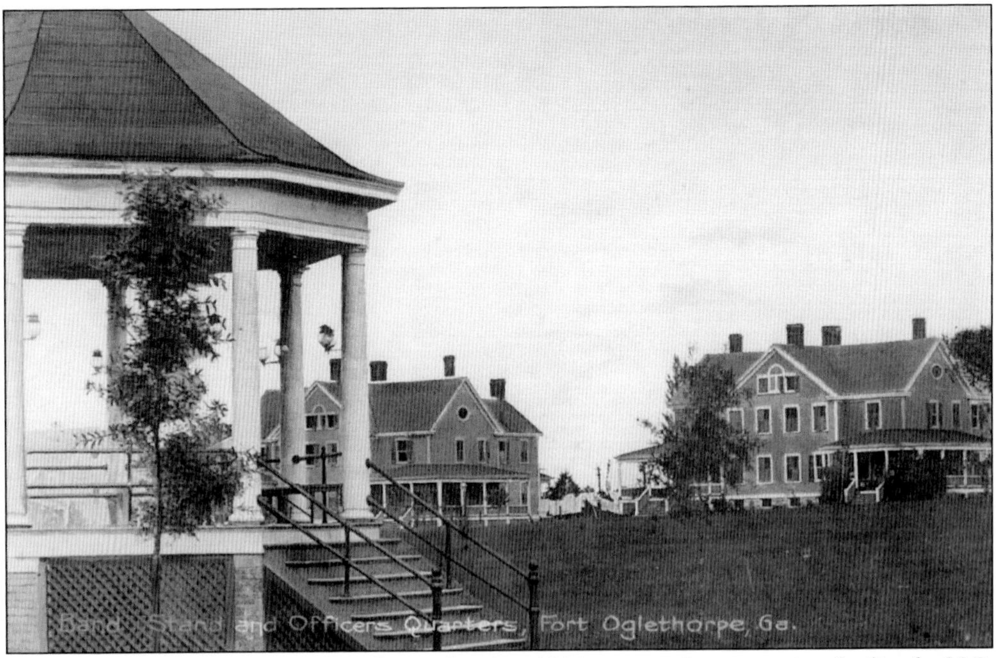

Fort Oglethorpe, begun in 1902 and completed in 1904, was used as a training facility for U.S. soldiers during World War I and World War II. The military base closed in 1947. With the bandstand and greenery, the camp hardly seems like a military installation.

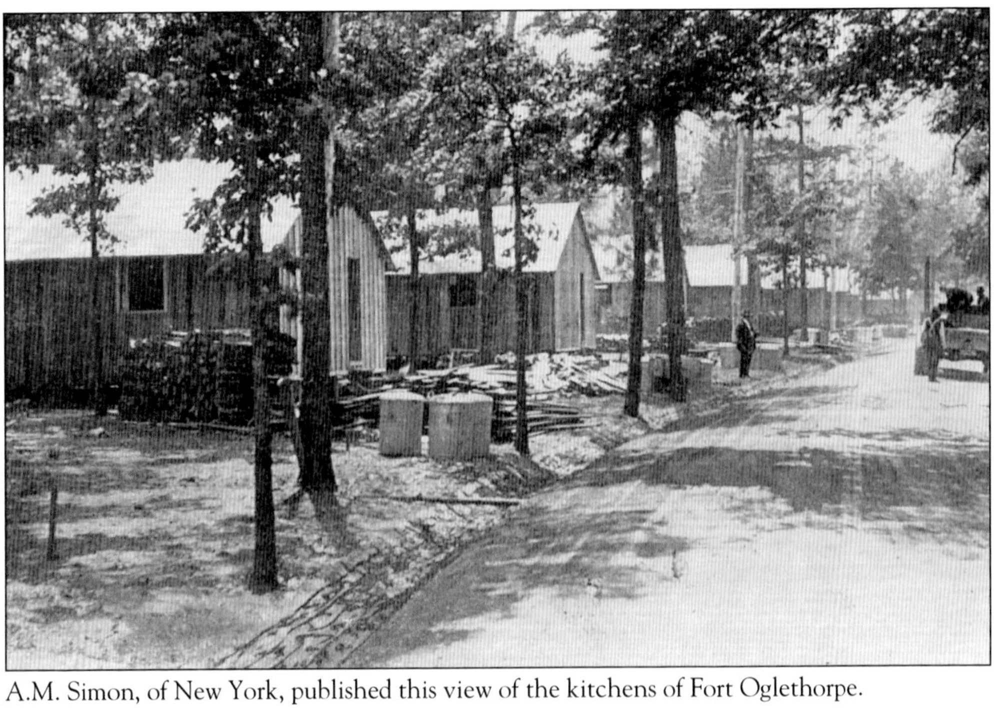

A.M. Simon, of New York, published this view of the kitchens of Fort Oglethorpe.

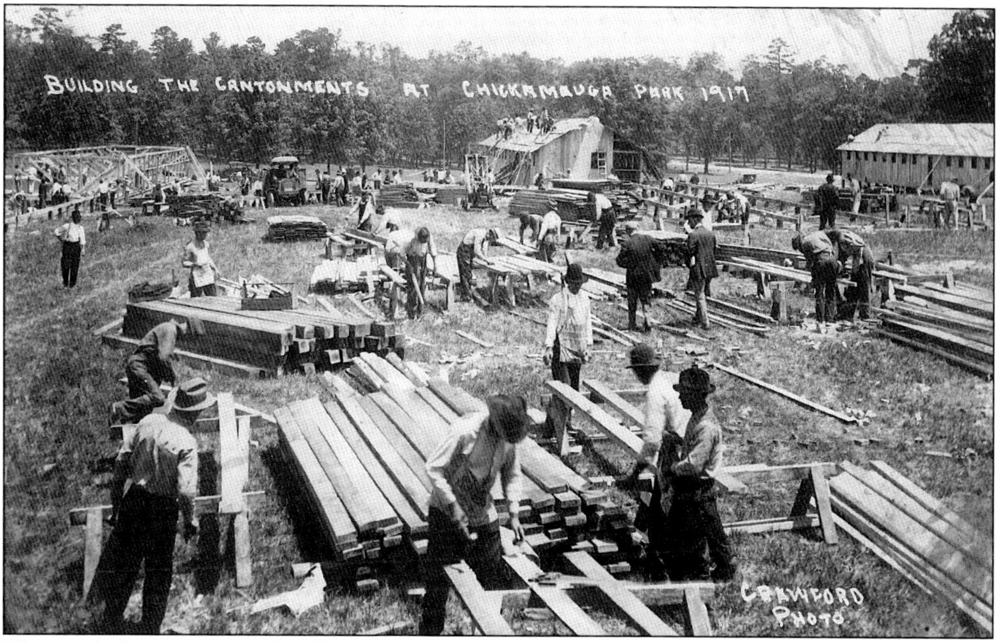

This real-photo post card, taken by "Crawford," shows the building of the cantonments at Chickamauga park (cantonments were temporary quarters assigned to troops).

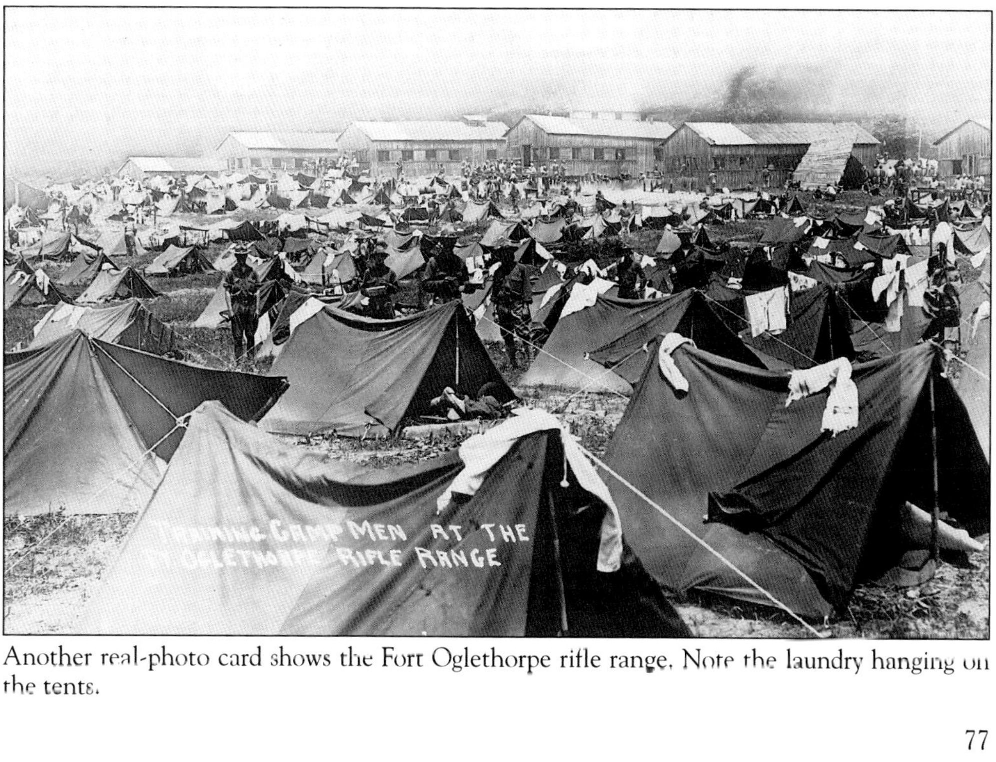

Another real-photo card shows the Fort Oglethorpe rifle range. Note the laundry hanging on the tents.

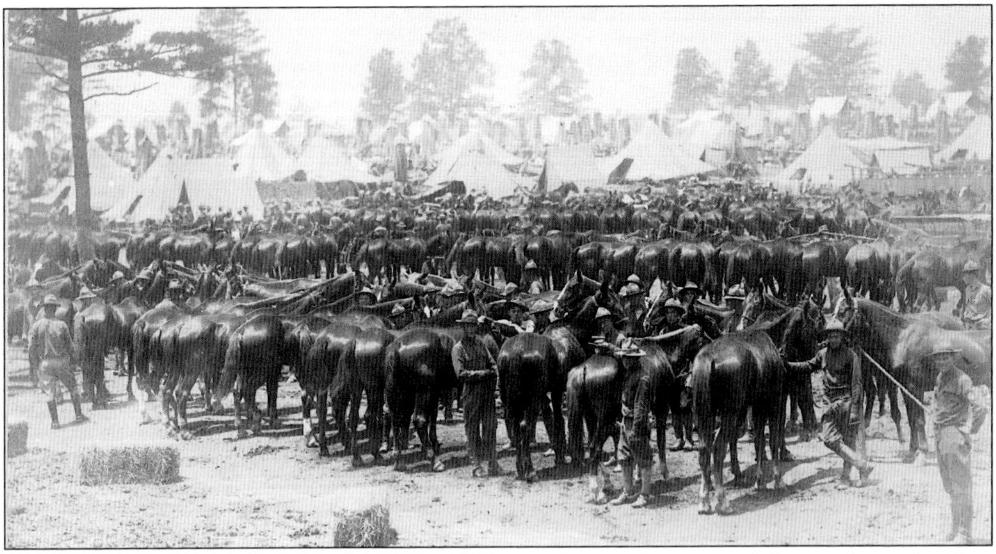

The U.S. Army's dependence on horses in 1917 is evident in this view of the cavalry picket line at Fort Oglethorpe.

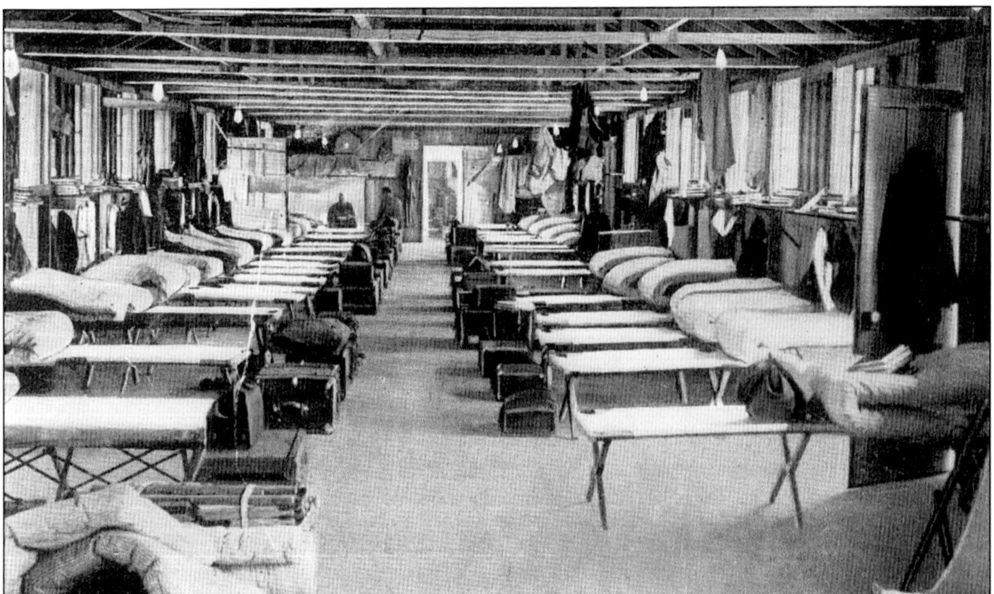

The T.H. Payne Company of Chattanooga, Tennessee, published this view of the sleeping quarters in one of the many barracks at Chickamauga Park.

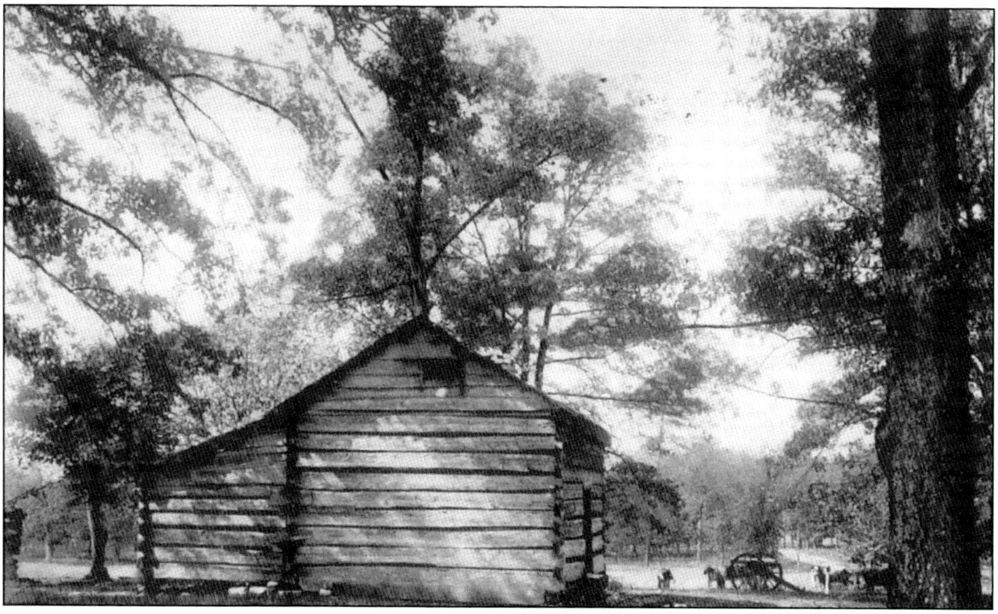

The sender of this c. 1909 post card wrote: "Chattanooga Ten. 10-17. Dear Grace. Papa is camping tonight in Chattanooga and had a delightful trip here. Weather fine and scenery just grand. Am real well and hope you are all well at home. I put in the day here tomorrow and leave at 6:15. Good Bye, Papa."

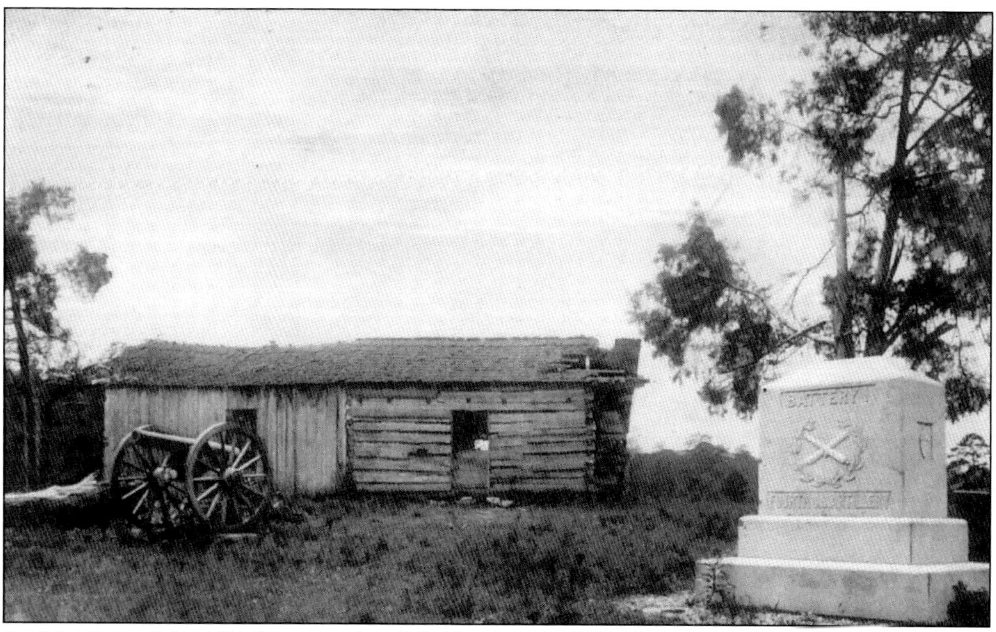

In this view of the Chickamauga battlefields, the "Old Snodgrass House" and a monument to the Fourth U.S. Artillery Battery are visible.

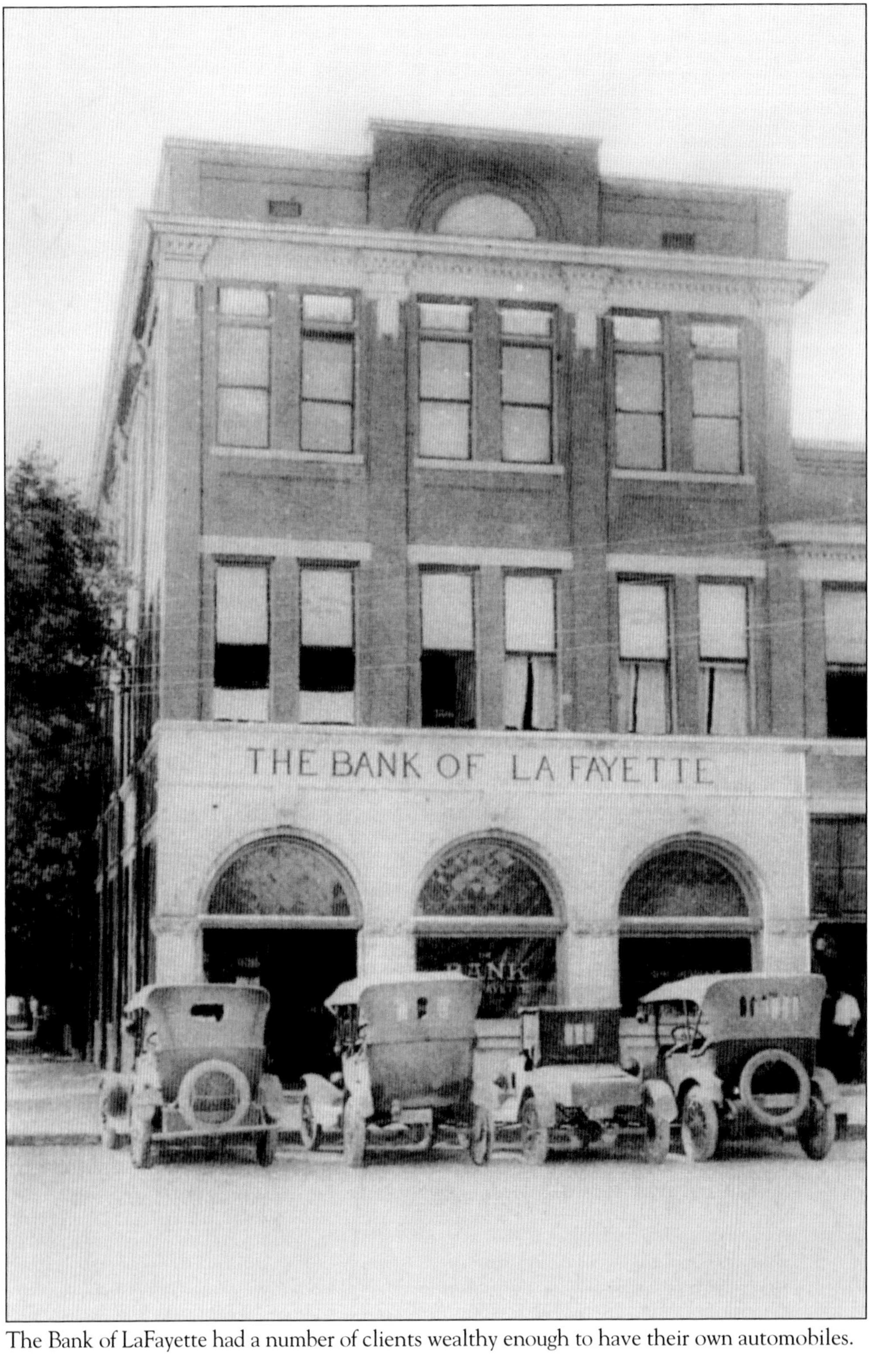

The Bank of LaFayette had a number of clients wealthy enough to have their own automobiles.

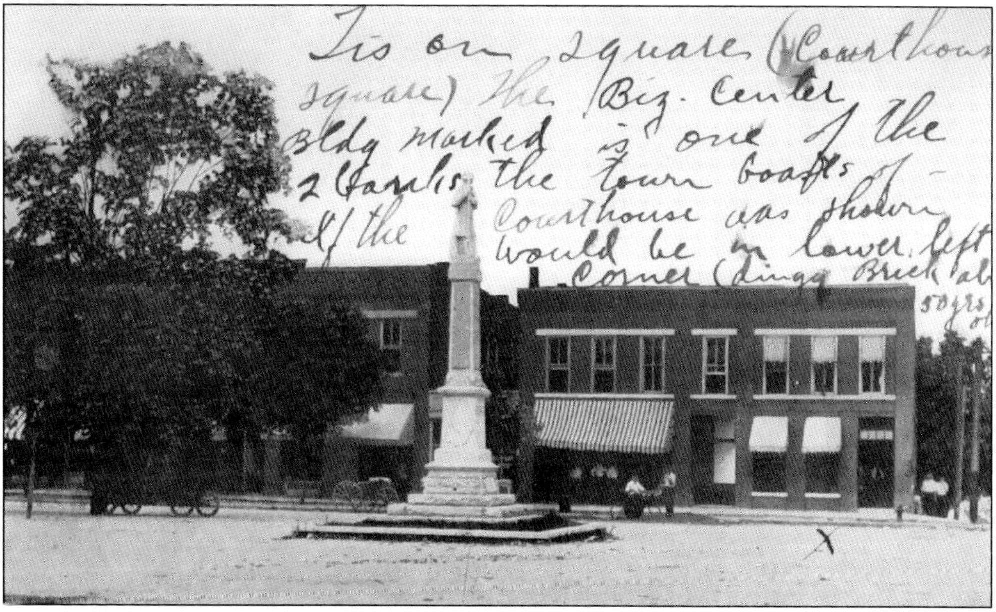

A Confederate monument in any town was always a favored subject for post card photographers and LaFayette's Monument was no exception. This *c.* 1912 card shows the monument standing in the middle of a dirt street. It was moved in 1968 to the front of the chamber of commerce.

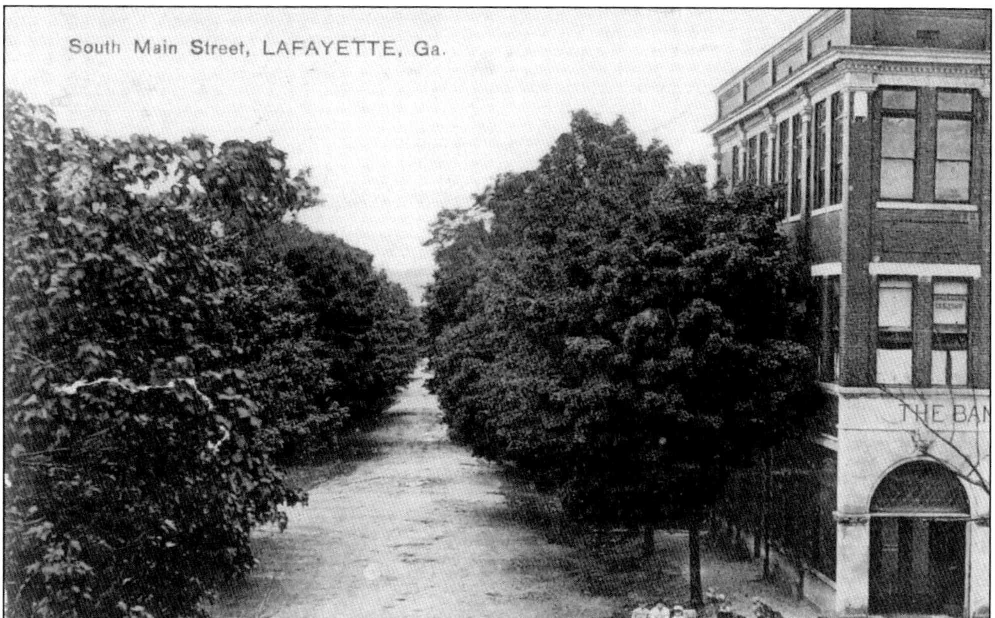

This view, published by Warthen's Drug Store, shows South Main Street in LaFayette. Note the large trees lining the street.

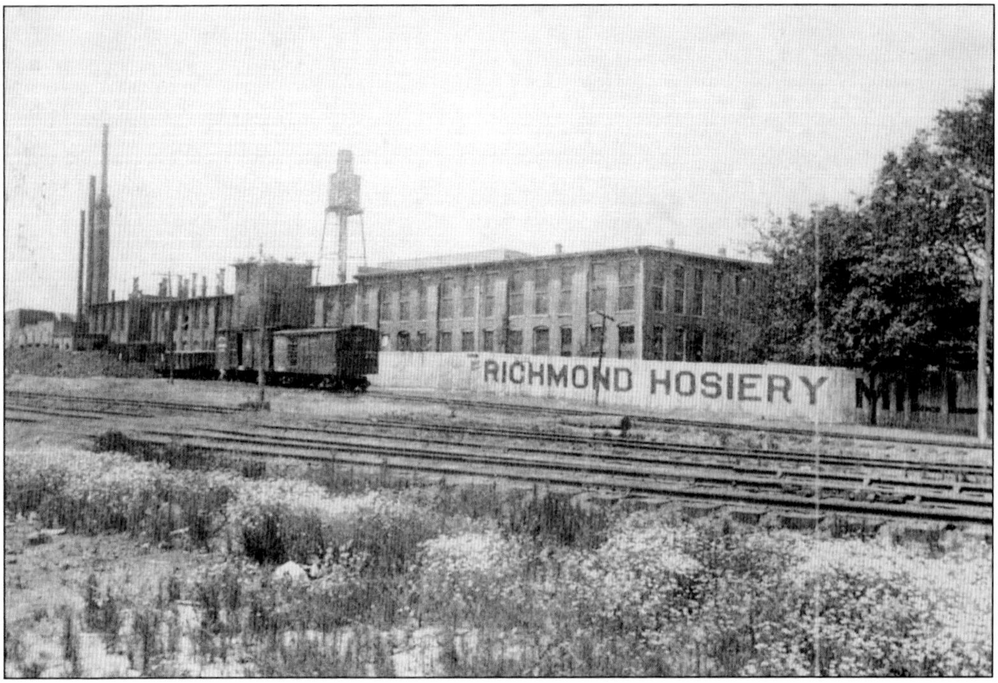

The MacGowan-Cooke Printing Company of Chattanooga published this *c.* 1911 view of the Richmond Hosiery Mills in Rossville.

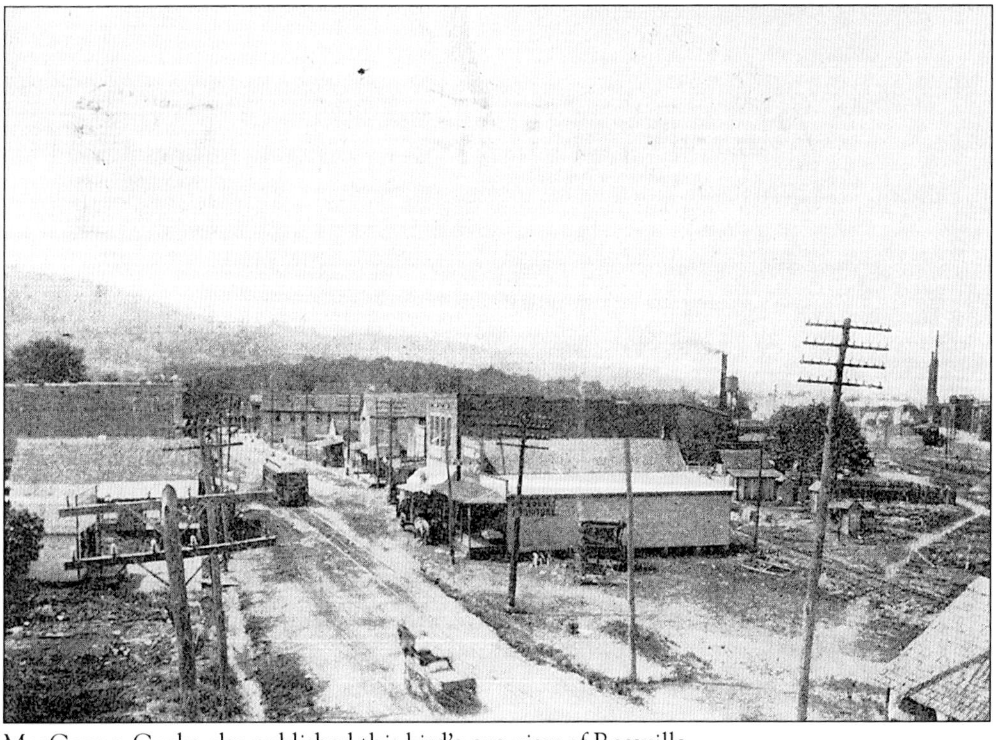

MacGowan-Cooke also published this bird's-eye view of Rossville.

Six

Fannin, Gilmer, Pickens, and Whitfield Counties

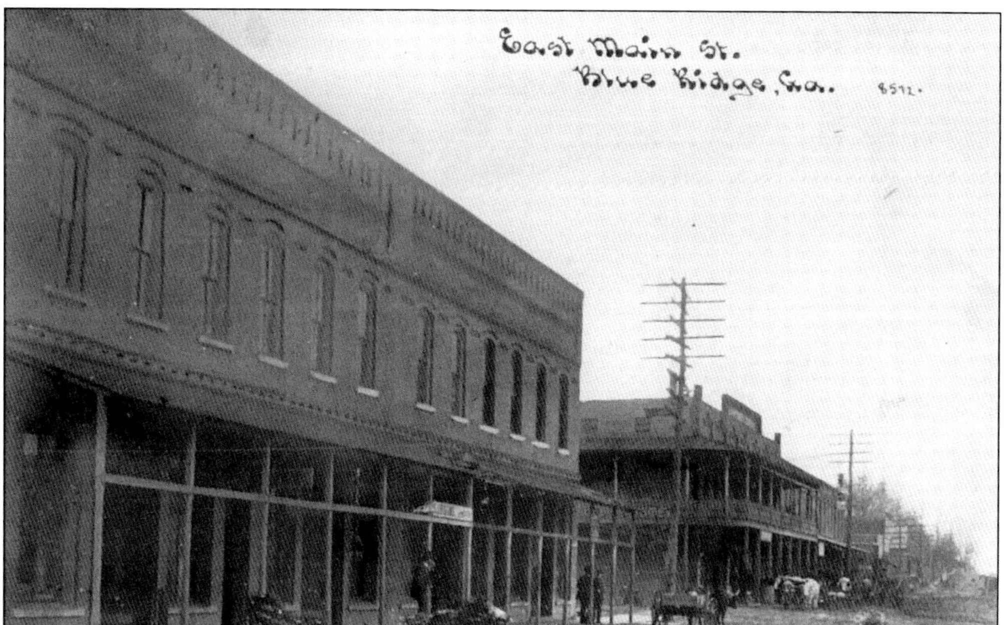

This view of East Main Street in Blue Ridge c. 1908 shows a landscape that, although beginning to look more urban, was still largely rural in nature.

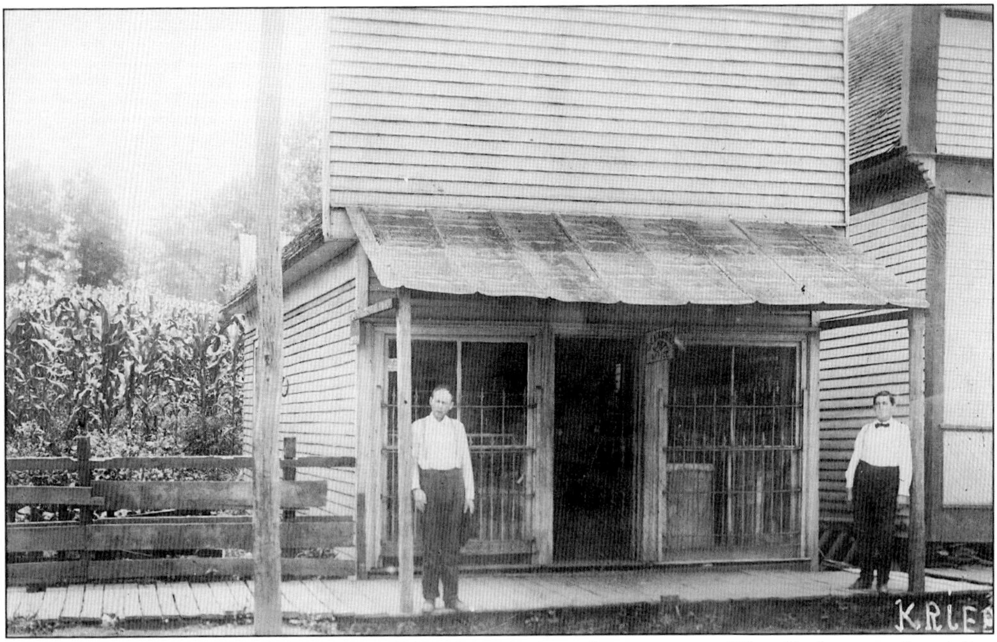

This real-photo post card shows Dr. C.B. Crawford, a pharmacist in Blue Ridge, on the right. The man on the left is unidentified.

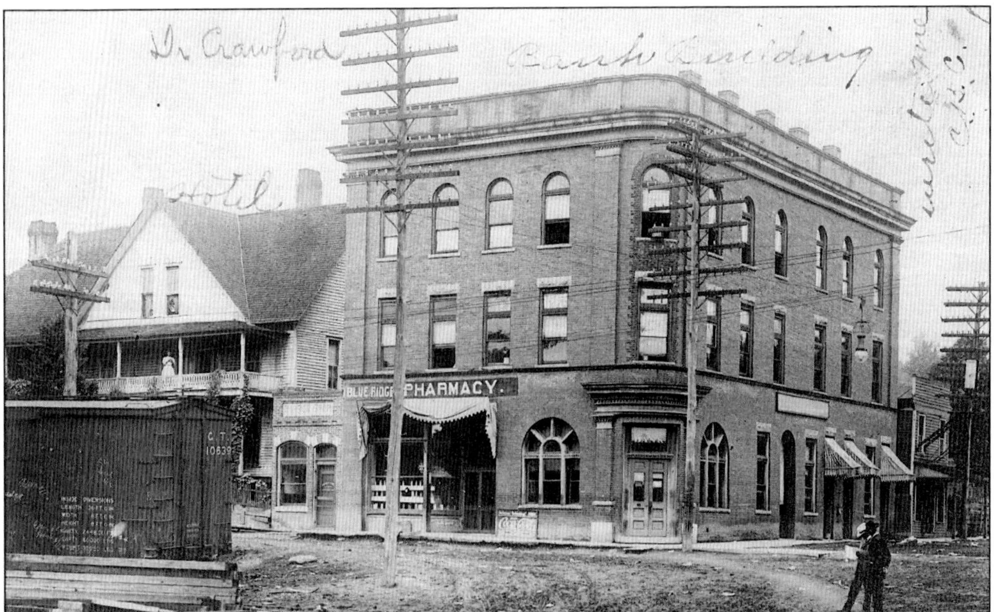

This 1906 real-photo view of Blue Ridge shows the hotel, barber shop, bank, and Dr. C.B. Crawford's pharmacy with a Coca-Cola sign out front.

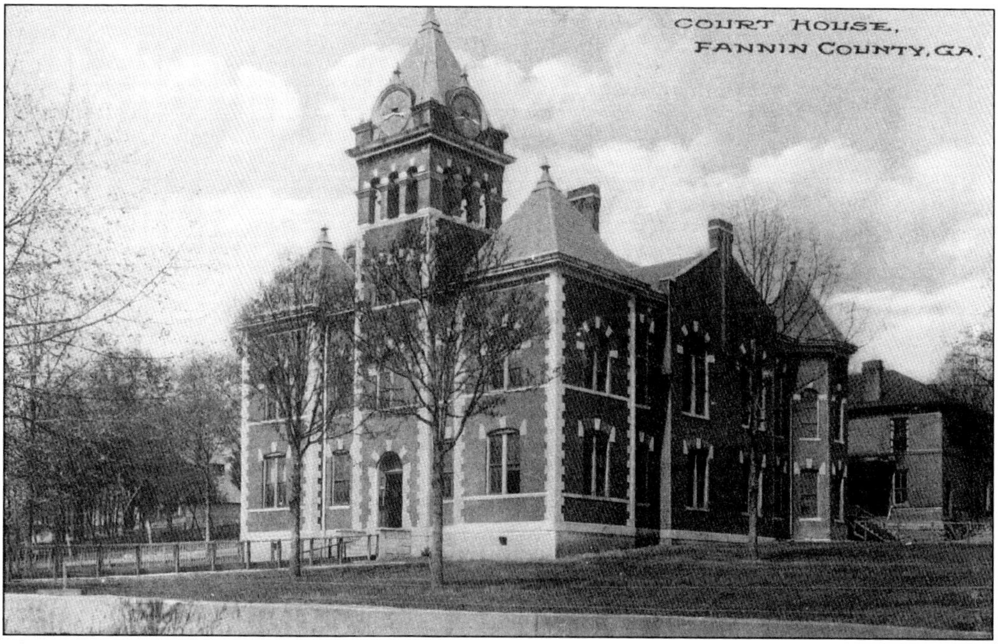

This Fannin County courthouse building in Blue Ridge was built in 1895 and burned down in 1936.

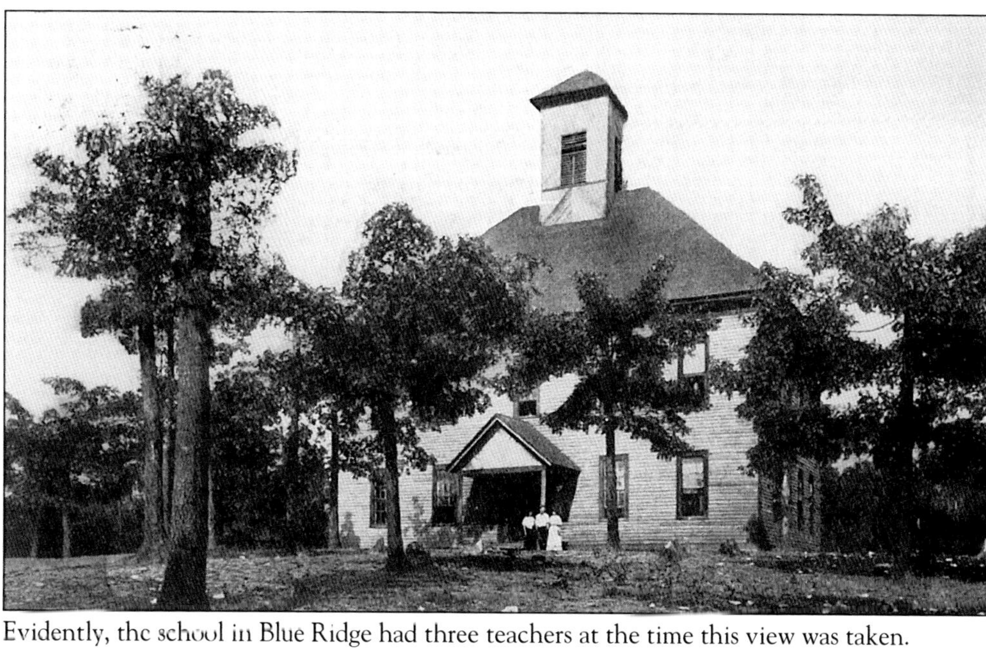

Evidently, the school in Blue Ridge had three teachers at the time this view was taken.

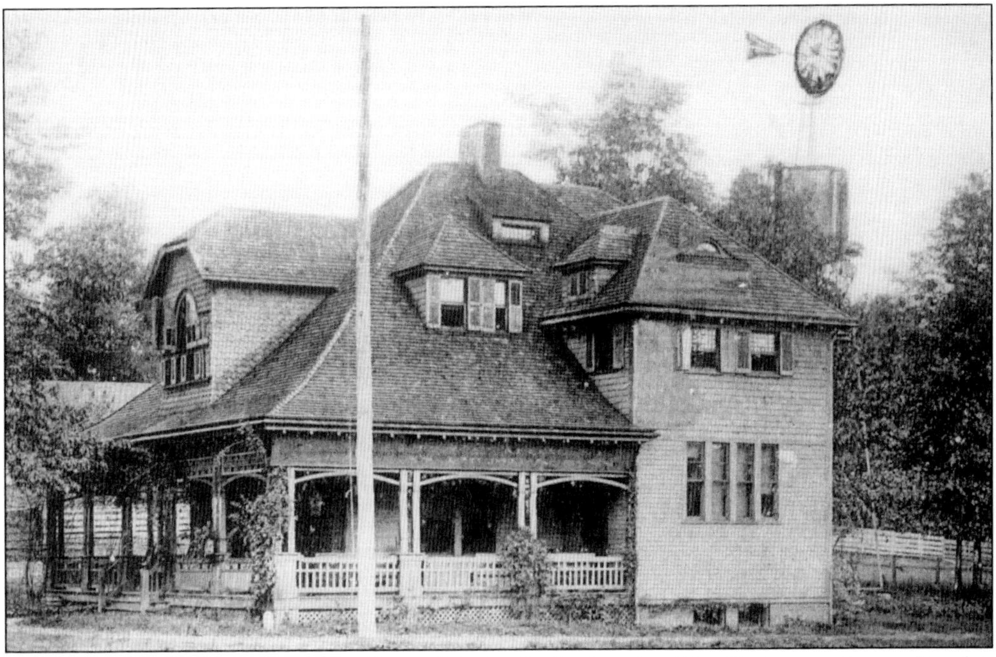

The YMCA building of the Louisville and Nashville Railroad in Blue Ridge was featured in this card, published by the Blue Ridge pharmacy. Note the windmill and water tower at the rear of the building.

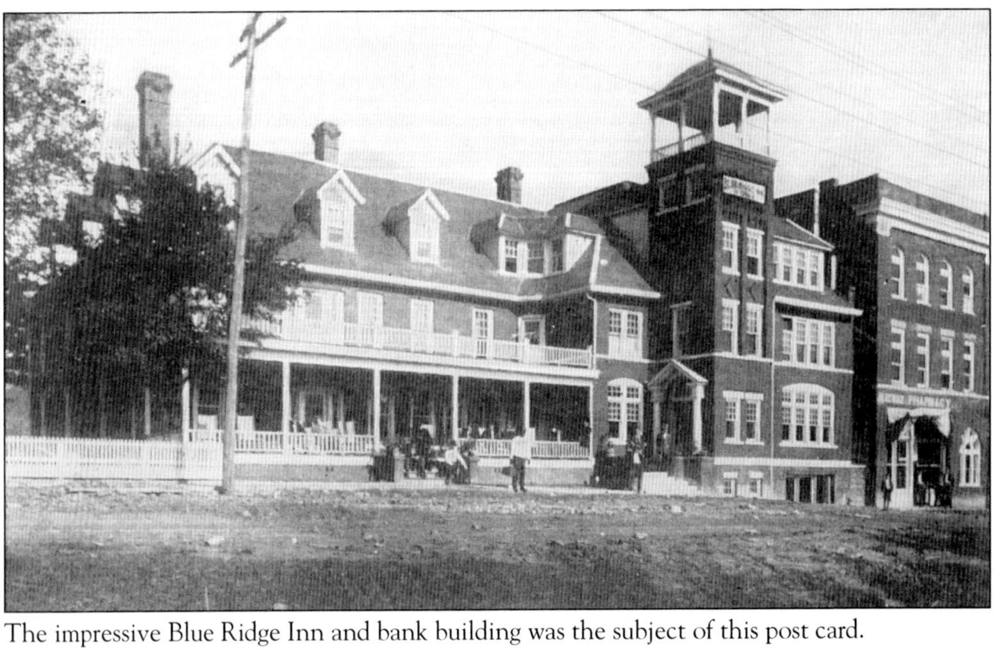

The impressive Blue Ridge Inn and bank building was the subject of this post card.

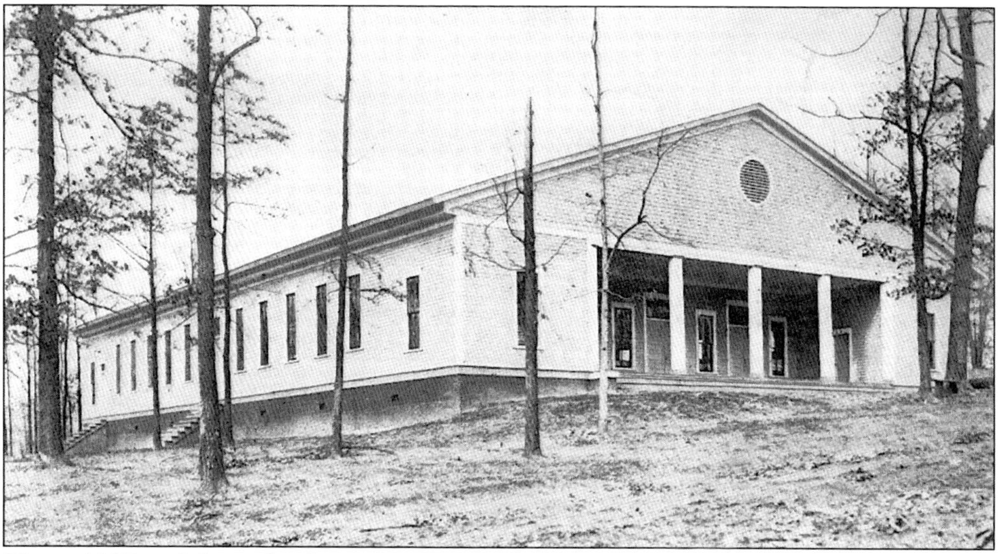

This c. 1907 card shows the Georgia Baptist Assembly auditorium in Blue Ridge.

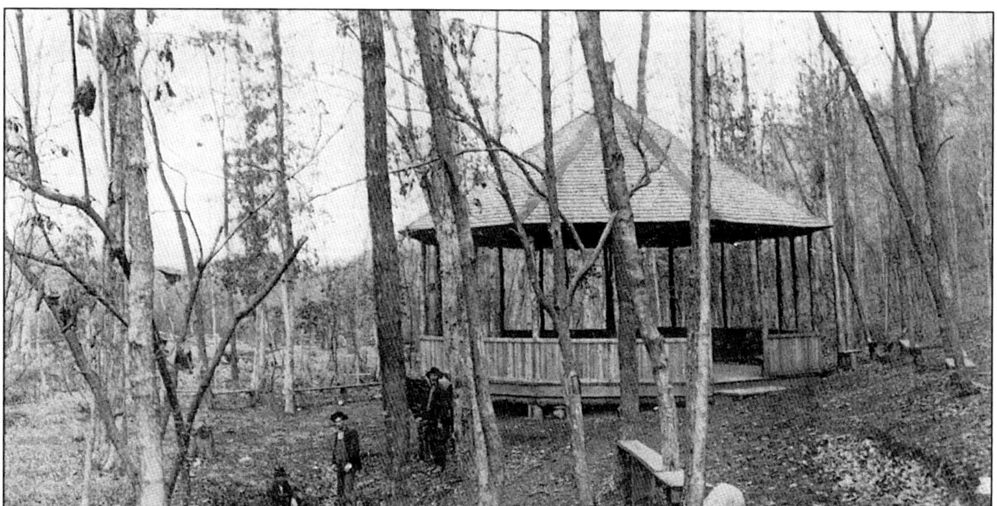

The rustic but attractive pavilion at the Georgia Baptist Assembly grounds is featured in this c. 1907 post card. The message: "You should see granny drinking water from this spring."

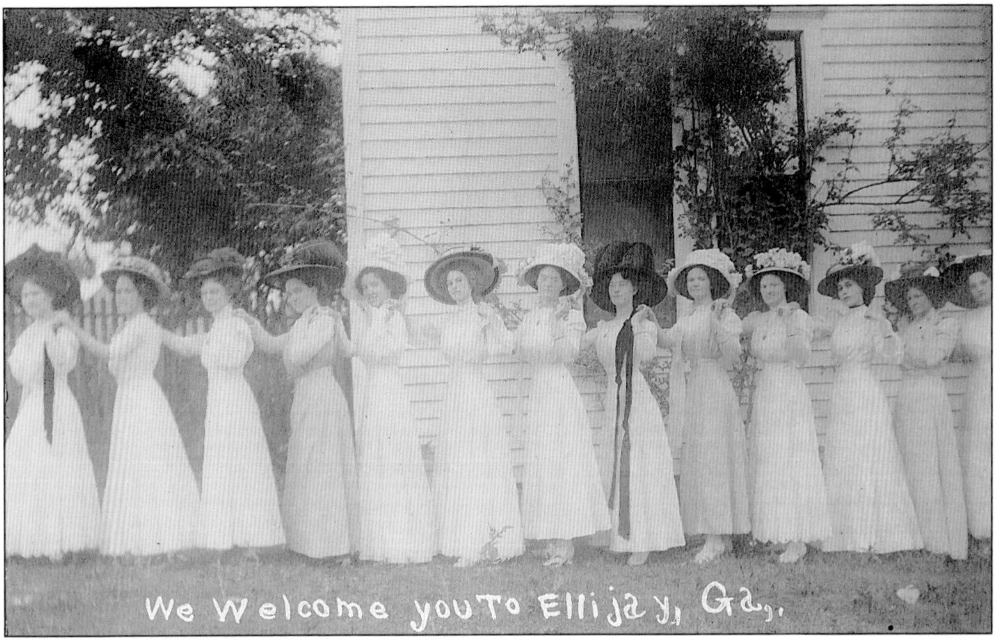

As the caption clearly indicates, these finely dressed ladies welcomed you to Ellijay.

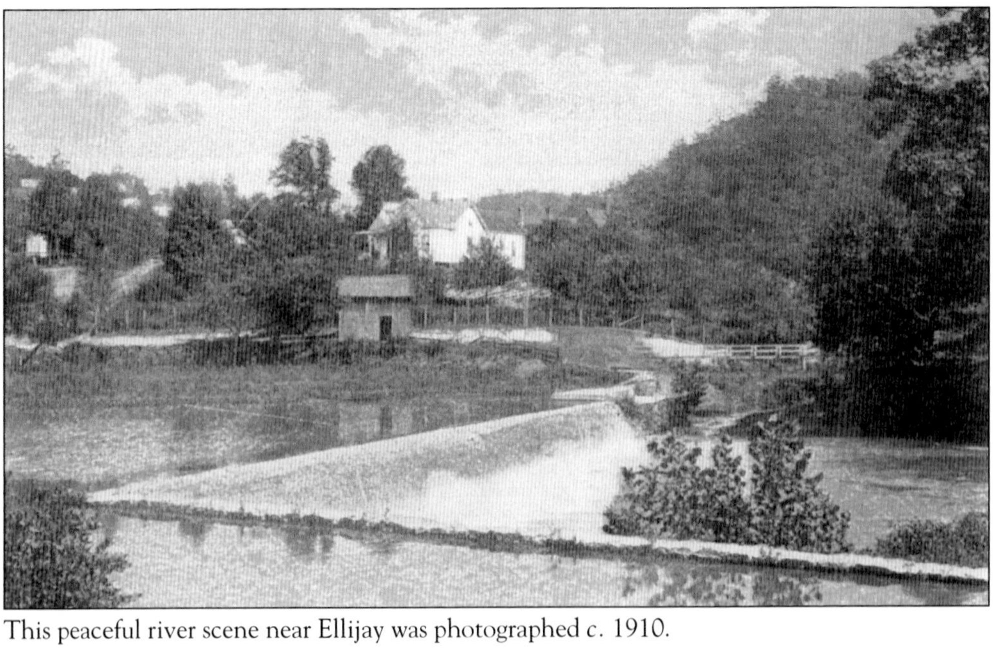
This peaceful river scene near Ellijay was photographed *c.* 1910.

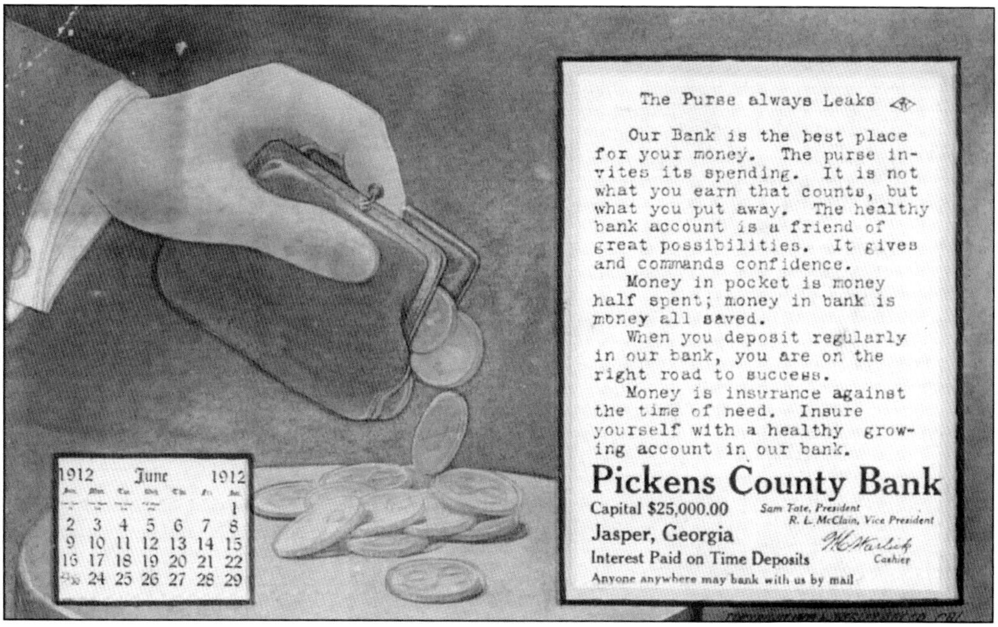

This 1912 advertising card from the Pickens County bank in Jasper advised customers to put their money with the bank because "the purse always leaks."

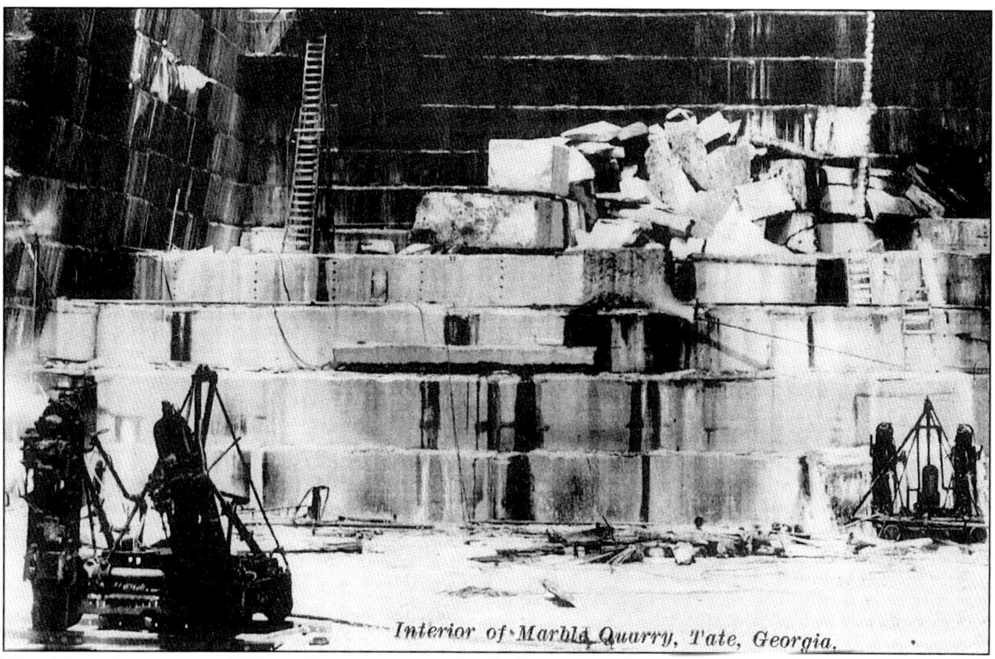

The Tate Company of Tate, Georgia, published this view of the interior of the marble quarry.

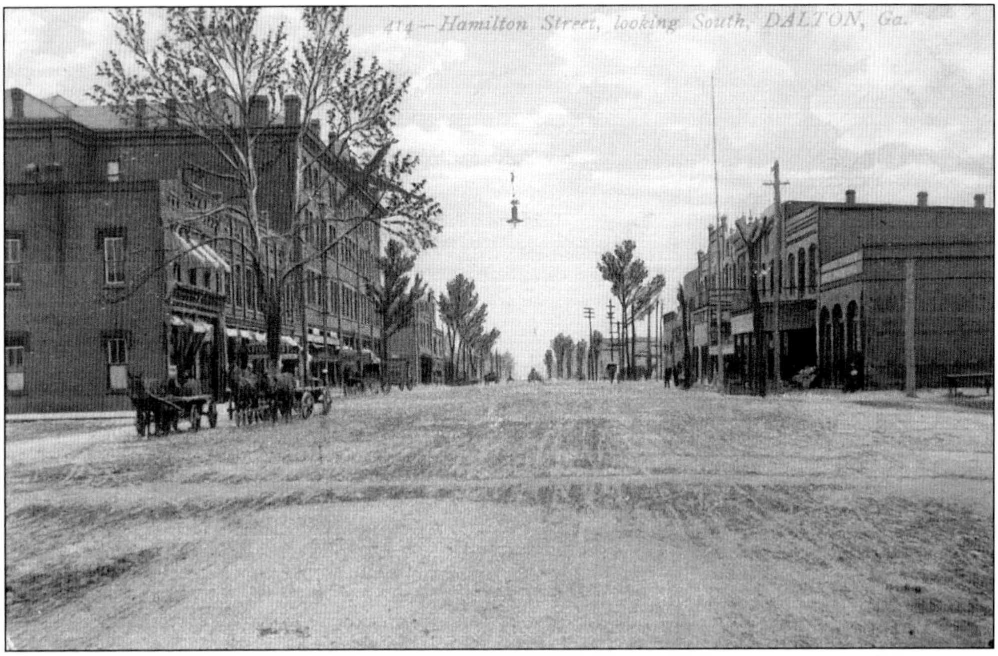

This *c.* 1907 card shows the south end of Hamilton Street in Dalton criss-crossed by wagon wheel tracks with an early streetlight suspended over the middle of the street.

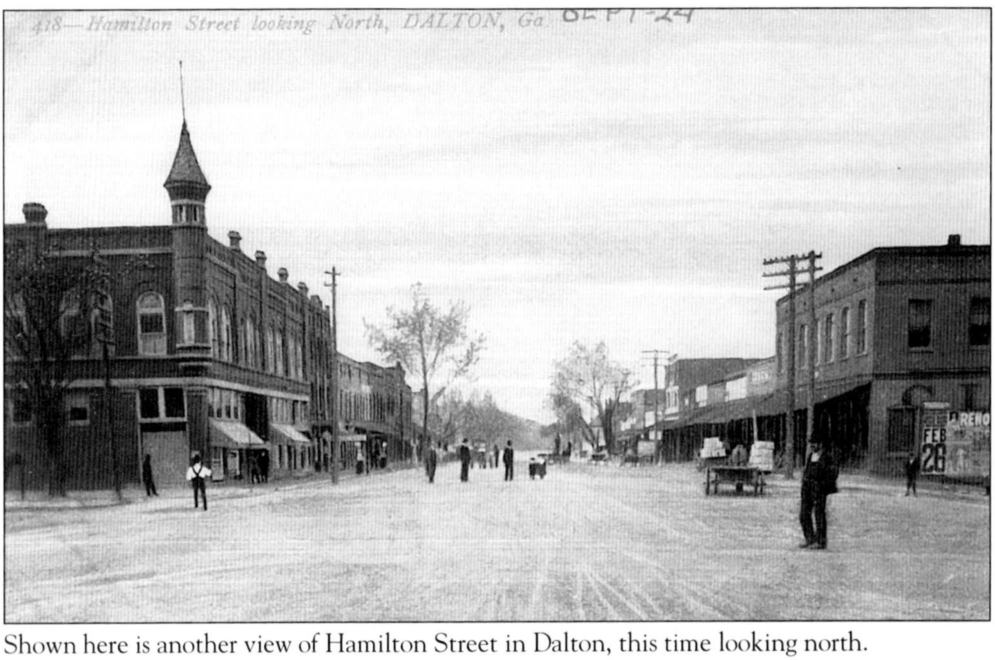

Shown here is another view of Hamilton Street in Dalton, this time looking north.

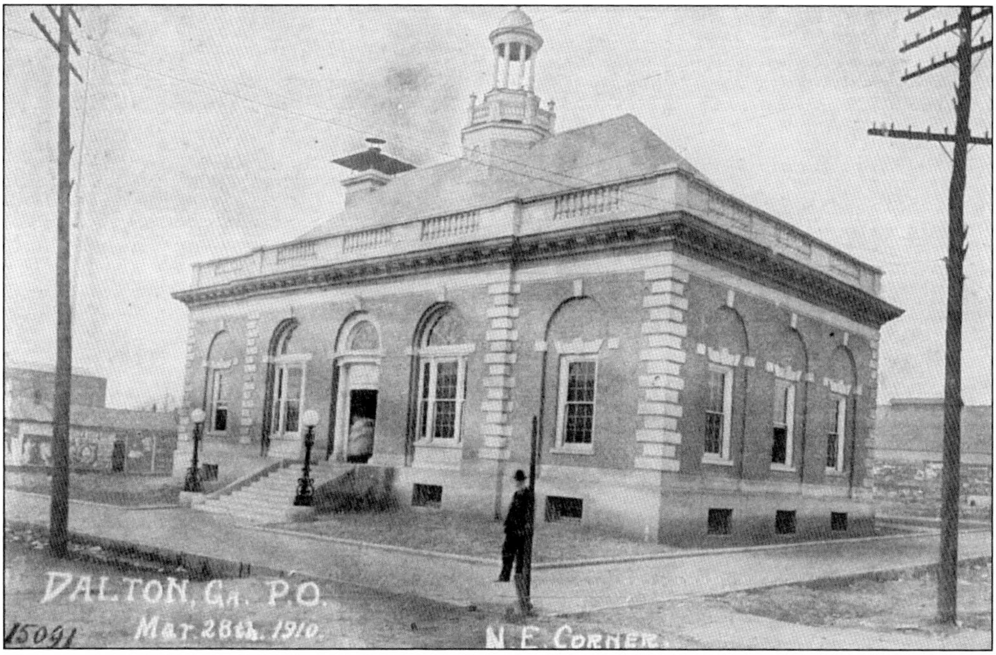

The sender of this card featuring the post office in Dalton was evidently recuperating from an illness. She wrote: "Dear Ethel: Was glad to get your card. This makes the fourth day I've been up. I am feeling stronger each day but have to rest several times during the day. I've been eating most anything and living on chickens. I think in another week I'll be able to go about as much as ever. Write again soon, both send love, Clara."

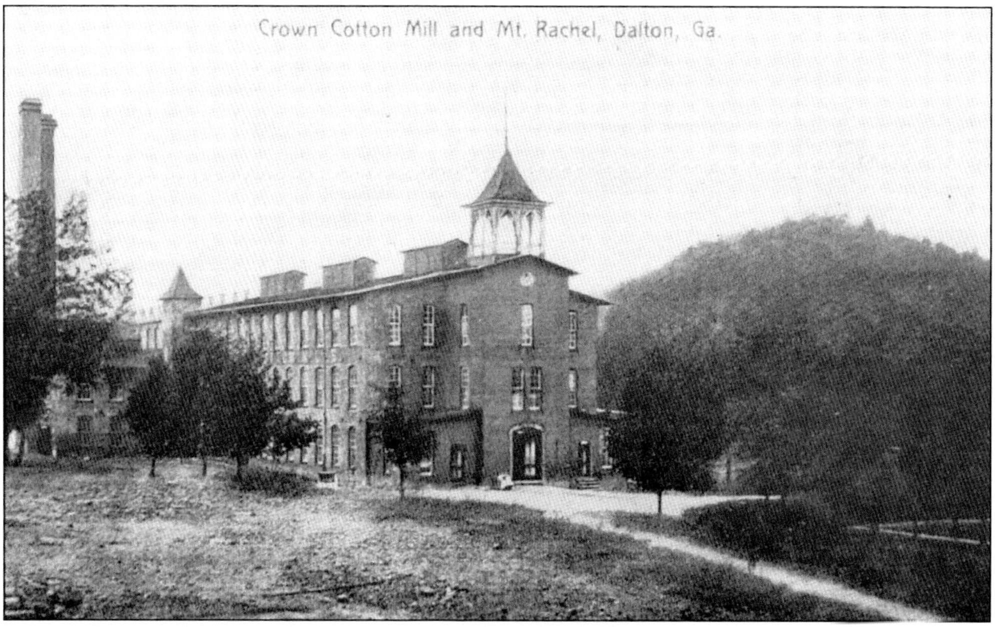

Post cards carried a lot of importance to some senders. The message on the back of this card reads: "This is to remind you that you are not forgotten."

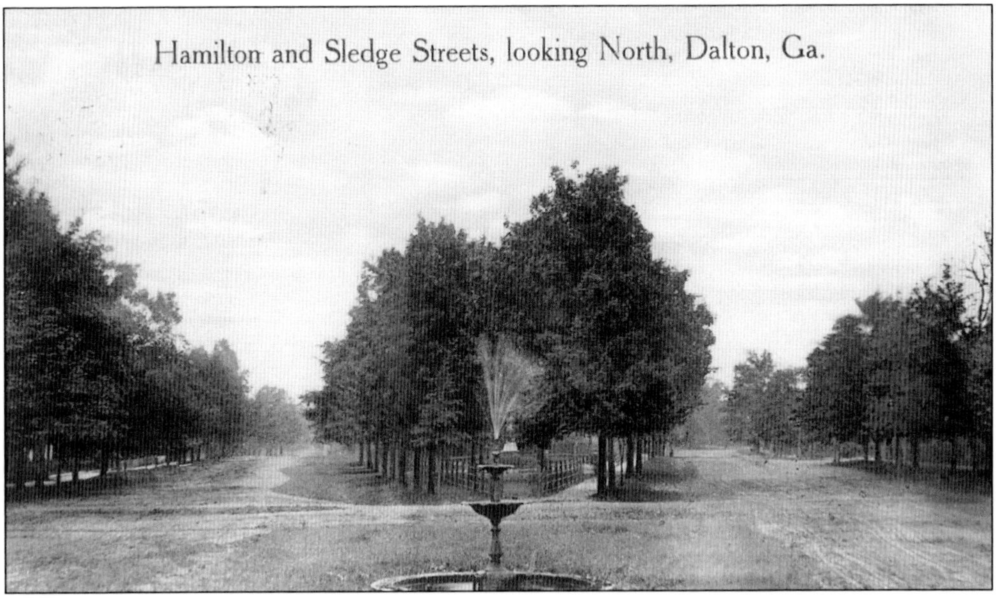

Note the fountain in this view of Hamilton and Sledge Streets in Dalton.

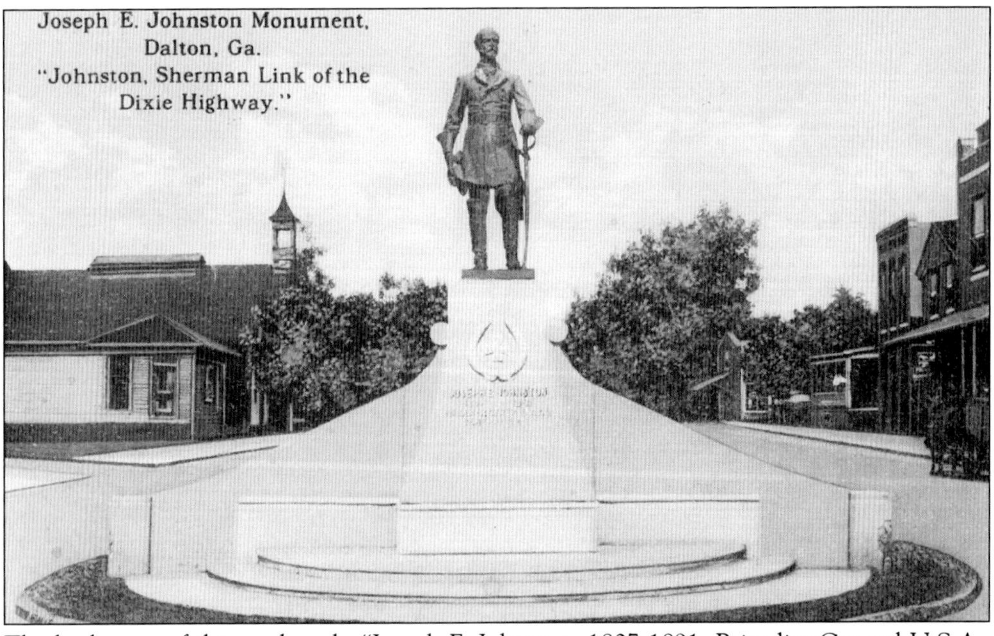

The back copy of this card reads: "Joseph E. Johnston, 1807-1891, Brigadier General U.S.A., General C.S.A., given command of the Confederate forces at Dalton in 1863. He directed the 79 days campaign to Atlanta, one of the most memorable in the annals of war. Erected by Bryan M. Thomas Chapter United Daughters of Confederacy, Dalton, Georgia, 1912."

Seven

FLOYD COUNTY

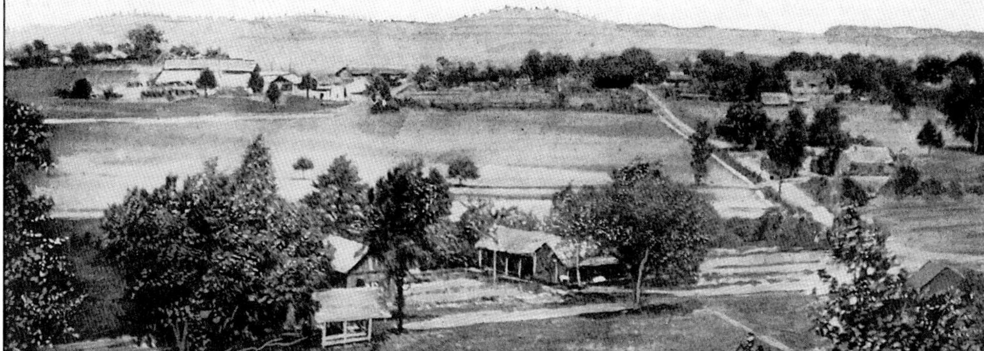

This bird's-eye view of Cave Spring was published by the Wright Drug Company of Cave Spring.

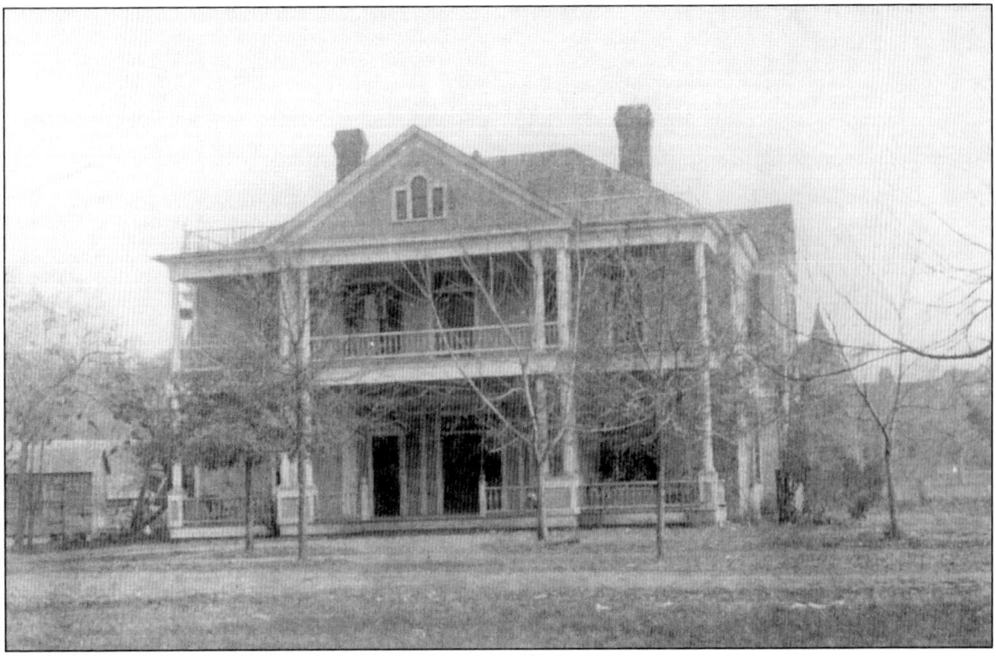

The Cave Spring Hotel was a huge two-story wooden structure.

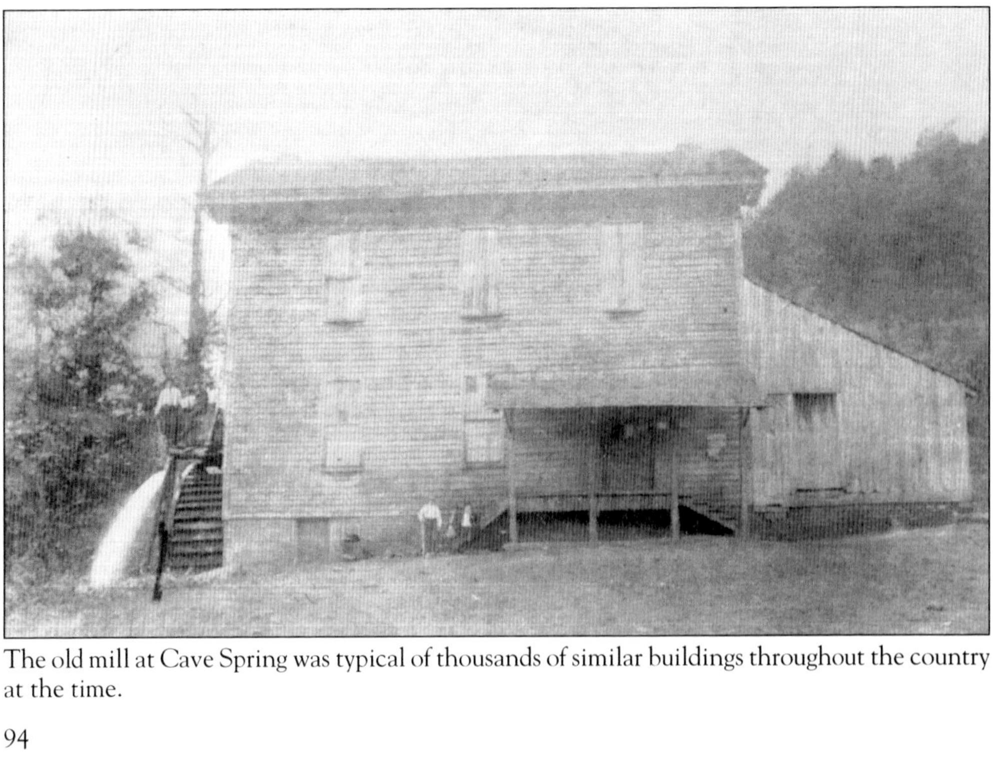

The old mill at Cave Spring was typical of thousands of similar buildings throughout the country at the time.

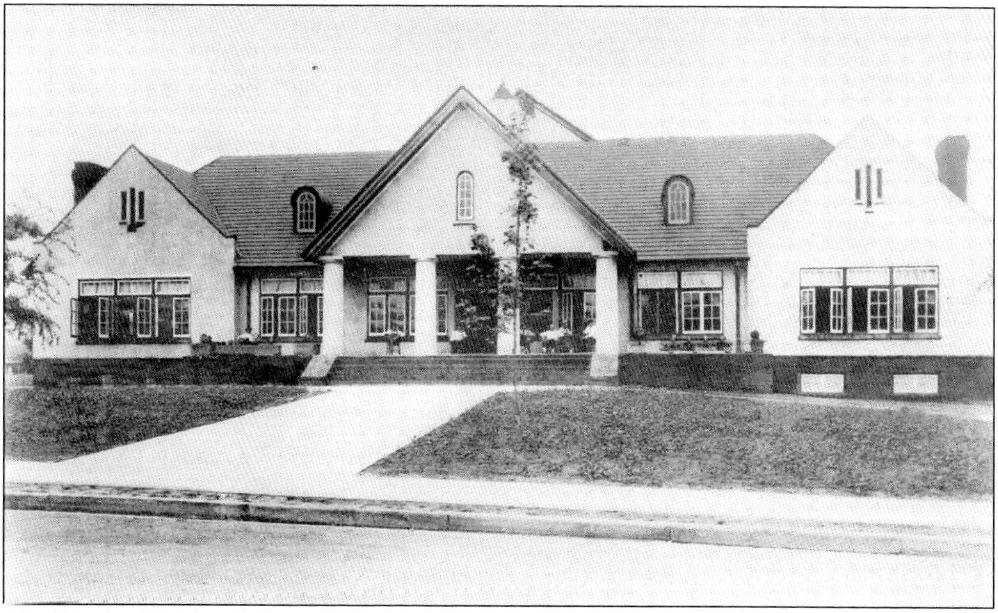

This hand-colored card shows the auditorium of the Massachusetts Cotton Mills in Lindale. On the back, the publisher stated that the company could print 2,000 cards of a view for $20.50.

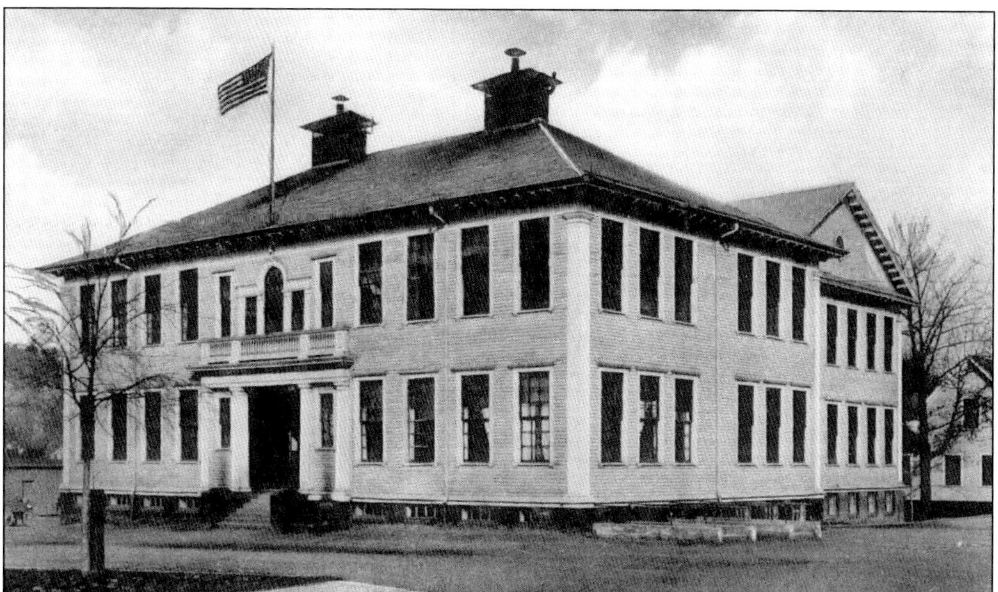

This is the public school of the Massachusetts Cotton Mills in Lindale. The sender of this card tried an earlier version of multi-level marketing. On the back she wrote: "Will you join our view card club? Just send a view card to each name on this card. Then send five card copies to five card collecting friends leaving off the top name and adding your name to the bottom."

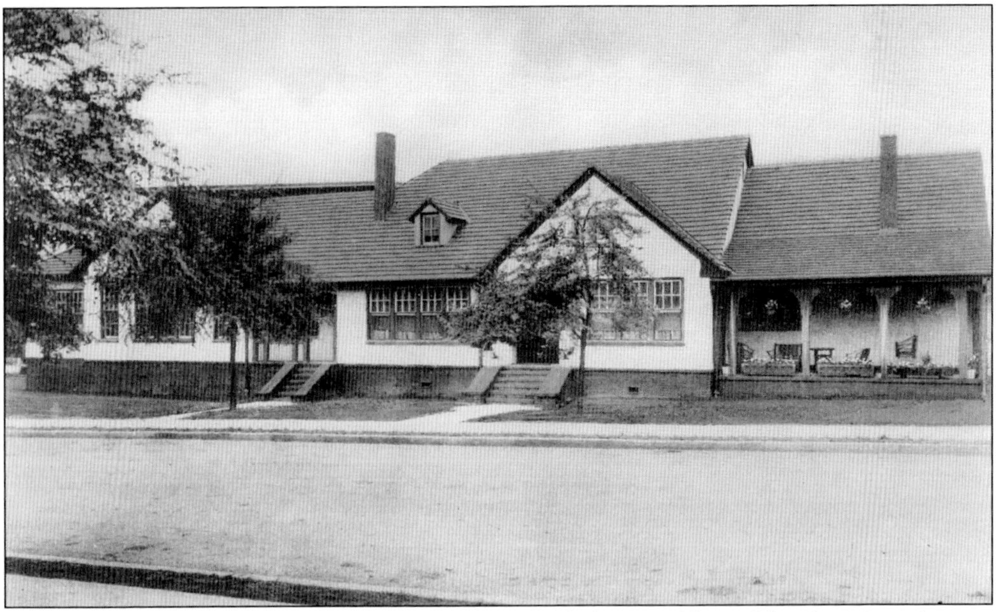

The issue of daycare for worker's children was already being addressed by the Massachusetts Cotton Mills in Lindale, as this post card of the kindergarten and day nursery shows.

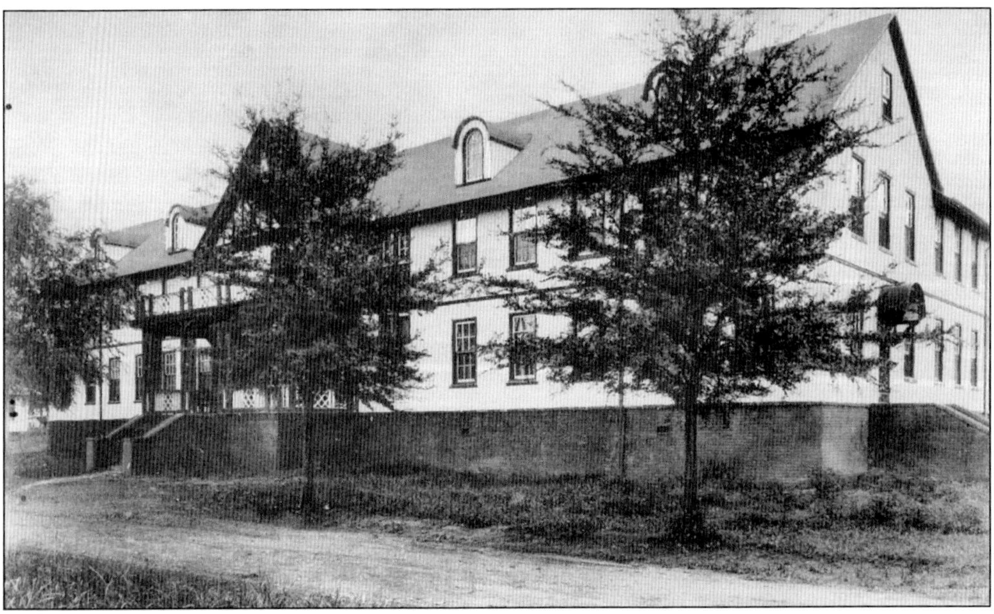

The cotton mill also featured a boarding house, as this post card shows.

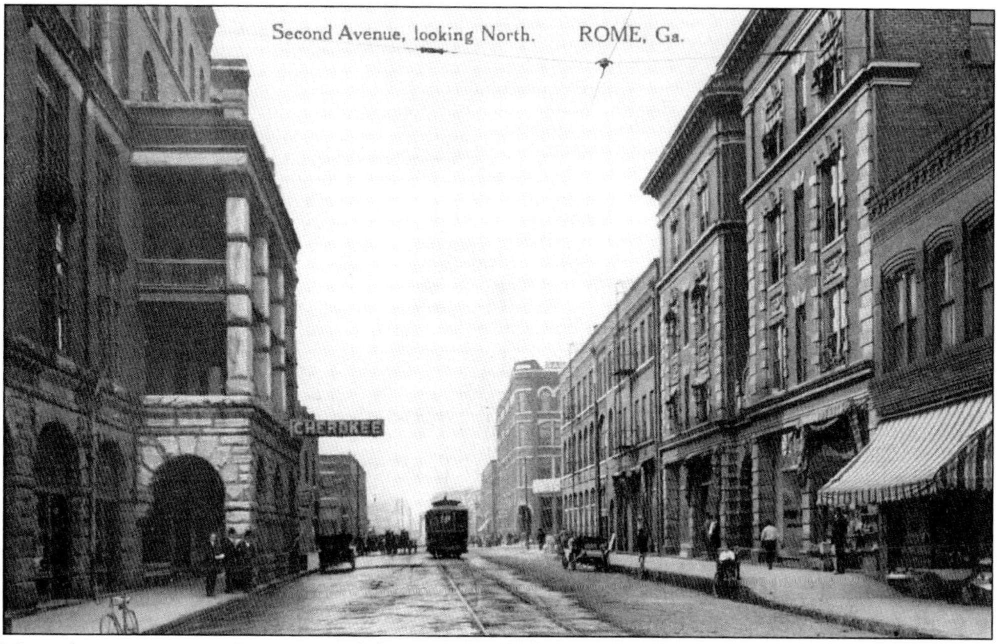

Note the streetcar in the center of this post card of Second Avenue in Rome, published by the Shropshire Bookstore Company.

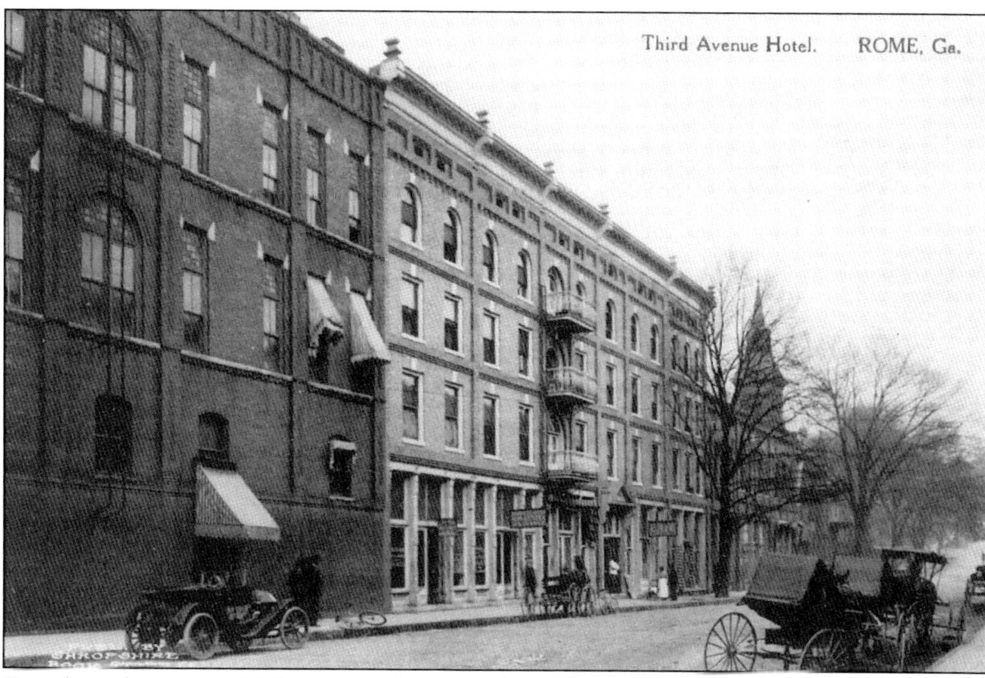

Cars share the street with buggies in this view of the Third Avenue Hotel in Rome.

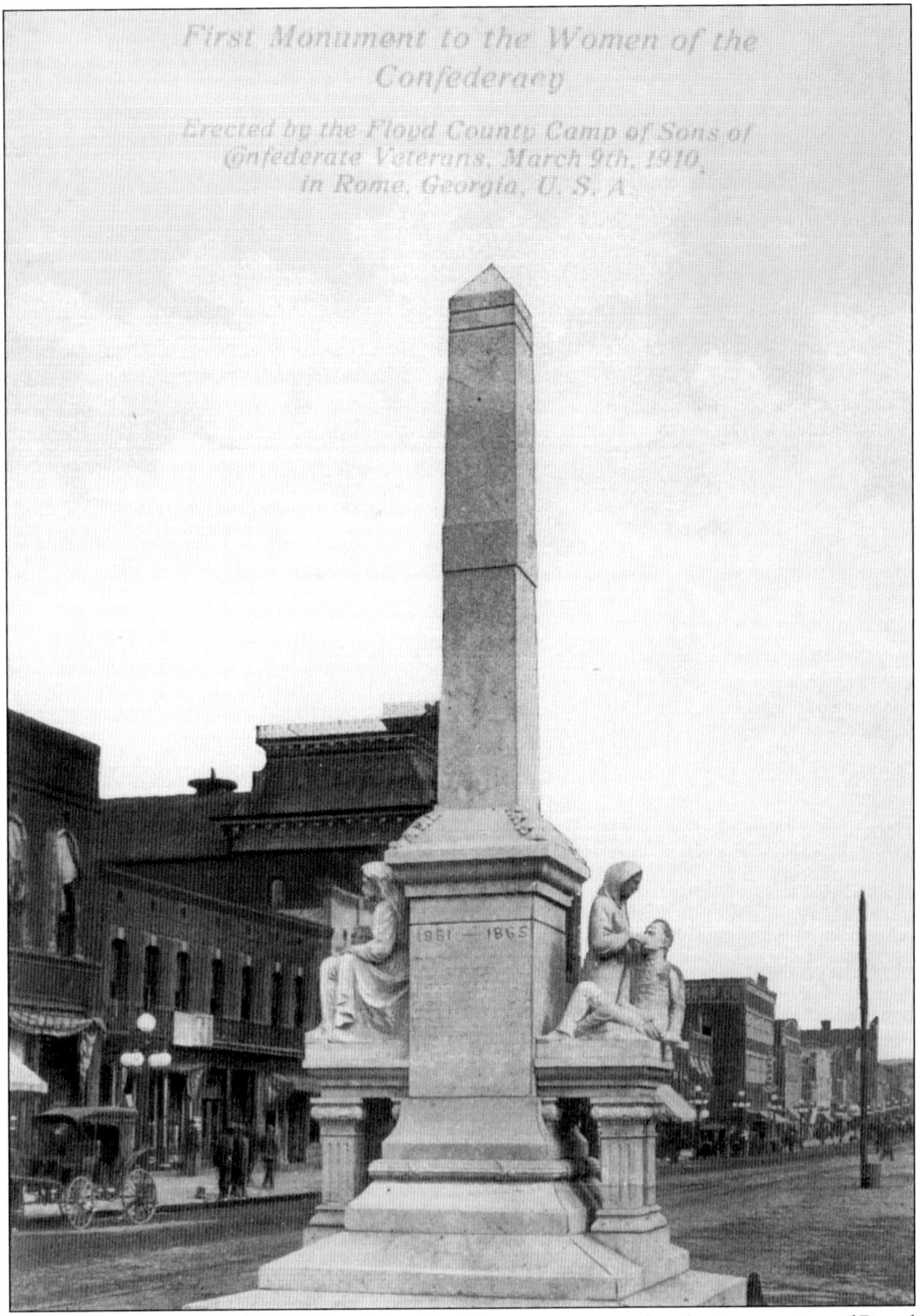

The First Monument to the Women of the Confederacy was erected at the intersection of Broad and Third Streets in Rome. In 1952, the monument was moved to the entrance of the Myrtle Hill Cemetery. The back copy includes copies of poems that were inscribed on the monument. The poems were written by Woodrow Wilson and G.A. Nunnally.

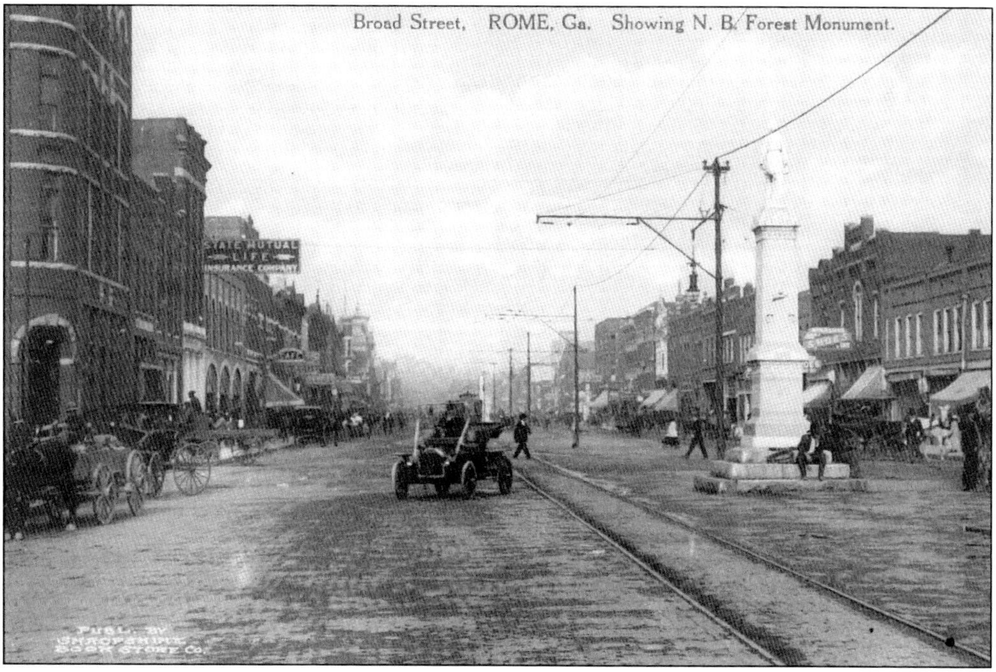

This post card featuring the Nathan Bedford Forrest Monument in Rome shows that, while it may have been a monument, the structure was also a good place to sit and watch the activity of Broad Street. As with the monument to the women of the Confederacy, an increase in traffic necessitated the removal of the Forrest Monument to the Myrtle Hill Cemetery in 1952.

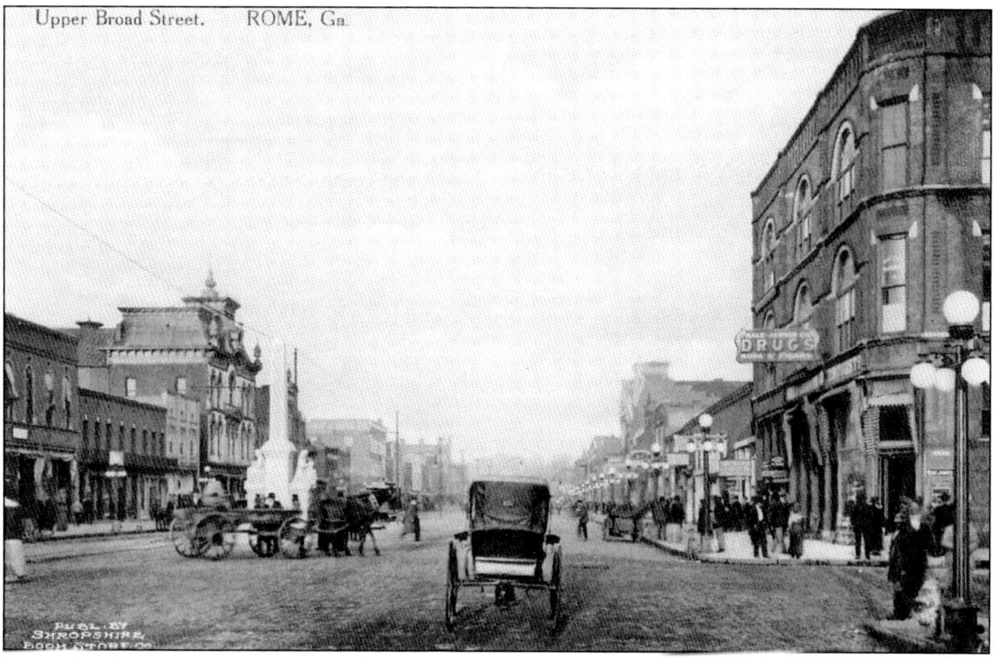

Note the elaborate streetlights in this view of upper Broad Street in Rome.

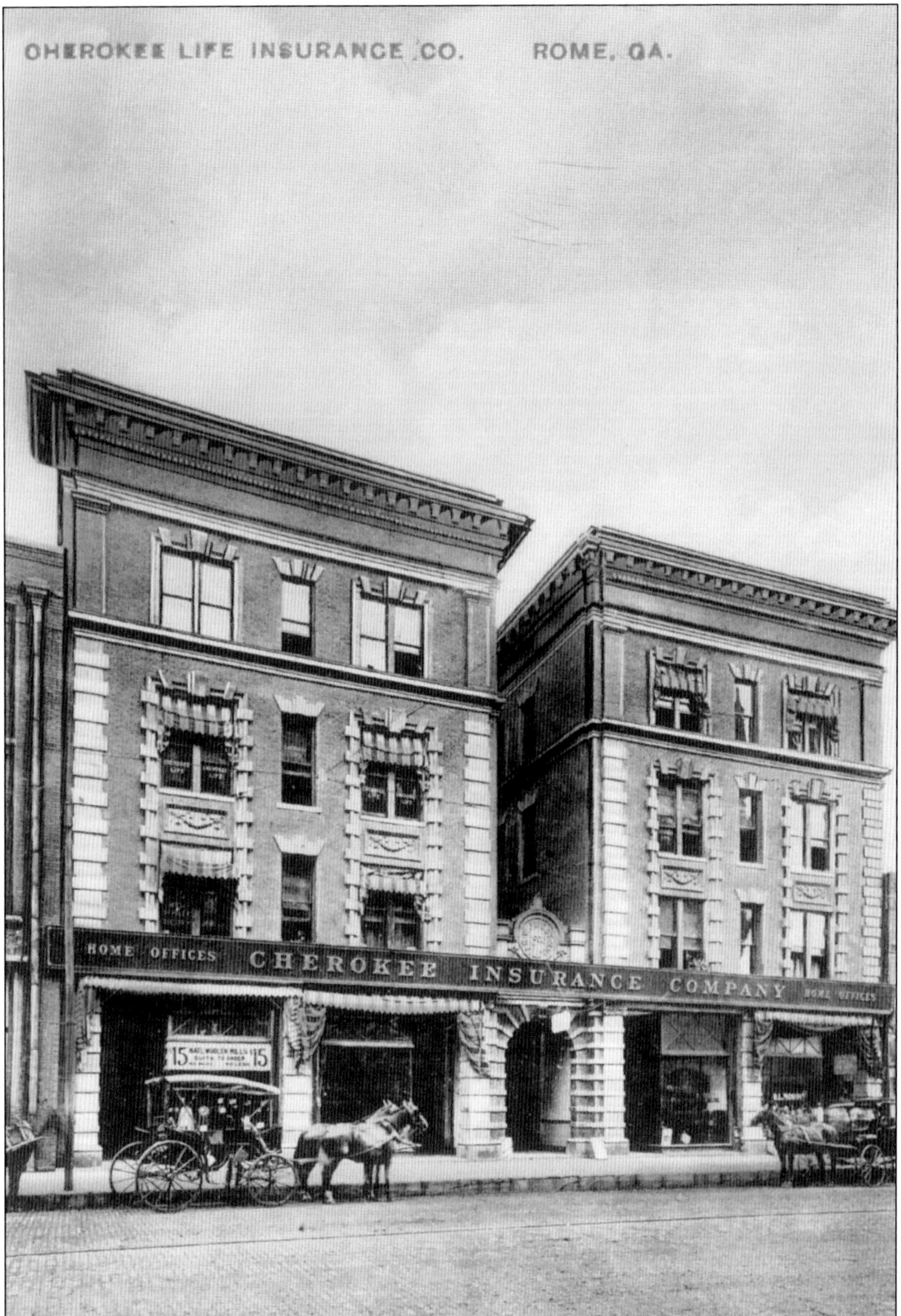

In this view of the home office of the Cherokee Life Insurance Company, one can see a sign advertising: "Suits to order for $15."

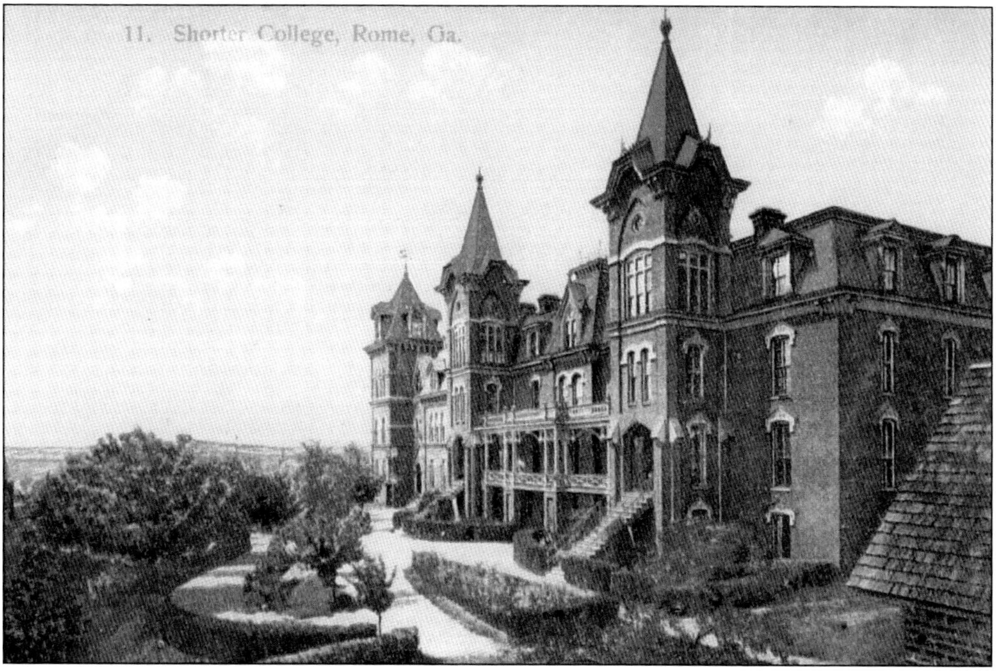

The lovely grounds of Shorter College in Rome are shown in this hand-tinted postcard.

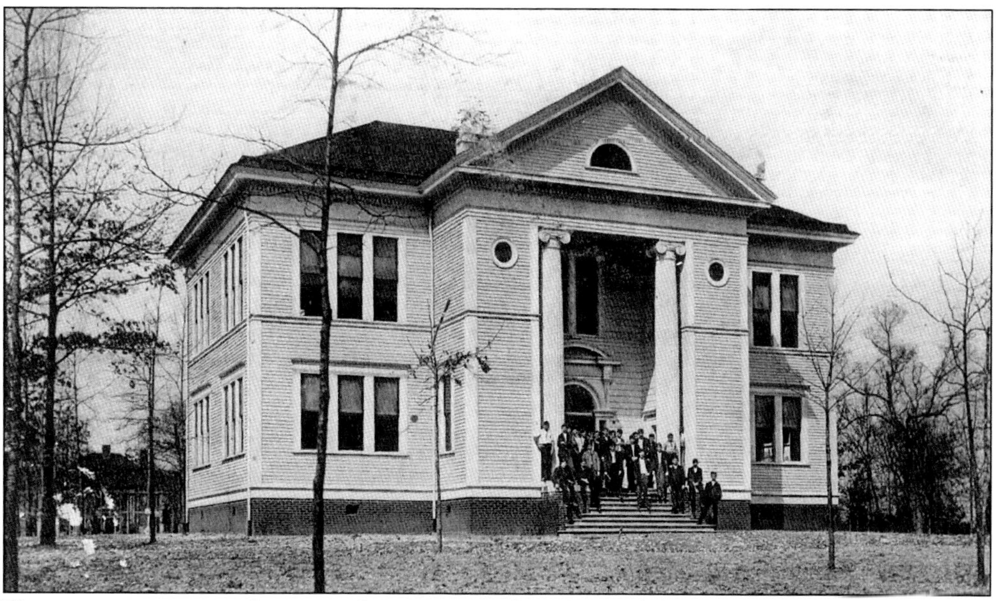

The imposing structure known as Recitation Hall at the Boy's Industrial School in Rome later became part of the campus of Berry College.

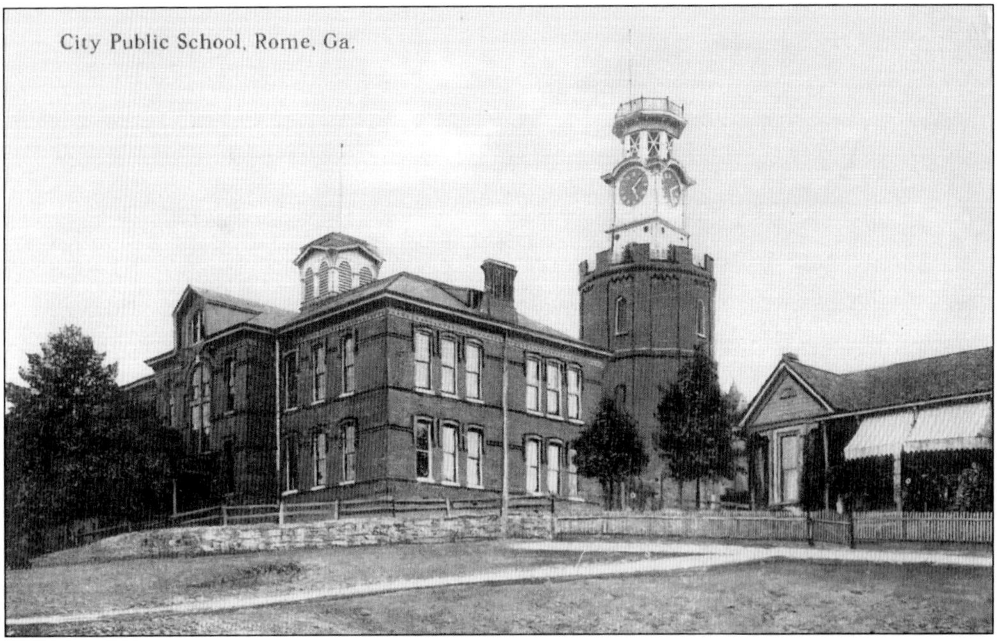

The elaborate city school building in Rome is shown in this c. 1912 view.

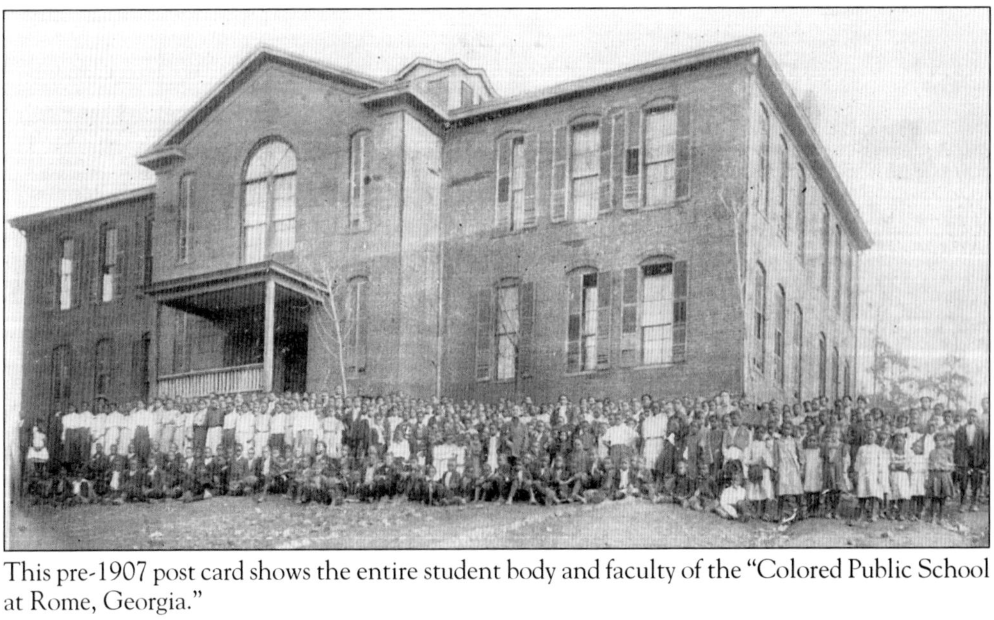

This pre-1907 post card shows the entire student body and faculty of the "Colored Public School at Rome, Georgia."

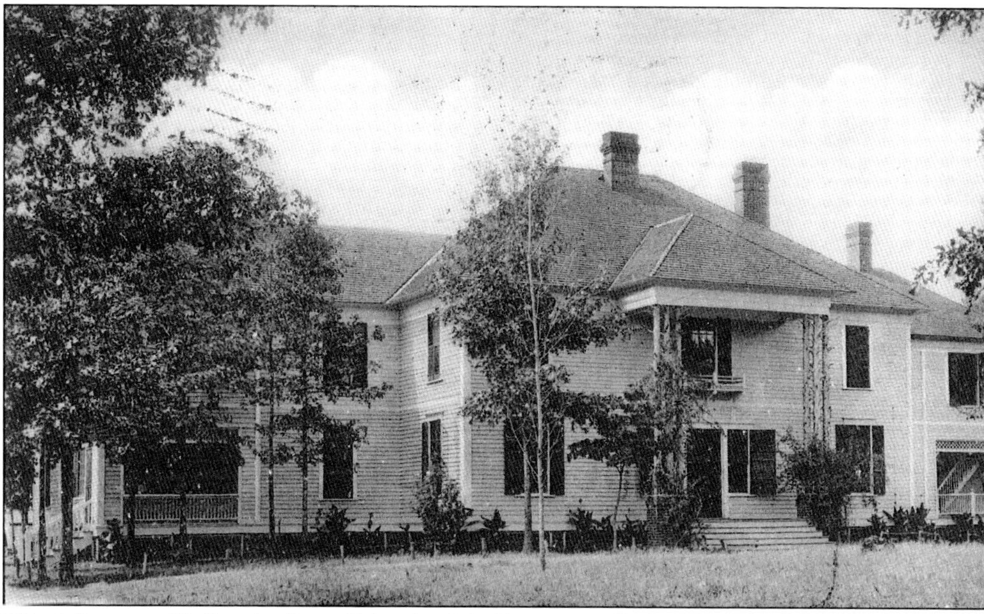

This is Brewster Hall at the Berry School in Mt. Berry, near Rome, Ga. The first floor of Brewster Hall served as a dining hall for students and living quarters were located on the second story.

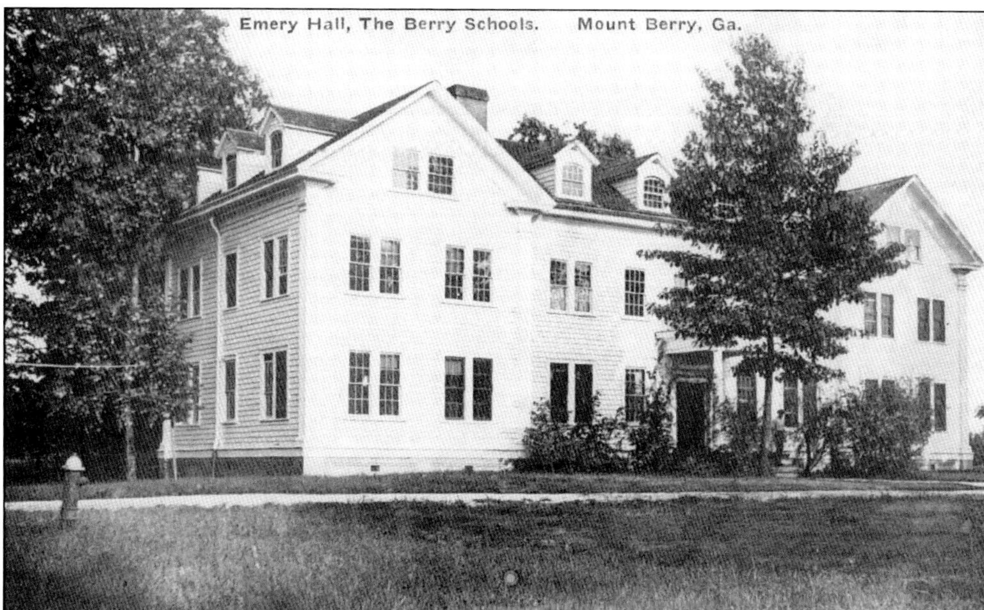

Emery Hall, at the Berry School, is featured on this post card.

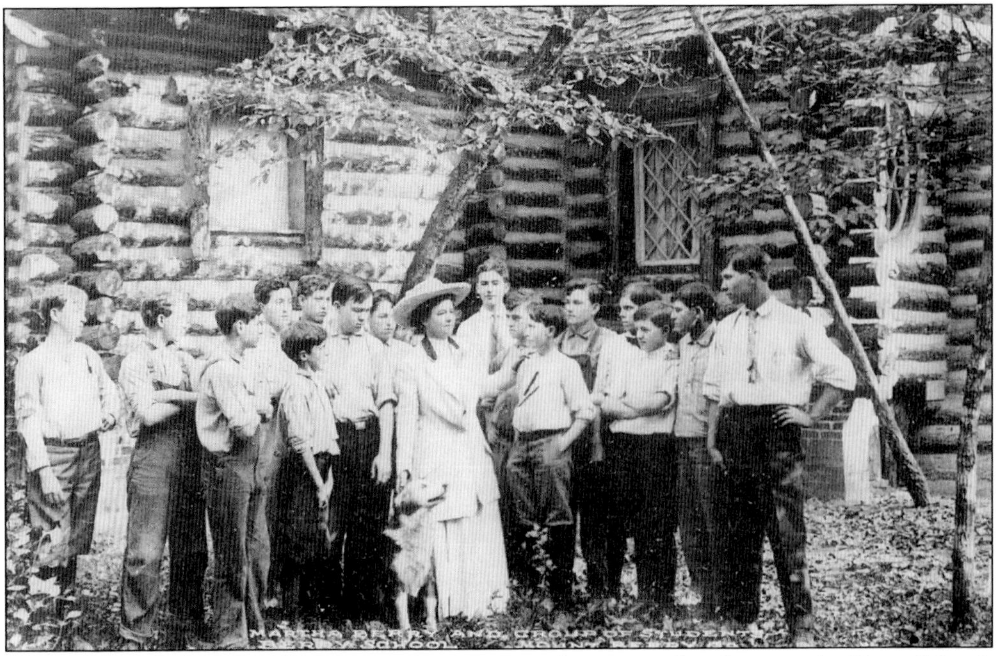

Martha Berry is shown with a canine companion and a group of students at the Berry School. Miss Berry was the daughter of a wealthy farmer and started the school in 1902 in a one-room cabin on his property to help educate poor mountain children. With more than 26,000 acres, the Berry School has the largest campus of any school in the U.S.

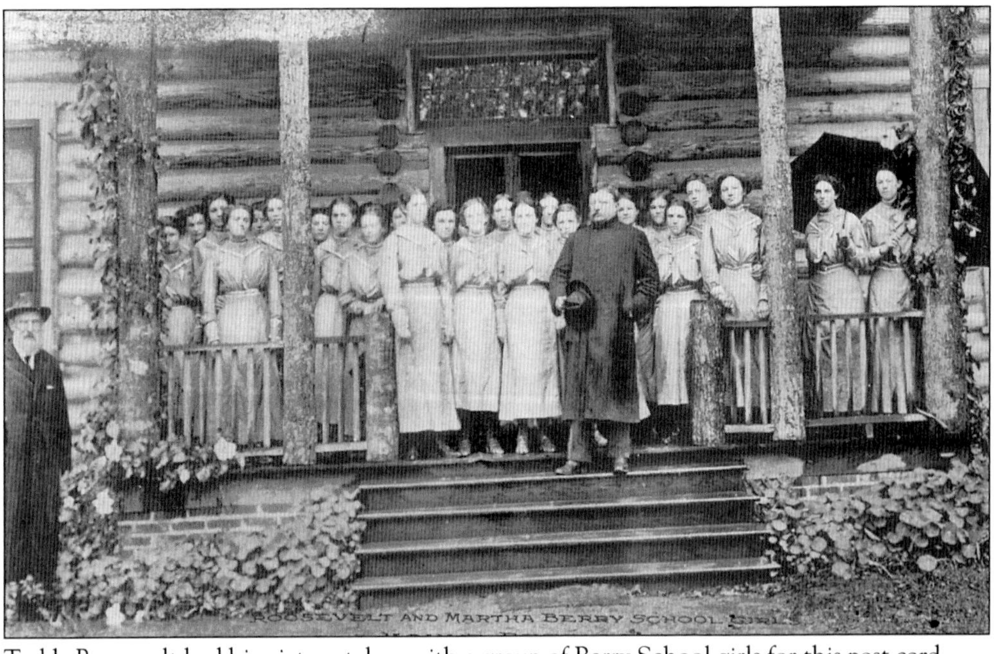

Teddy Roosevelt had his picture taken with a group of Berry School girls for this post card.

Eight

Forsyth, Gwinnett, Newton, and Rockdale Counties

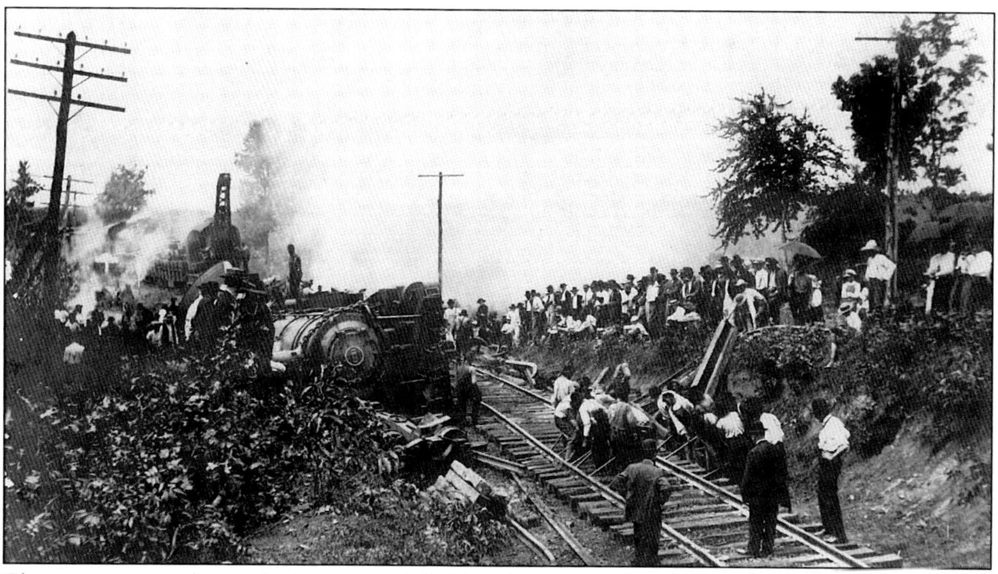

The message on this real photo reads "38 Derailed one mile south of Buford 8/23/08. Engine 1231, Engineer Dewberry."

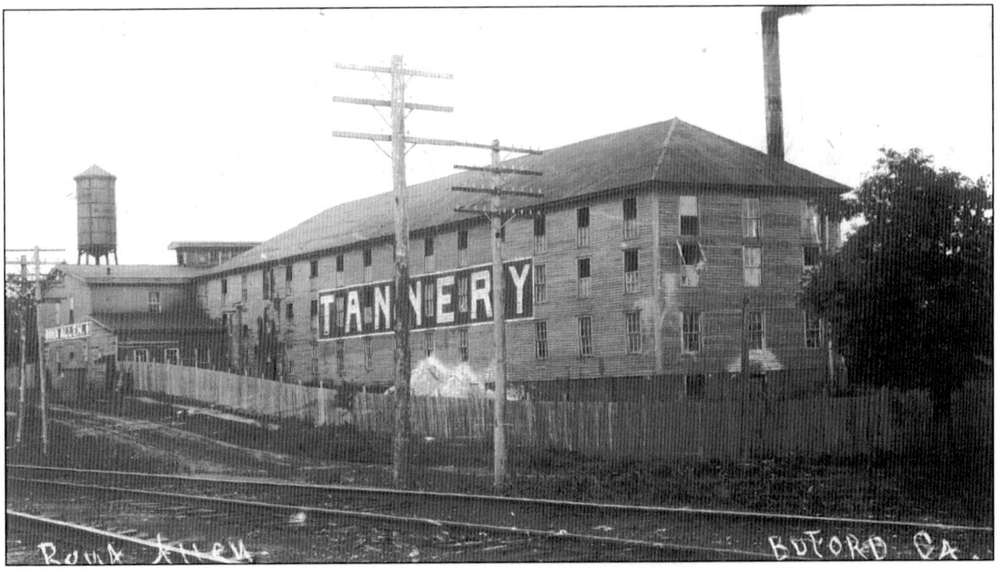

The Bona Allen Tannery in Buford was housed in a large building.

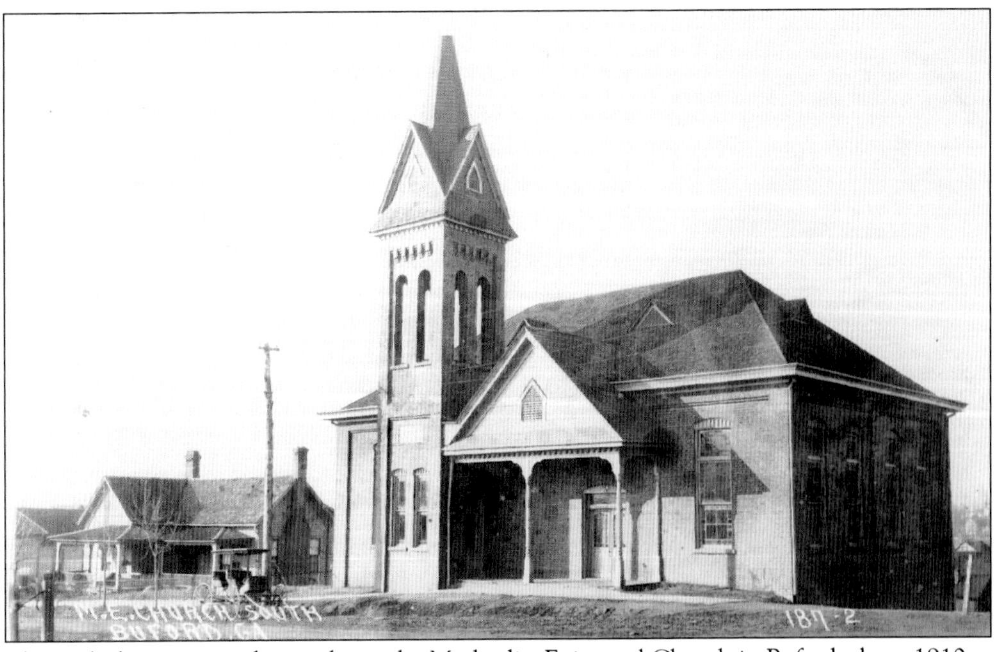

This real-photo postcard view shows the Methodist Episcopal Church in Buford, about 1910.

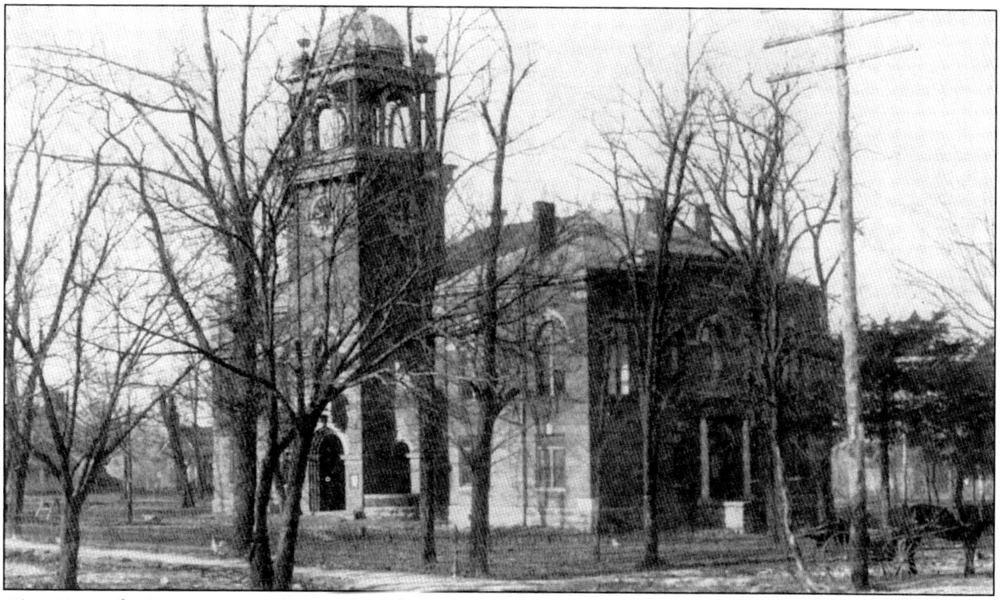

This Forsyth County courthouse building in Cumming was built in 1905 but was the victim of a devastating fire in 1973.

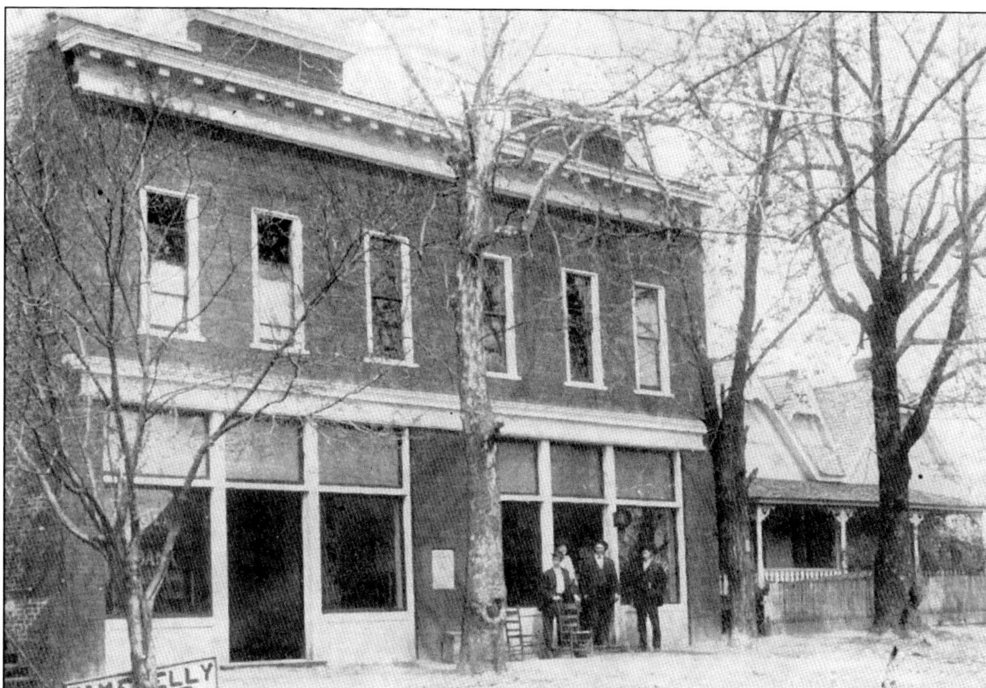

This scene in Cumming shows the Farmers and Merchants Bank, the Cumming Drug Store, and Dr. J.A. Otwell's residence.

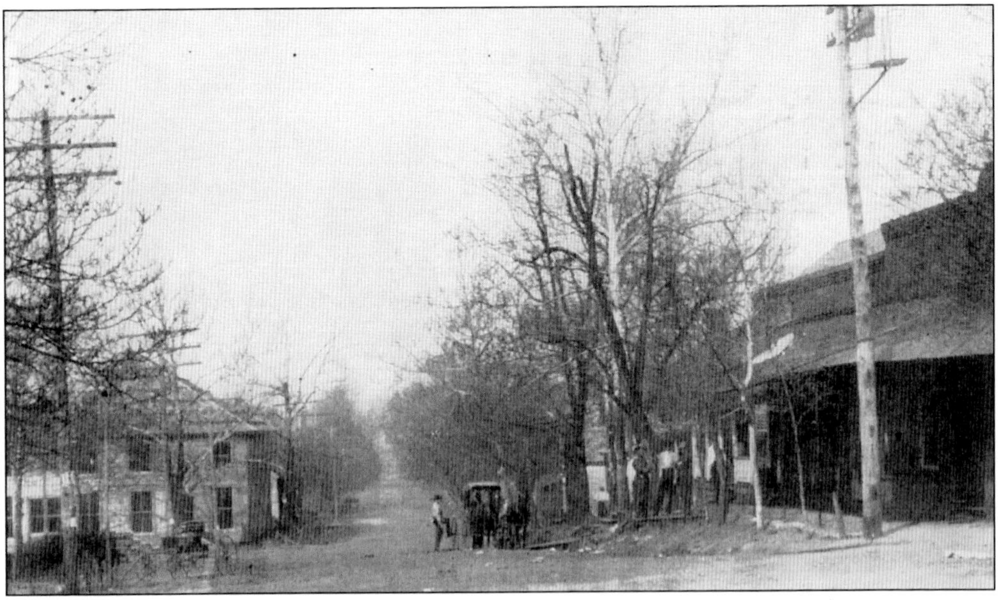

Though the streets are unpaved and carriages seem to be the main means of transportation, an electrical transformer is visible in the upper right of this view of West Canton Street in Cumming.

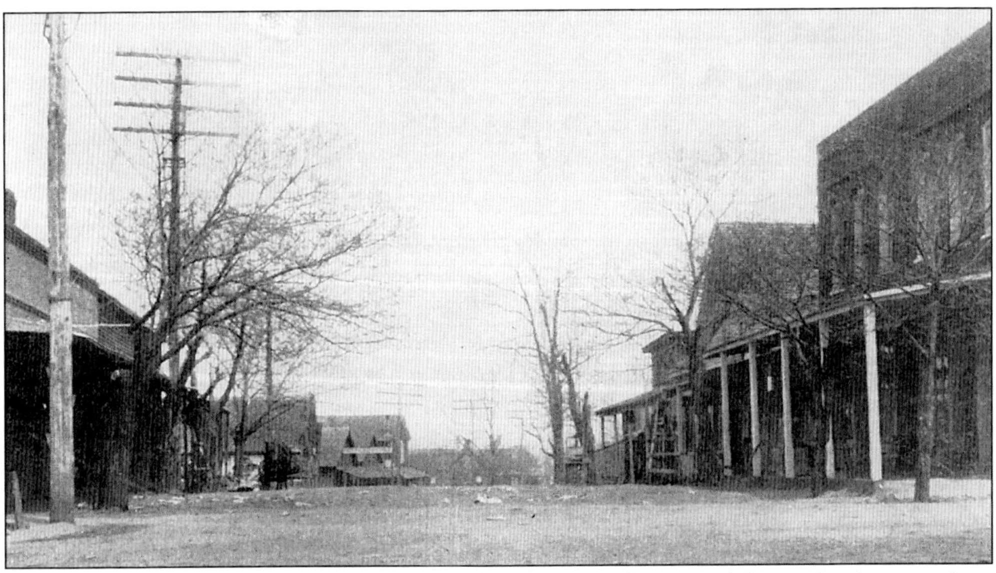

Dahlonega Street in Cumming seems deserted in this *c.* 1907 postcard, but early photographers often picked such a time because of the long exposure required by their film. Too many people, vehicles, and animals could result in blurred images.

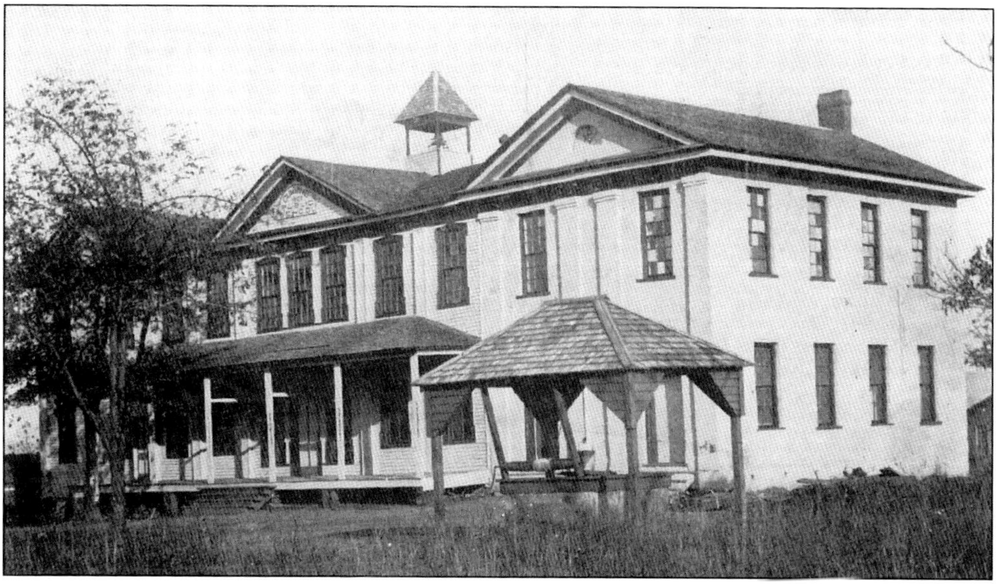

The Cumming Grade School featured a covered well and windlass, as shown in this view.

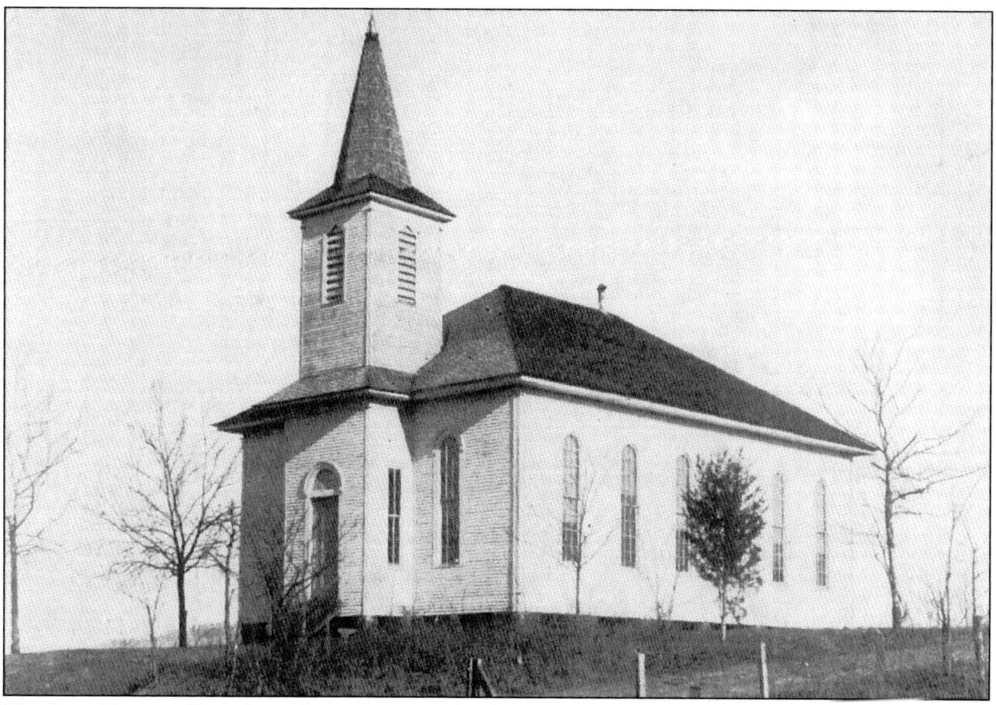

The First Baptist Church in Cumming stands alone in this view, another of the many published by the Cumming Drug Store.

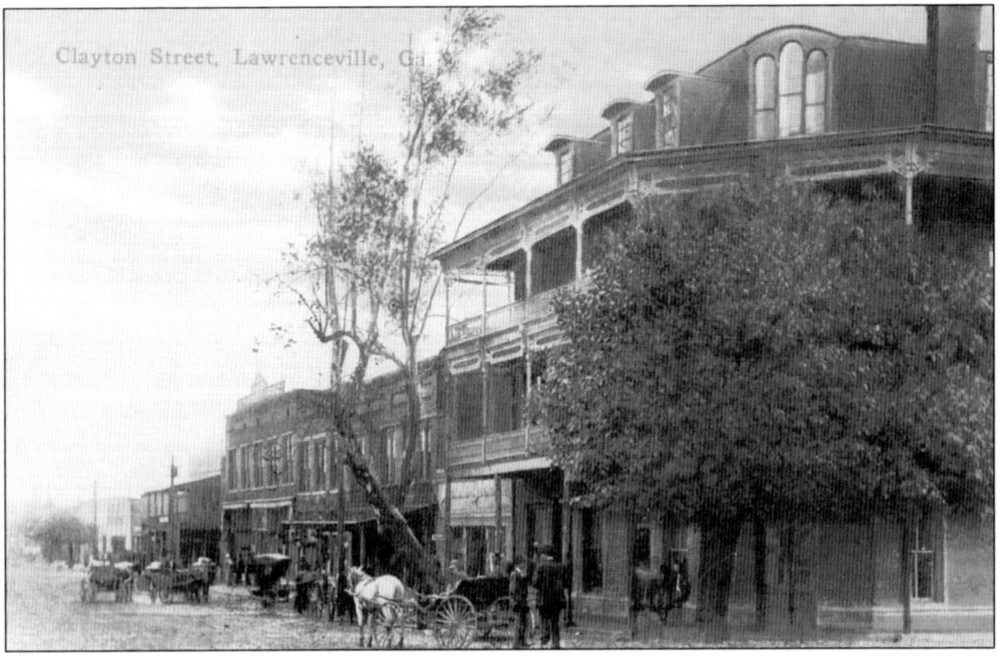

Clayton Street in Lawrenceville is shown here about 1912.

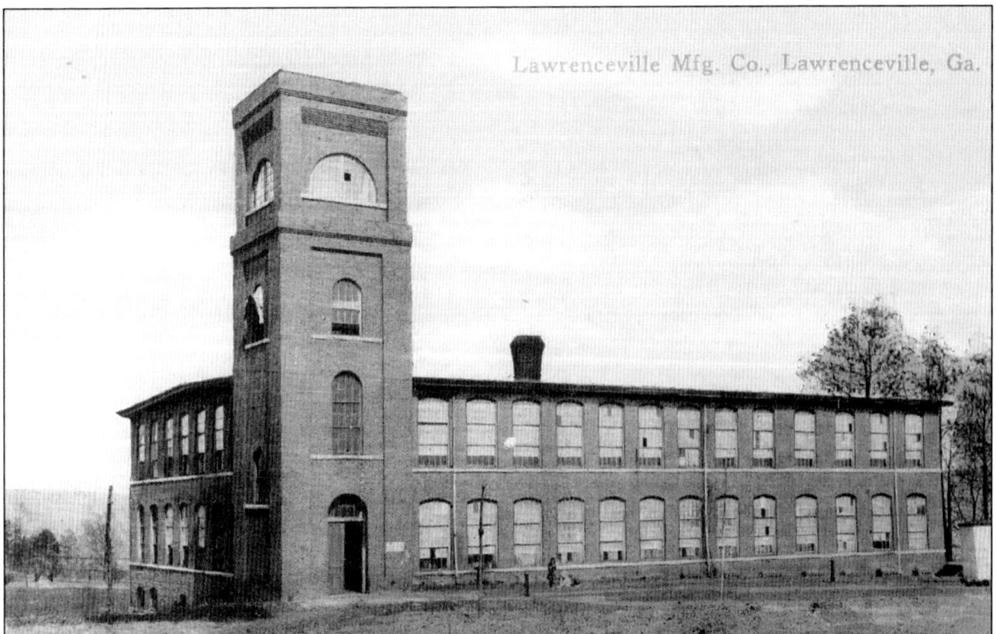

The multi-storied Lawrenceville Manufacturing Co. building was where cotton yarn was manufactured.

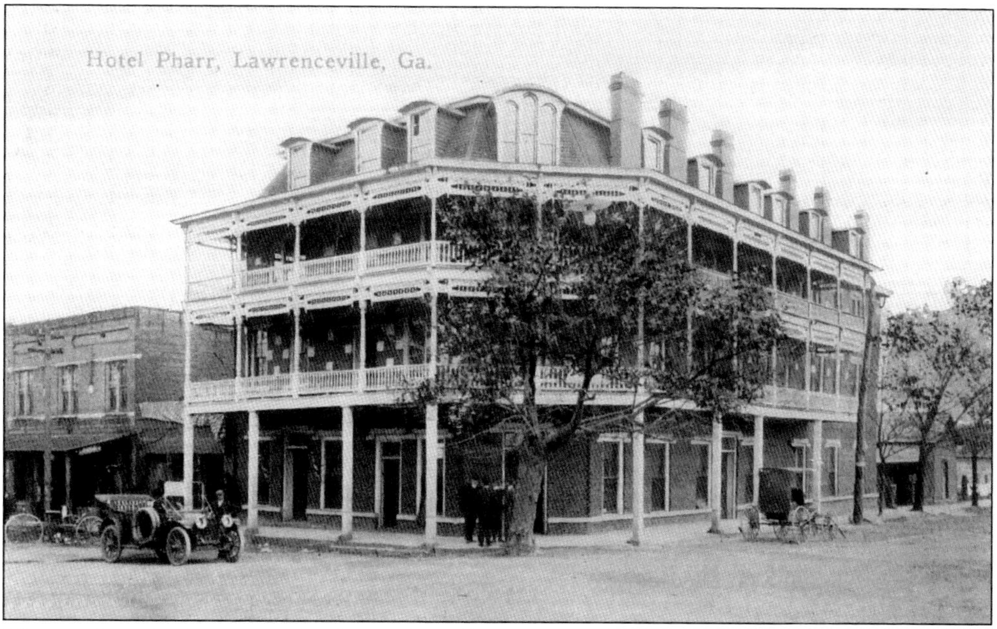

The sender of this post card of the Hotel Pharr wrote: "Are you sick, or have you entirely forgotten me?"

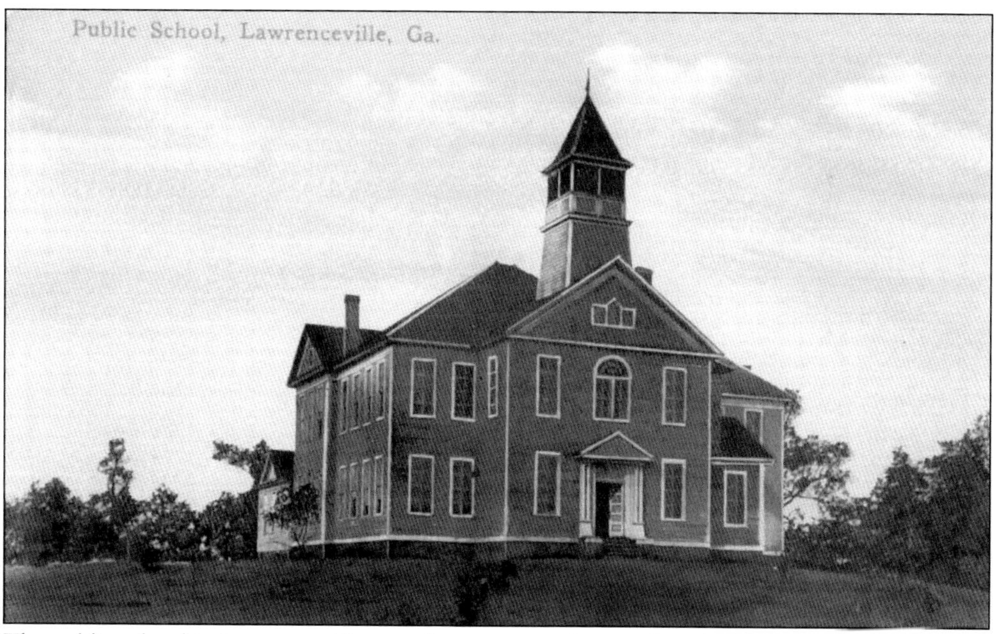

The public school in Lawrenceville must have appeared somewhat foreboding to young students on their first day at school.

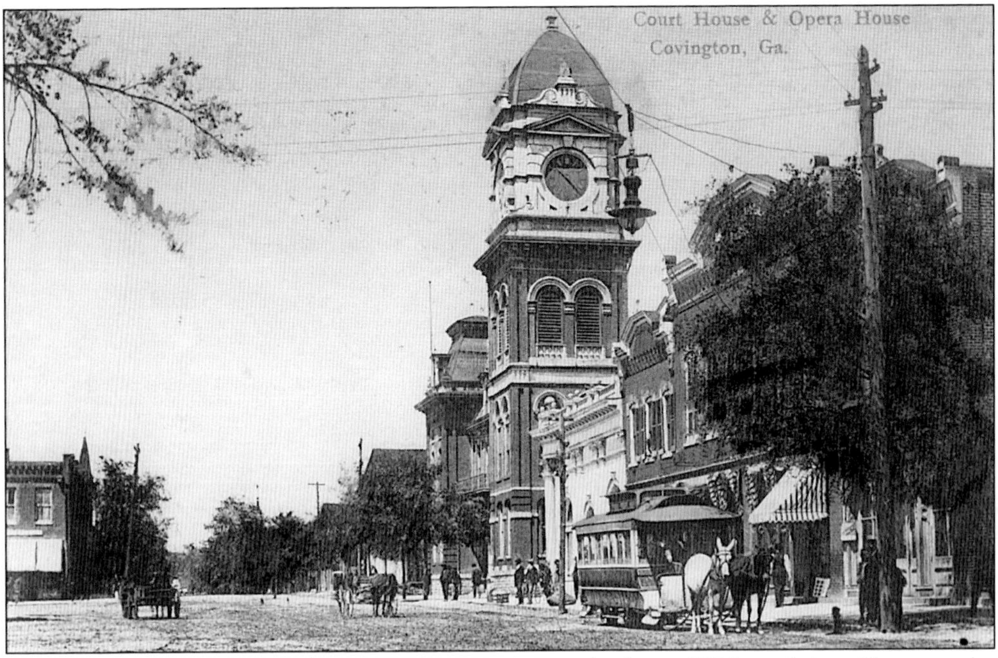

The Newton County Courthouse in Covington was built in 1884, and it still serves the community. The sender of this post card wrote: "I am at Covington waiting for the train, will spend the night in Atlanta and leave in the morning for the mountains. Ida."

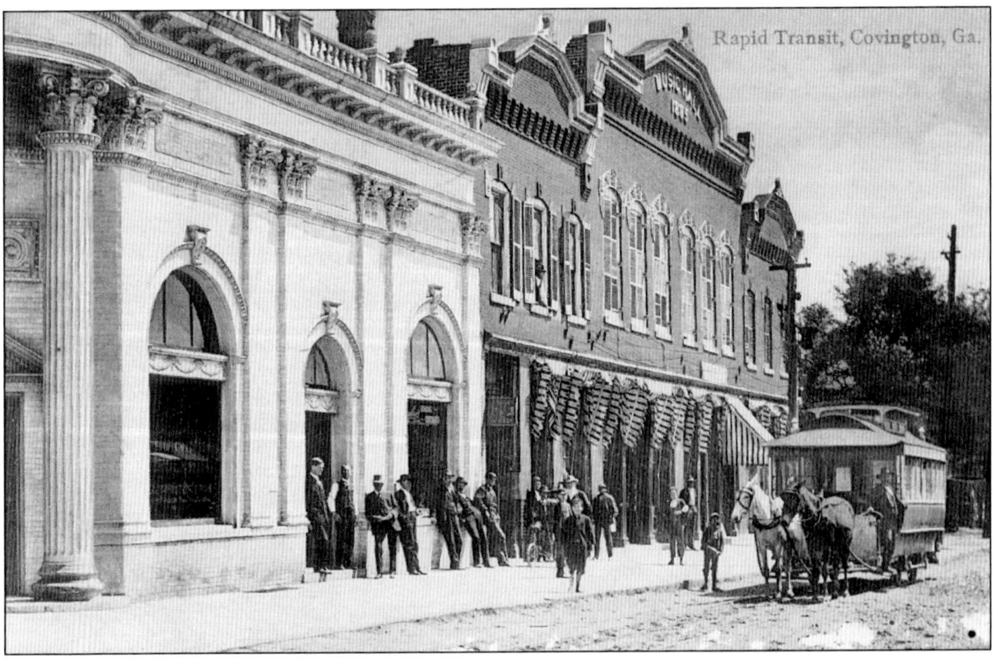

A horse-drawn streetcar was humorously referred to as "rapid transit," according to this view in front of the Opera House in Covington.

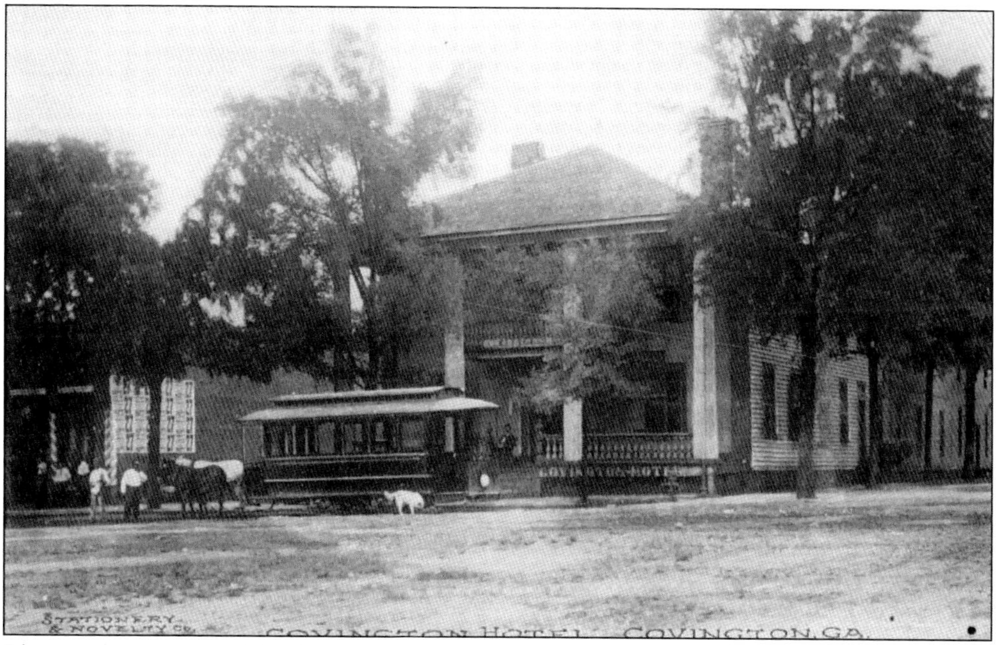

The stately Covington Hotel featured streetcar service from the hotel through town.

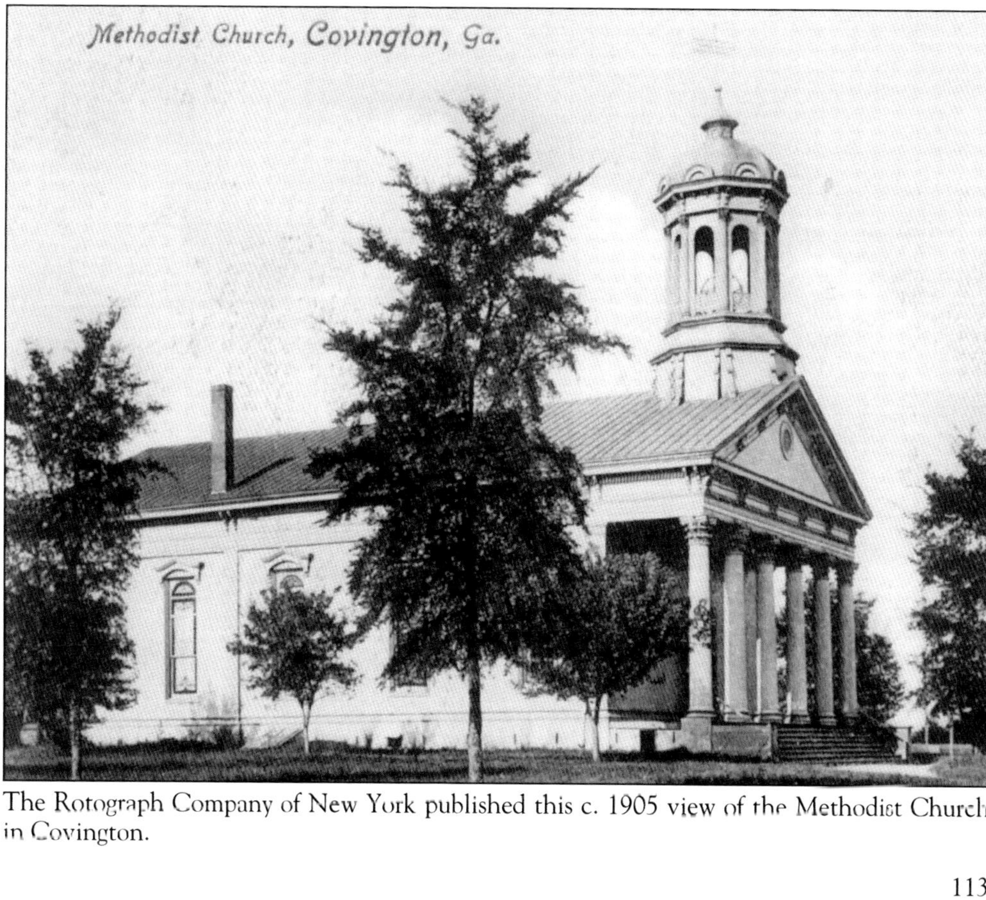

The Rotograph Company of New York published this c. 1905 view of the Methodist Church in Covington.

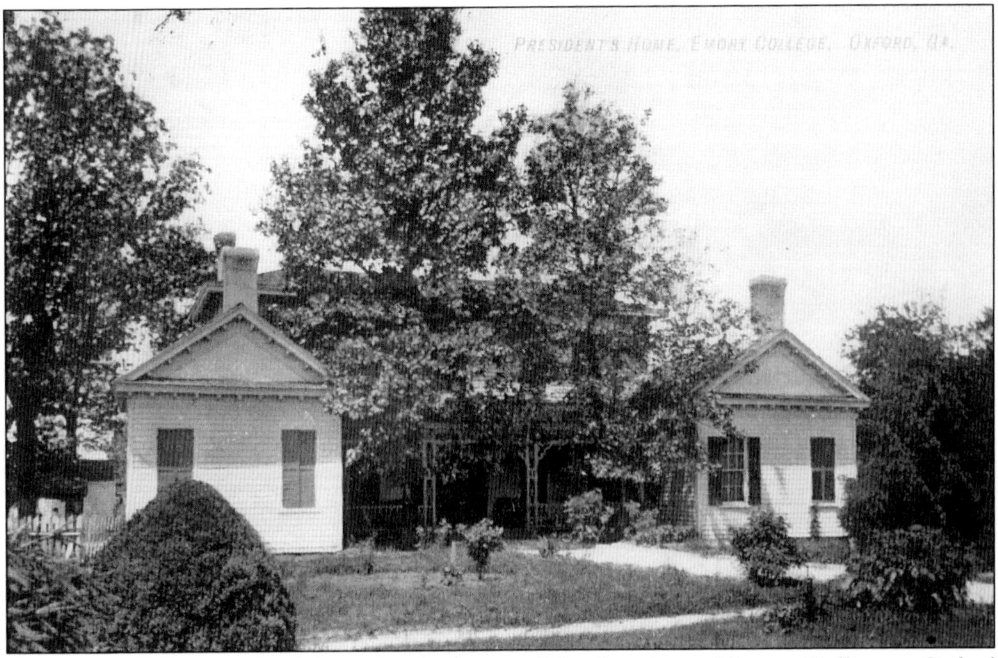

The sender of this post card featuring the home of the President of Emory College at Oxford wrote: ". . . would have written you sooner but really Pearl I am so busy . . ."

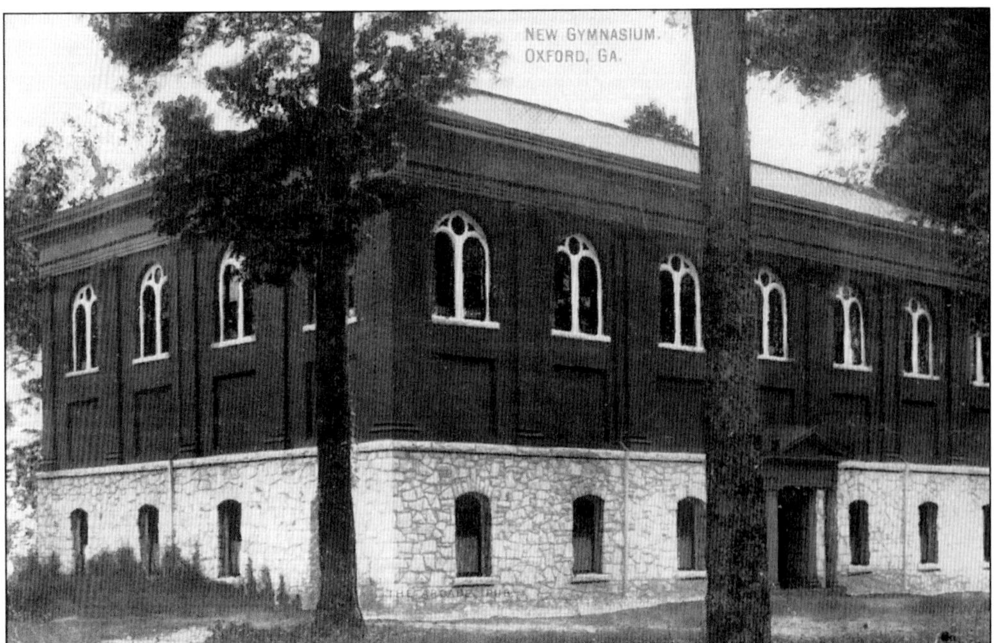

The sender of this card, like many others, seems a little starved for attention, but still courteous. He wrote: "Would you object very seriously to writing me just a line or two? J.B."

This is a pre-1907 view of the Emory College Chapel at Oxford.

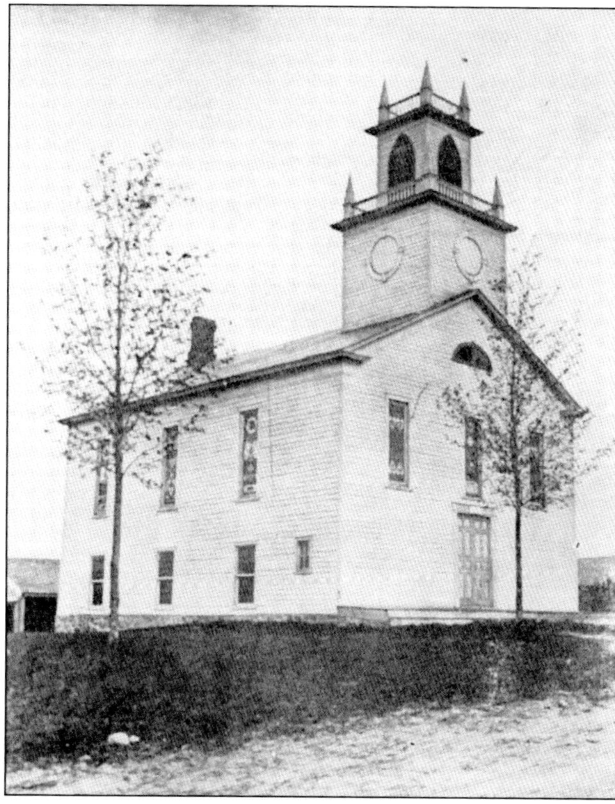

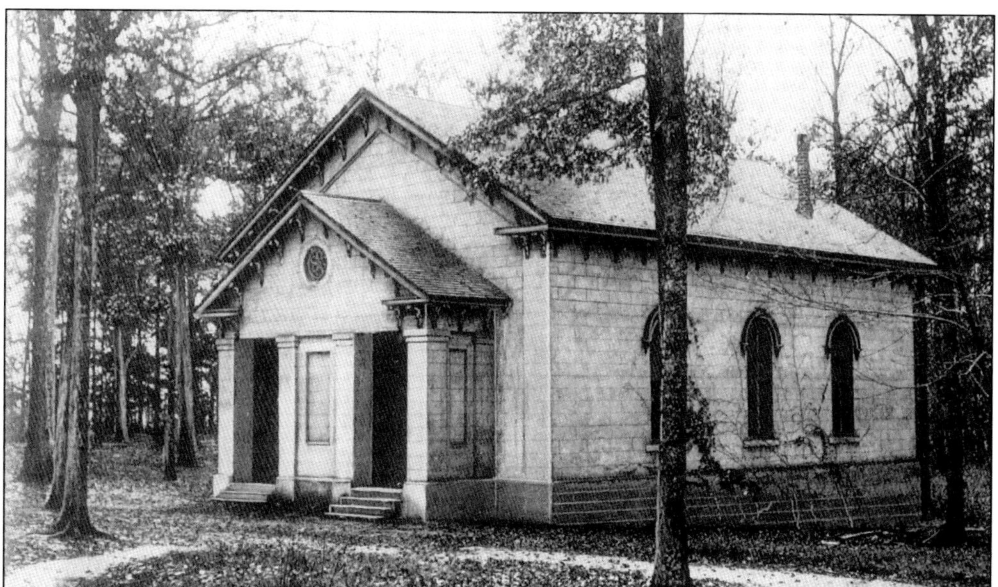

A later view identified as Emory Chapel shows a masonry building, which apparently replaced the earlier wooden structure.

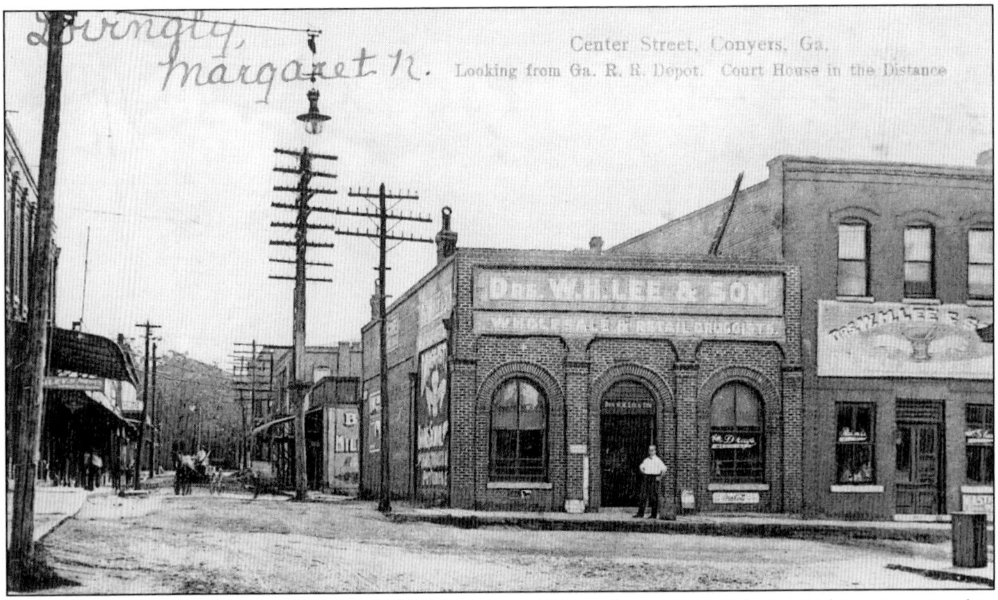

Note the impressive signs for Drs. W.H. Lee and Son, wholesale and retail druggists, in this view of Center Street in Conyers.

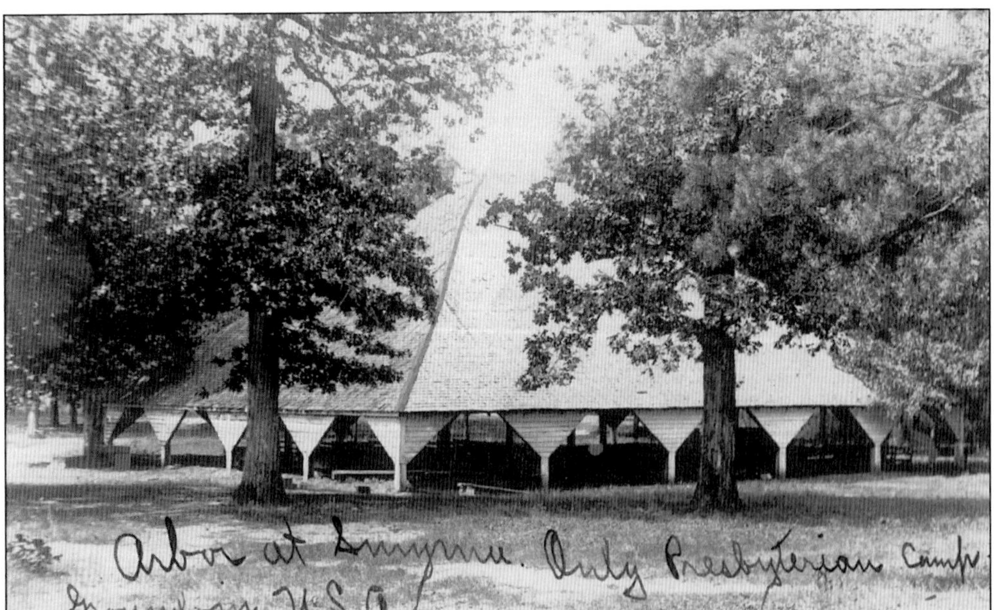

According to the sender of this card, in 1907 the Arbor at Smyrna was the "only Presbyterian campground in the U.S.A." The camp still exists just west of Conyers.

Nine

Haralson, Paulding, and Polk Counties

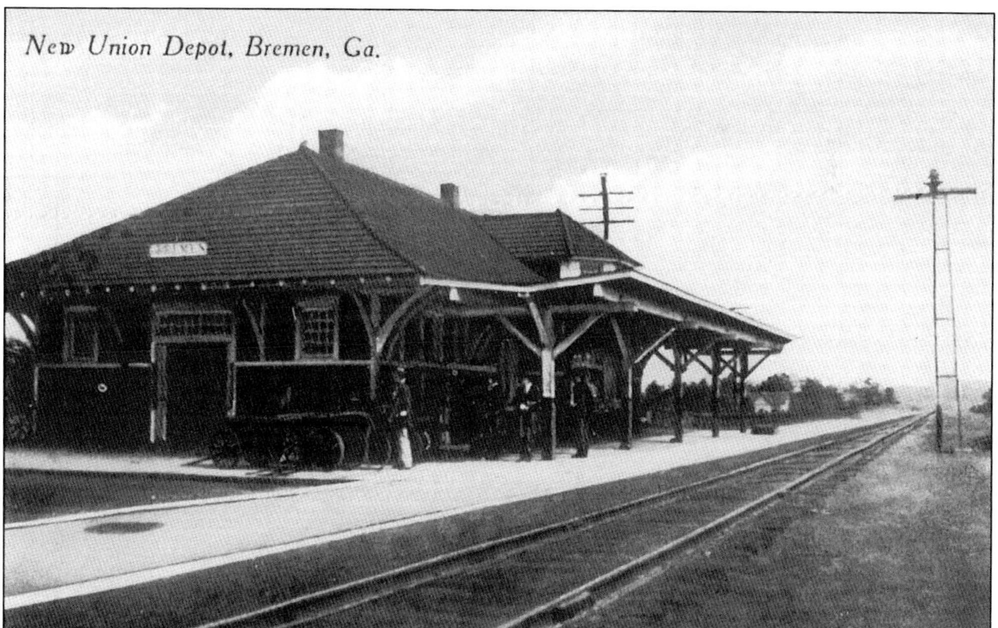

The New Union Depot in Bremen is shown here about 1910. Bremen was served by the Central of Georgia Railway and the Southern Railway.

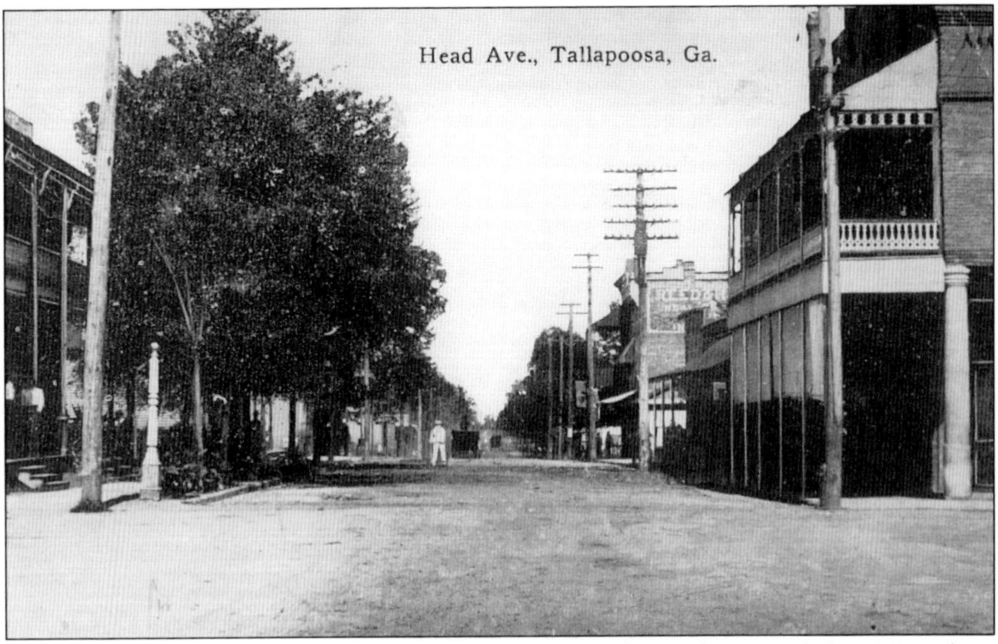

This is a c. 1912 view of Head Avenue in Tallapoosa. The card was mailed to Muscadine, Alabama, with this message: "Dear Ellen: Am awfully disappointed because you are not coming here to stay. You must come and spend a few days with us once in a while anyway. What are you doing with yourself, picking cotton? Am afraid it is going to rain before I can get back to town. With Love, Alma."

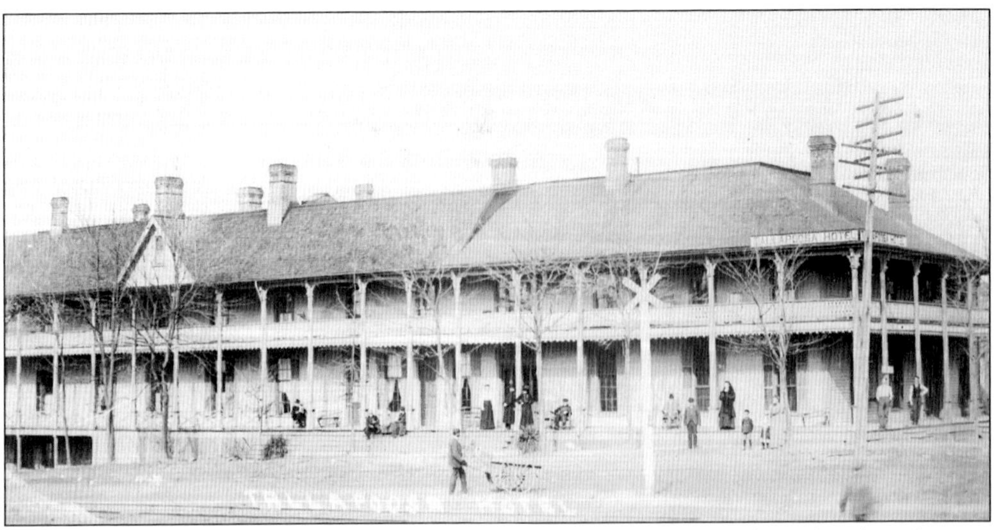

This real-photo post card, c. 1906, shows the Tallapoosa Hotel along the railroad tracks near the depot. The message reads: "Hello Alice. I am back at Tallapoosa. Want to come up one night this week? Tom."

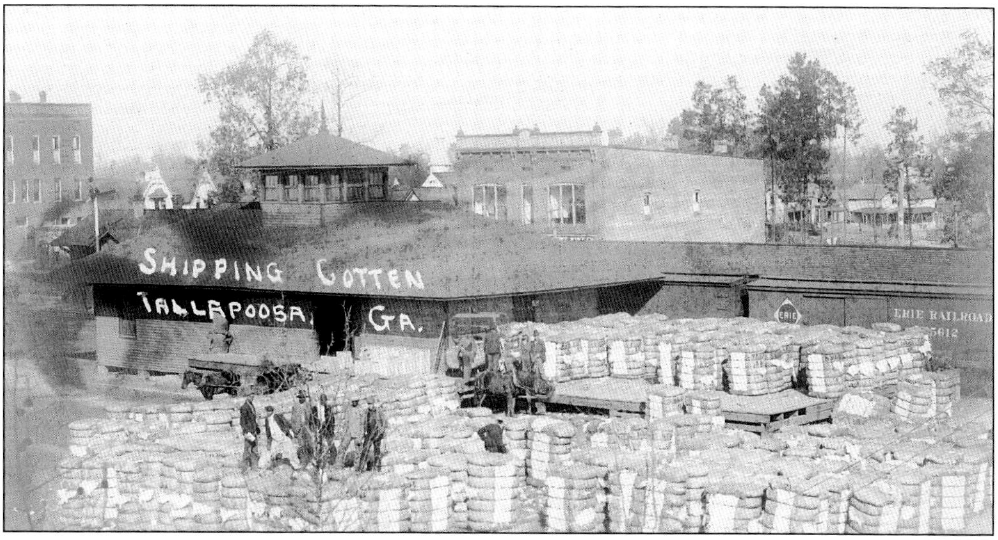

According to the publisher of this c. 1906 post card, this scene shows "cotten" being shipped in Tallapoosa. In fact, the dock at the railroad depot could hold only a small part of the cotton.

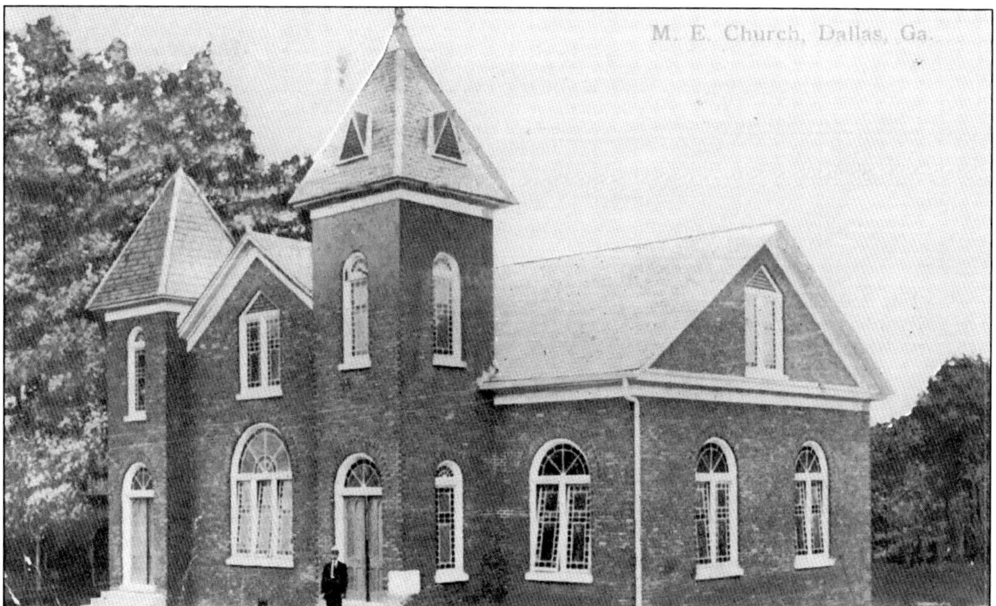

The C.A. Hart Company of Dallas, Georgia, published this view of the Methodist Episcopal Church in Dallas.

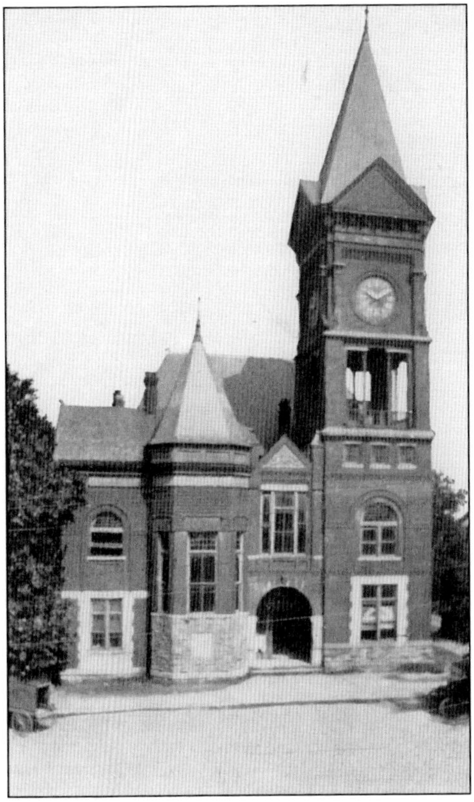

The Paulding County courthouse in Dallas was built in 1892. The building underwent extensive renovation in 1956 and remains in service.

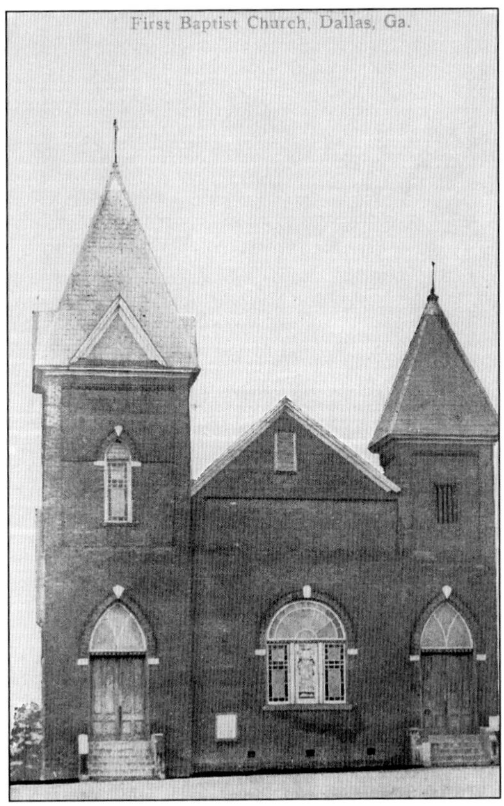

Another card published by the C.A. Hart Company shows the First Baptist Church of Dallas.

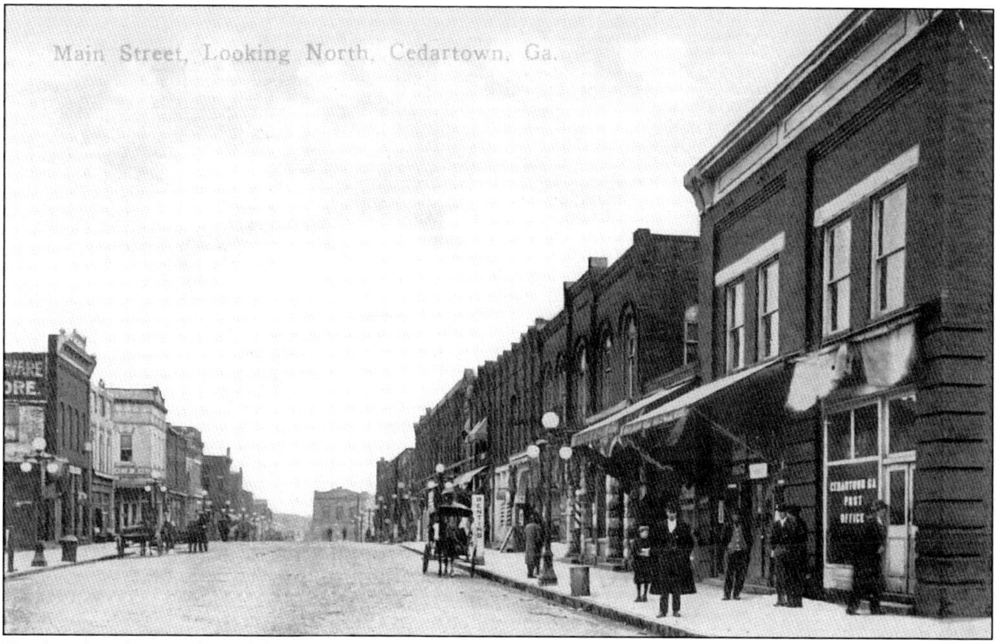

Evidently, the sender of this card showing Main Street in Cedartown was a member of a troupe or team of some sort. He wrote: "5-18-17. Dear Clara: We rode 221 miles today. Got here at 2 o'clock. We have an open date tomorrow and leave at 6:10 in the morning for Chattanooga, where we stay all day. Will send you a card from there. Bye-Bye, Papa."

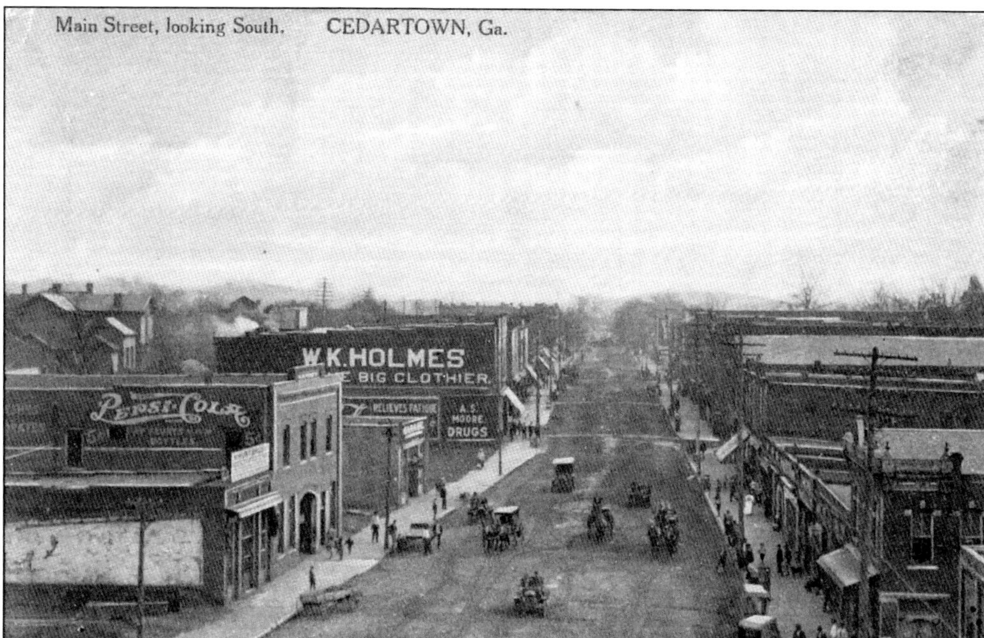

In a switch from the norm, this view of Main Street in Cedartown shows a large sign advertising Pepsi Cola instead of Coca-Cola.

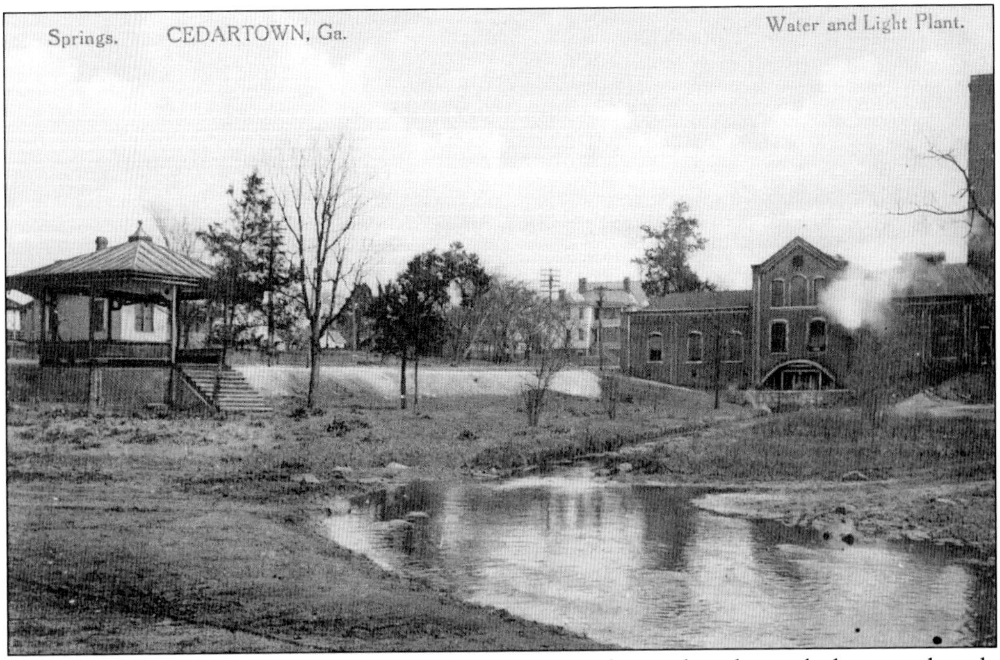

The springs and water and light plant in Cedartown are featured in this real-photo card made about 1914.

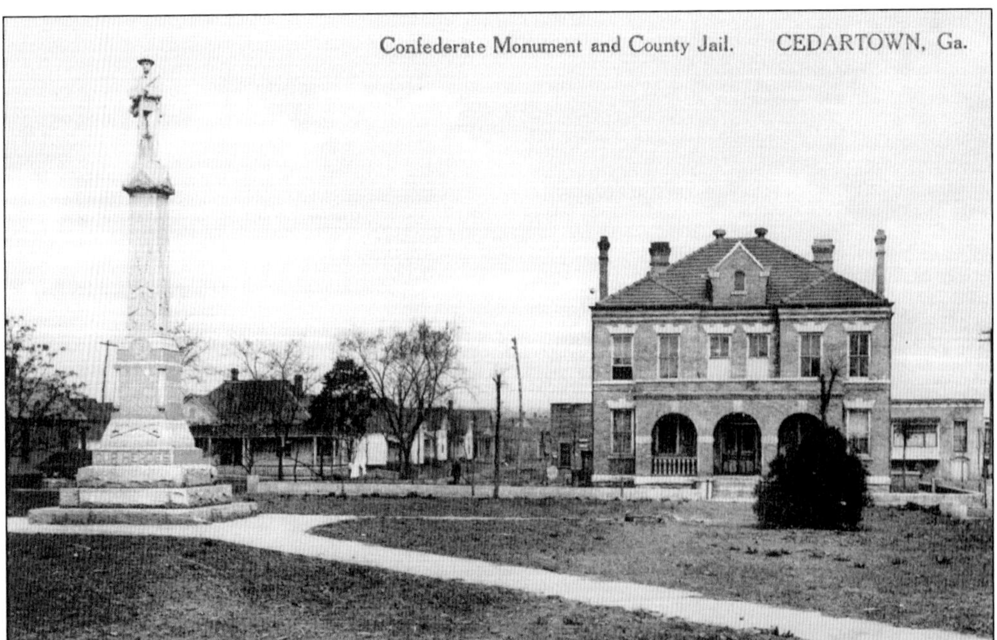

The Confederate Monument in Cedartown was erected on the Polk County courthouse square in 1906 by the United Daughters of the Confederacy.

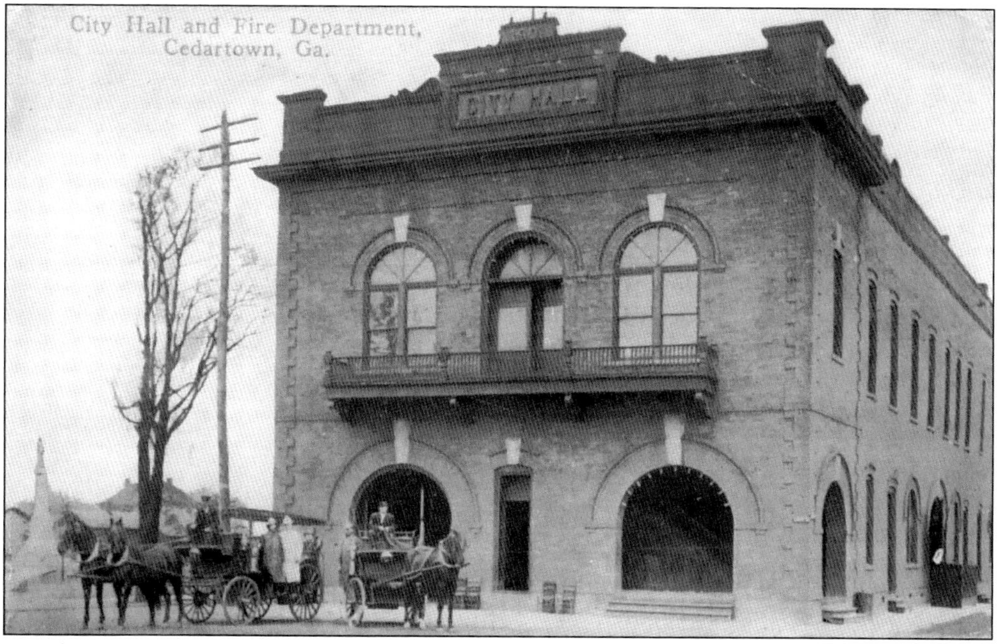

Proud members of the Cedartown Fire Department posed outside the city hall and fire department building for this post card.

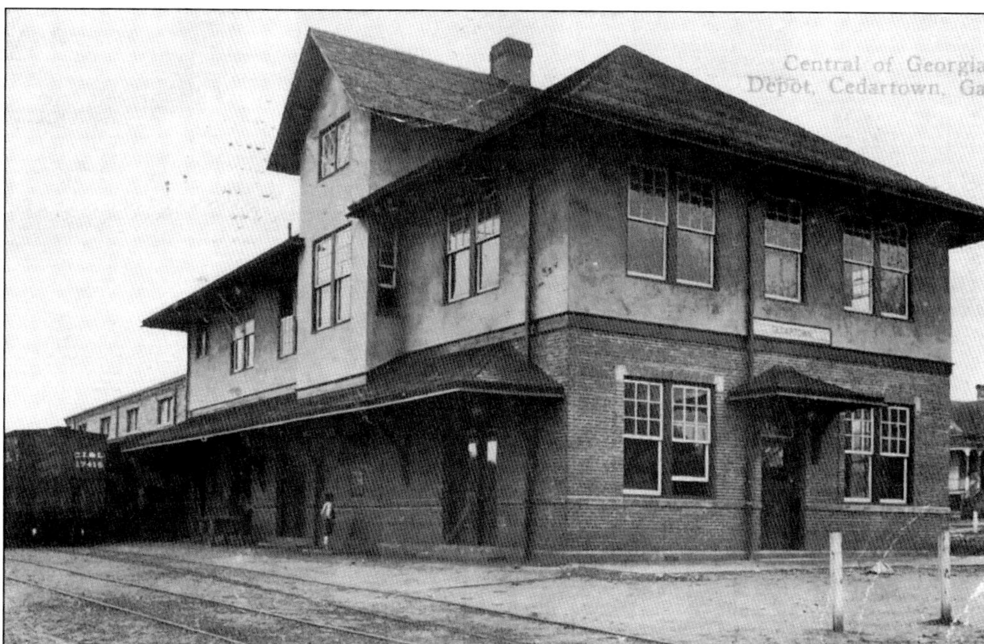

The Central of Georgia Depot at Cedartown is the subject of this c. 1912 post card. Note the boy reading the train schedules.

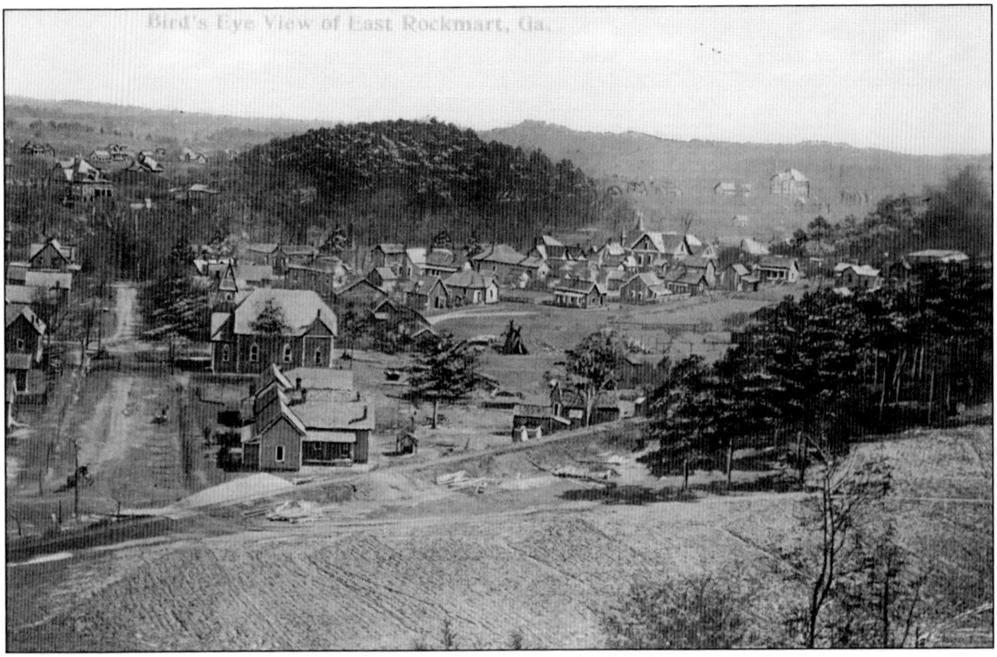

This bird's-eye view of Rockmart manages to show both the city and the pastoral setting surrounding it.

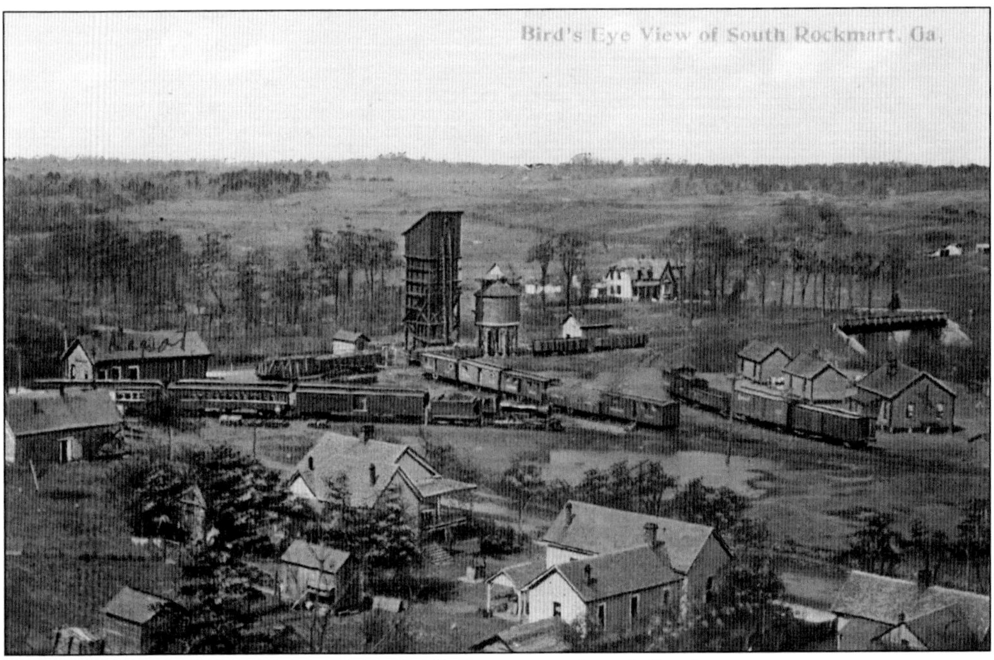

The railroad depot is the focus of this bird's-eye view of south Rockmart.

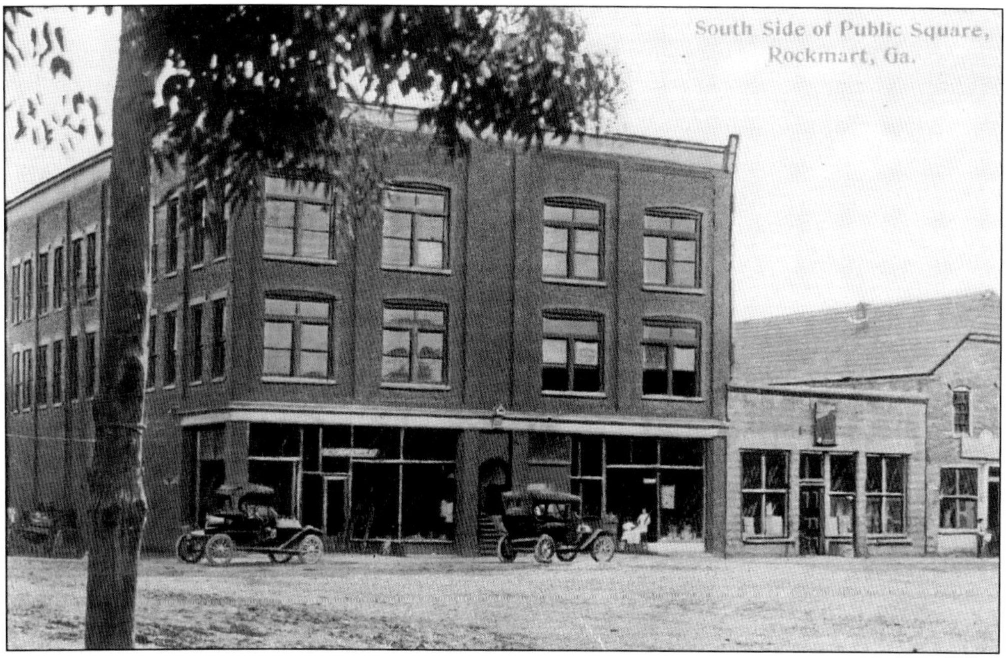

The sender of this post card featuring the public square in Rockmart in 1912 was short and to the point. He wrote: "Will be here all this week. 5/20."

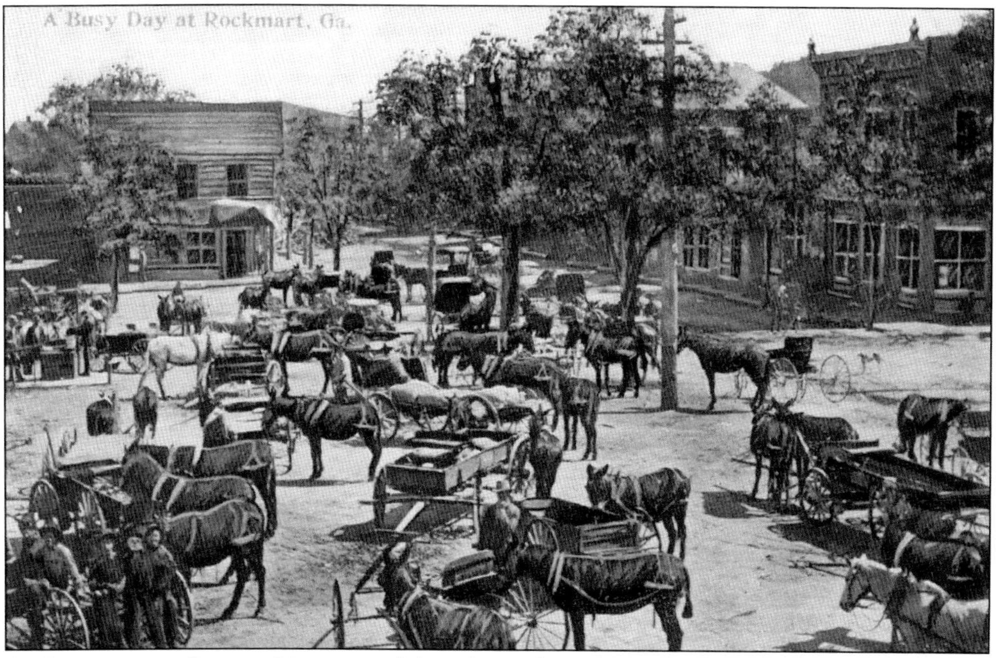

As the caption indicates, this post card does show a busy day in Rockmart. The group of men in the lower left corner seem to be posing for the camera.

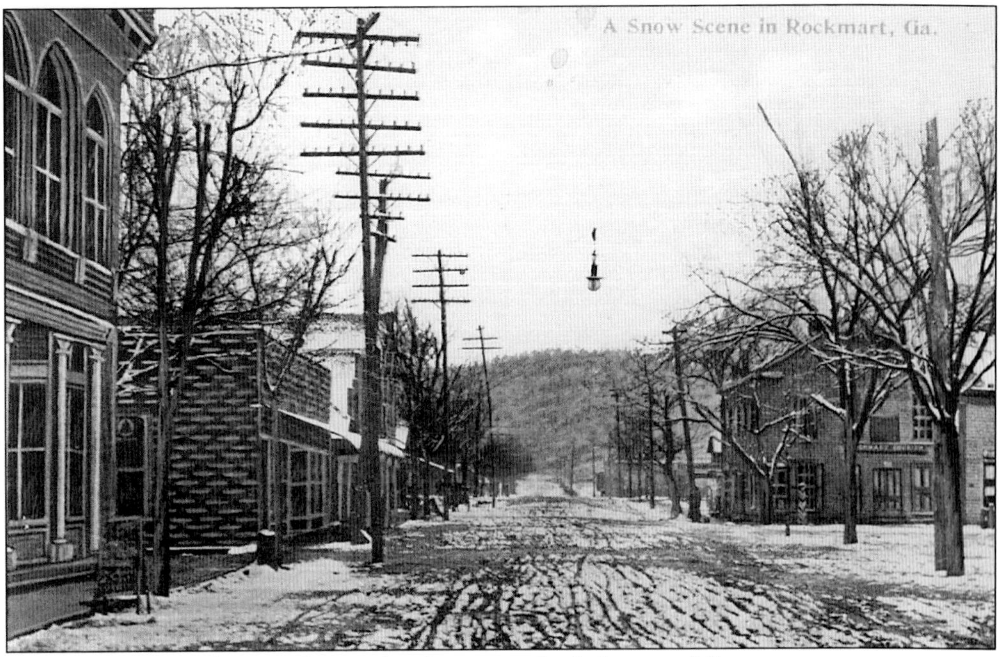

An opportunistic photographer took advantage of a light snowfall to capture a snow scene in Rockmart.

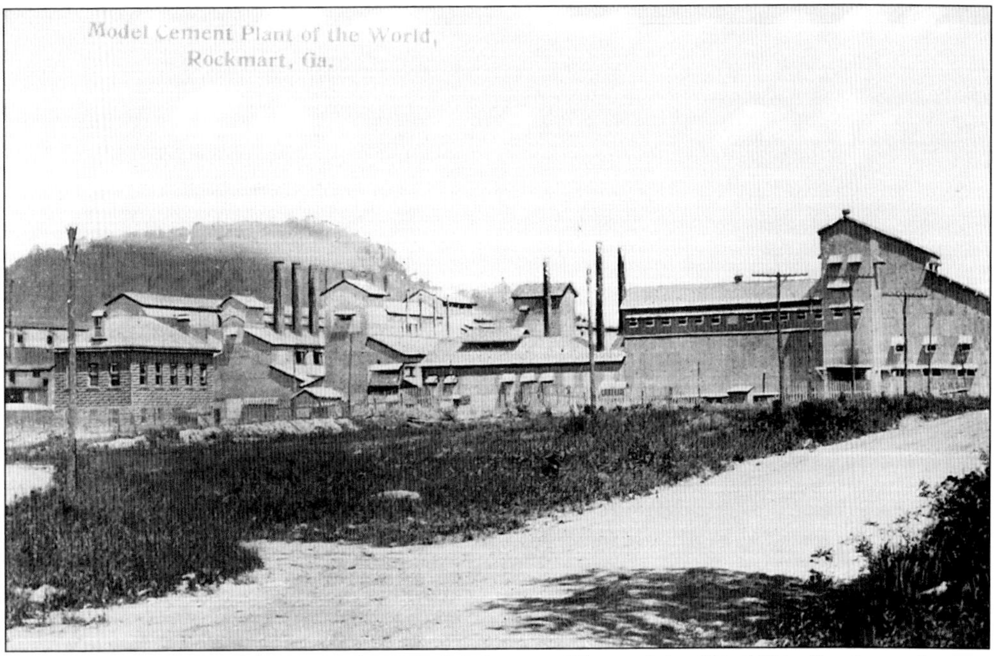

The sender of this card featuring the "Model Cement Plant of the World" in Rockmart had an unusual message to send. He wrote: "Will not get your letter until Sunday. Will answer then."

Bibliography

Anonymous. *1909–1910 Business and Professional Directory of the Cities and Towns of Georgia*. Atlanta, Georgia: Young and Company, 1910.

Garrett, Franklin M. *Atlanta and Environs, A Chronicle of Its People and Events*, Vols. I and II. Athens, Georgia: University of Georgia Press, facsimile reprint, 1969.

Jordan, Robert H. and J. Gregg Puster. *Courthouses in Georgia*. Editing and design by Patti Anderson and Mary Jackson. Norcross, Georgia: The Harrison Company, 1984.

Krackow, Kenneth K. *Georgia Place-Names*. Macon, Georgia: Winship Press, 1975.

McKenny, Frank M. *The Standing Army: History of Georgia's County Confederate Monuments*. Alpharetta, Georgia: W.H. Wolfe Associates, 1993.

Winn, Les R. *Ghost Trains & Depots of Georgia (1833–1933)*. Chamblee, Georgia: Big Shanty Publishing Company, 1995.

INDEX